The World Economy and Financial System

Levent Sümer

The World Economy and Financial System

A Paradigm Change Offering a Sustainable Approach

palgrave
macmillan

Levent Sümer
Boğaziçi University
Istanbul, Türkiye

ISBN 978-3-031-27529-6 ISBN 978-3-031-27530-2 (eBook)
https://doi.org/10.1007/978-3-031-27530-2

This Palgrave Macmillan imprint is published by the registered company Springer Nature Switzerland AG
The registered company address is: Gewerbestrasse 11, 6330 Cham, Switzerland

To Nur & Rana

Foreword

For more than a century now, capitalism has been successful in increasing economic welfare globally. Communism as an alternative could not even compete. But capitalism is still unloved. The current state of the capitalist system is easily blamed for being the root cause of most financial and economic crises in the current century. After the global financial crisis of 2008, criticisms of capitalism have turned louder with many experienced intellectuals now discussing how the system is broken and in need of fundamental reform.

After the demise of Bretton Woods in early 1970s, which also marks the start of the fiat money regime, and waves of financial deregulation after 1980s, the global economic system changed fast with many unintended consequences. First of all, extreme "financialization" is the best one-word description of the capitalist system today. Finance has become a game in itself, a game so big that the size of global financial markets today cannot be explained by any function of real economic activity. As such, it has become more harmful than useful for societies. Secondly, environmental damage is an unfortunate direct consequence of activities enabled and financed by the current system. The world is now in search of ways to reverse the catastrophic trend of climate change. Thirdly, distributions of wealth and income have become more unequal than ever seen in recorded history. Furthermore, this inequality seems to have worsened as a result of most public policies designed to solve financial crises during the last few decades. We have seen this after 2008 and again today after the pandemic's economic damage. More debt of all kinds appears as the easiest solution to economic problems and it is blindly chosen by policymakers. But then more debt makes lenders, the minority, richer and borrowers, the majority, poorer in due time. This is a simple mathematical fact with huge undesirable social and political consequences.

The current global system fails to meet the aspirations of billions of people around the world. People have largely lost their trust in institutions. Central banks are fast becoming topics of tabloid media. Hopes of better economic conditions have diminished and sense of financial insecurity is wide spread. Governments have lost their trust in other governments. Discontent is everywhere. Uncertainty about the future has become the new psychology. Concentration in the financial industry and increasing control power of a few corporations are further warning signs of an unpredictably abysmal future.

The merits of a free-market system driven by private ownership and backed by property rights should not be questioned. The problem with capitalism today is that it has deviated from such a free-market model. Ownership and control are increasingly concentrated and this hinders competition, which is the main building block of free markets. Paradoxically, this is mostly the result of various regulations since 1980s to achieve deregulation! Therefore, piecemeal solutions to known problems cannot be the proper approach. A fundamentally new approach is needed, which prioritizes prevention of deviations from a free-market model. As this book properly discusses, the centrality of profit maximization has to be modified under a new paradigm to emphasize the ethical basis of free markets. Policymakers, regulators, business people and academicians must change their mindsets and models to realize that the only morally acceptable purpose of production, trade, and finance must be the happiness of people and societies. As disagreeing parties cannot agree on what they disagree about, the current state of capitalism has to be reformed from scratch and as if it did not exist. Levent Sümer deserves praise for this book, and its careful reading is likely to trigger new and wise ideas about the future of our world.

Prof. Vedat Akgiray
Boğaziçi University
Istanbul, Türkiye

Preface

I do not like being pessimistic and seeing the glass from its empty side, but the world economy is on the knife-edge nowadays. In the post-COVID-19 era, I am not sure if we can use the word "post", yet as we experience many extensions, versions, or variants of new forms of dangerous or fatal viruses, the world has been experiencing a high inflationary period similar to the 1970s. After a global recession in 2020 with a 3.3% global GDP decline, the global economy was in a recovery period in 2021, but the geopolitical conflicts, one of which resulted in an ongoing war between Russia and Ukraine, completely changed the global economic outlook and the growth projections were revised downward again by IMF and World Bank. Monetary expansion policies of major central banks including the Federal Reserve (FED) and European Central Bank (ECB) during COVID-19 which helped rising inflation were finally replaced by the decision of increasing interest rates to fight against inflation which now may put the global economy into another recession, or worse, a stagflation risk and thereafter a global financial crisis. Despite the recent declines in global food and energy prices, inflation in many developing and emerging economies is still the first major issue to overcome to be optimistic about the future of the world economy.

It is known that past crises resulted in very deep socio-economic consequences. Beyond the wrong or late economic decisions taken or policies employed, the situation of the economy is very correlated with political moves and decisions. While sometimes the crises were initiated by the negative consequences of war or a political decision, for instance, the high inflation after the Vietnam War or the 1973 oil crisis and thereafter high inflation after the Yom Kippur War, on the other hand, a crisis was ended by a big war such as the end of Great Depression with the start of the World War II. In that context, what the global economy is experiencing now may either be a dramatic consequence of the current political conflicts and ongoing wars or in the worst-case scenario may trigger a new global war to end the crisis. Although a new catastrophic conventional global war is not a close scenario to happen, it is a fact that biological, technological, and even trade wars among many states have already been ongoing.

Past economic and financial crises revealed that in addition to their specific characteristics and causes, many financial crises have common features, and it seems like policymakers do not learn lessons from past crises. Slowed down international trade due to trade wars even before the great lockdown in the pandemic, sanctions applied even before the Russia-Ukraine war, never-ending debate about the Brexit effects on the EU and the global economy since 2016, rising inflation rates due to late moves of central banks, year by year historically high-recorded global debt, social, and economic impacts of refugee problems caused by civil or cross-national wars, the negative impacts of consumerist mindset incepted by capitalism, and in contrast, hundreds of millions of people living under poverty lines which increase the income inequality gap among nations and people are some of the significant warnings of a new global economic crisis. The policymakers, unfortunately, are unable to find alternatives for the global financial system to replace the Bretton Woods agreement which collapsed in 1971. Thus, in order not to experience deeper financial crises, sustainable steps are needed to be taken urgently.

First, we need to resolve the basic dilemma of overspending and hunger. Why does the world is wasting around USD 1 trillion worth of food (33% of the food annually produced) yearly while each day 25,000 people, including more than 10,000 children, are dying from hunger and related causes? While the statistics report that only a quarter of the wasted food amount can feed 840 million hungry people in the world, 854 million people are estimated to be malnourished. Second, we need to find a solution to the distribution of wealth among nations and societies considering that the total wealth of 2,153 people in the world is more than the total wealth of 4.6 billion people. No more words needed to say about that. Third, we need to question the meaning of our lives, what our needs are, what makes us happy, what money is for, and how conflicts can be avoided.

The starting point is a paradigm change. The mindsets shall be shifted from egocentric consumerist perspectives to sharing-oriented approaches. This change is both easy and at the same time difficult, indeed. It is easy because as suggested in this book, the steps to be taken are very clear and straightforward; *develop*, *balance*, *save*, and *share* what you have. On the other hand, it is complicated because one of the toughest challenges of humankind is changing traditional habits and managing egos.

This book is an outcome that carries the experience of more than 20 years of my professional and academic life. It is aimed that the new sustainable economic and financing approach introduced here which put humans in the center and replaces the growth-oriented economic mindset with a sustainable development approach will spark a change in the global economic and financial system.

Istanbul, Türkiye

Dr. Levent Sümer

Acknowledgments

Writing a book needs great effort and dedication. While you put your knowledge, experience, and vision into words and focus on the ideas and models you develop, you need support from your family, friends, and sometimes from professionals. Even though you are the one who puts his name on the cover of the book, the joint efforts of many people lie behind that great achievement. I would like to extend my special thanks to Prof. Vedat Akgiray, the author of Good Finance, who inspired me to write this book and always encouraged and supported me with his valuable comments and advice. My very special thanks and gratitude go to my dear father, Hıdır Sümer, who enlightened my way and became a role model for me; my beloved mother, Sevgi Sümer, who was always there for me with her prayers and unconditional love and support; my brothers, Mehmet and Gökmen, whom I always felt their encouragement and continuous support during each phase of my professional and academic life. I would like to thank Dr. Fatih Kiraz and Burak Pilavcı for their comments, recommendations, and correction of my errors before publishing this book, and thanks to all the anonymous names I did not mention here for their support. I would also like to extend my deep thanks to Tula Weis, Wyndham Hacket Pain, Susan Westendorf, Shreenidhi Natarajan and Chitra Gopalraj of Springer Nature for their full support from the beginning of the process till publishing. This book would not be completed without their kind assistance. My last but most special and endless thanks go to my beloved wife, Nur, and my lovely daughter Rana for their unconditional and never-ending support while I was writing this book day and night and stealing from the time we may spend together.

Contents

About the Author

Dr. Levent Sümer graduated from Istanbul Technical University, Civil Engineering Department. He got his master's degree in Construction Engineering and Management from the Illinois Institute of Technology, and he holds a Ph.D. degree from Boğazici University with the interest-free financing model he developed for large investment projects by combining interest-free real estate capital market instruments with pension funds.

Dr. Levent Sümer is the Chairman of SMR Strategy, an international investment and management consultancy company. Before establishing SMR Strategy, he worked for reputable companies at C-level positions. He has also been part-time lecturing at Boğazici University Executive MBA and Construction Engineering and Management Master Programs. As a guest lecturer and a keynote speaker, he gave many lectures and speeches at many reputable organizations and wrote articles for newspapers and journals. Project management, real estate finance, Islamic funds, pension funds, sovereign wealth funds, and political economy are his interests and research areas.

List of Figures

List of Tables

CHAPTER 1

Introduction

It was early in the morning in the US and late afternoon in Europe when the world was shocked by the terrorist attack in New York City on September 11, 2001. When I saw the World Trade Center (WTC) being hit by an aircraft and smoke rising on the top of the twin towers on the TV screen, the first thing that came to my mind was the social and humanitarian impacts of it. While watching people jumping out of the windows of the towers and seeing them running away from fire, smoke, and dust on the streets, humankind was witnessing a big tragedy. Anyone who carries mercy in his heart would not be reckless to this heartbreak event. When we realized that the attack was targeting more than the WTC, then, I thought about the political aspects of 9/11, the reasons behind the attack, and how the US domestic and foreign policy would respond to that. The attack was a new milestone for global politics and the world would not be the same again. While following the news, I was also thinking about the causes of the collapse of the twin towers from a civil engineering perspective. Beyond the social and political impacts, I was also curious about the economic consequences of the attack and how the US and in general the world economy would get affected by such a big shocking event.

The 9/11 attack had initial negative effects on the US economy which was already suffering through a recession after the dot-com bubble. The New York stock exchange fell 7.1% on the first open day of the stock

L. Sümer, *The World Economy and Financial System*,
https://doi.org/10.1007/978-3-031-27530-2_1

market after the attack, and 143,000 jobs were lost in a month only in New York City. 60% of job losses were in the finance and air transportation industries (History.com, 2022). However, there was a very fast bounce back in markets and business. According to the Bureau of Economic Analysis (BEA) analysis (2022), at the end of the year, the US Gross Domestic Product (GDP) increased over the previous year by about 1% and 2.7% in the last quarter of 2001.

While some conspiracy theorists claimed that the attack was used by the existing US government to gain power over the Middle East and American citizens, the death of 2996 people from 78 nations was an undeniable fact (Safrany, 2013). Similar conspiracy theories were also discussed in history. For instance, some theorists claimed that Adolf Hitler used the fire of the German Parliament in 1933 to increase his power (Boissoneault, 2017). Another conspiracy theory was about the creation of the coronavirus, which affected the whole world in the last two years, as a biological weapon produced in a lab (Lynas, 2020). Whether these theories are true or not, the political moves are somehow integrated with economic developments and may lead the power holders to make wrong decisions that may negatively affect the whole world.

Frederic Bastiat (1850) in his essay "That Which is Seen, and That Which is Not Seen" explains the broken window parable and states that spending on improving should not be replaced by spending on repairing. In the war economy, which is considered a political-economic reflection of the broken window fallacy, money is used to create weapons and later to repair the damages of the war instead of creating consumer goods and services. In that context, the idea of a broken window fallacy may mislead nations to declare war, support a war, or use such attacks by one side or the other to improve the economy and gain power. Indeed, such an approach does not actually bring long-term sustainable economic improvement but losses of innocent lives.

The current economic situations of states or future gains aimed are also considered the reasons behind declaring wars on other nations. Such terrorist attacks or some political moves that increase the tension are also used for finding a reason for initiating the first spark of the war. The assassination of Archduke Franz Ferdinand of Austria and his wife ignited the first spark and started World War I. Indeed, the economic and political rivalry of states on both sides of the Atlantic, the effort to overcome existing international trade barriers, and the aim to ensure the security of energy, raw material supply, and the flow of inputs for the industry are generally accepted as the main economic causes of the war (Willmott, 2003). From that perspective, the war was not just militarizing the active workforce of unemployed youth, but it is also a significant financing ability for many countries. The wars had two main components: destruction and construction which both needed financing.

The US was not involved in the early periods of World War I, and yet, it was the one that changed its direction and became one of the main beneficiaries of it due to the large export volume it reached by selling products to the countries in the war. World War I indeed made the US become the new economic power of the world, but after a decade the global economic crisis, the Great Depression, rose in the US and lasted around another ten years. Ironically, the start of another global war, World War II, ended the Great Depression, but that war, for instance, was financed through debt and higher taxes in the US. Economic consequences of war on the US economy report published by the Institute of Economics and Peace (2015) underlines that, although the US economy grew during the war and unemployment fell to as low as 1.45%, both consumption and investments declined, which made us remember the Broken Windows fallacy again.

World War II was followed by many regional wars and revolutions including the Arab–Israeli War, Korean War, French–Algerian War, Cuban Revolution, Vietnam War, Soviet–Afghan War, Iran Revolution, Iran–Iraq War, Persian Gulf Wars, Bosnian War, Arab Spring, Libyan Civil War, Syrian Civil War, Ukraine Orange Revolution, the latest Russia–Ukraine War, and several others. In addition to 9/11, many terrorist attacks were made in metropolitan and rural areas such as bombings in Paris, London, Istanbul, or any third-world country which we may never hear about it on the news. Two destructive World Wars and many regional wars that the world experienced in the last century resulted in more than hundreds of millions of deaths of innocent people. Many terrorist attacks brought fear and uncertainty to many nations.

In the last century, the world faced serious financial crises, one of which was the Great Depression in 1929 and the other was the Global Financial Crisis in 2008. The frequency of those crises increased in the last few decades, and each new crisis had a worse impact than the previous one. As Akgiray (2019) states, the world experienced 66 financial crises between 1980 and 2017. This number was more than the total financial crisis experienced in the previous 400 years. Two big economic and financial crises as well as many regional financial crises including the

1973 oil price shock, the 1982 Latin American debt default, the 1987 Black Monday stock market crash, the 1989 US savings and loan crisis, the 1990 Japanese real estate bubble, 1994 Mexican peso crisis, 1997 Asian financial crisis, 1998 Russian financial crisis, 2000 dot-com bubble, 2001 Türkiye banking crisis, 2009 European debt crisis, 2020 COVID-19 pandemic-based recession, and many others had negative impacts on the financial markets, disrupted the global financial system, increased inequality, and decreased the welfare of the societies.

Within the last century, in which the modern financial systems are structured, the states aimed to standardize the system by bringing some rules and regulations. The gold standard which was used until the 1929 Great Depression had ended with import tariffs applied by many states after the global economic crisis. At the end of World War II, IMF and World Bank were established as a result of the Bretton Woods agreement signed in 1944. With this agreement, the USD was fixed to 35 USD per ounce value of gold, and other currencies were pegged to the USD (Ghizoni, 2013). The stability brought by this agreement lasted until the mid-1960s. The rise in the inflation rates after Vietnam War resulted in the suspension of the system by the US in 1971. The collapse of the Bretton Woods system did not untie the global currencies completely, and the USD kept being the reserve currency of the world with around a 60% rate (Amadeo, 2020). There had also been some attempts to find an exit from the hegemony of the USD in the global financial system. In the last decade, many countries decided to use their currencies in international trade. For instance, while Türkiye and Russia agreed on using the Russian Ruble and Turkish Lira, China and Pakistan also agreed to trade in Yuan to get rid of the USD in bilateral trade. In fact, Brazil, Russia, India, China, and South Africa (BRICS countries) have been discussing developing a new reserve currency to replace the USD (Liu & Pappa, 2022, Russia Briefing, 2022).

On the other hand, the involvement of technology in the finance industry started shaping financial services. Financial technology, known as Fintech, describes the new technologies that seek to improve and automate the delivery and use of financial services. Specialized software and algorithms that are used on computers and smartphones are utilized to help firms, businesses, and consumers better manage their financial operations and processes. Digital currencies are defined as a form of fintech that may transform the financial sector in payment, lending, trading, and investment areas. The common use and rise of cryptocurrencies made central banks consider issuing digital currencies.

Despite the recent latest sharp declines in their values, the rise of cryptocurrencies is being discussed whether they may replace all the state-oriented currencies. For example, China launched a digital yuan app in September 2022. The digital yuan, also known as e-CNY and officially called the Digital Currency Electronic Payment (DC/EP), is a digitized version of China's legal currency which was issued by China's central bank to be used for high-frequency, small-scale retail purchases and transactions (Huld, 2022). Although some other central banks are also considering issues with digital currencies, today, cryptocurrencies are still not considered stablecoins, because they are not tied to any real-world asset, and they may crash at any time just like some of them collapsed recently. For instance, Terra Luna was crushed from USD 120 to almost zero within a day, and Bitcoin, the most well-known and the largest cryptocurrency in volume, fell from its historically top value of around USD 67,000 to USD 18,000 within the last year (Investing, 2022). The future of cryptocurrencies in that sense is still questionable, but the development of financial technologies seems to change the future of the finance industry.

The last century also witnessed serious pandemics that killed millions of people. From 1918 till now, Spanish influenza, Legionnaires disease, HIV, AIDS, SARS, Ebola, Zika, and coronavirus disease (COVID-19) were recorded as the main pandemics that the world suffered from (Honigsbaum, 2020). The pandemic had also serious economic, social, and political impacts.

All these wars, terrorist attacks, pandemics, economic and financial instabilities, and crises made me think about the integration of politics, economics, finance, social life, and the flaws of the world economy and financial system. Whether we accept it or not, or whether the tie is weak or strong in different countries, politics and economics are interconnected to each other. The question to be answered here is how the social and environmental dimensions are integrated into these relations and whether the current financial system is strong and stable enough to stand out against such global devastations. It is a fact that the finance industry is in a transformation phase, and after COVID-19, capitalism has been being questioned, but it is obvious that the consequences of such catastrophic events show that the current economic and financial system is not capable enough to address the crises and needs to be replaced by a sustainable system that may be—not all but most of—the citizens of the world can benefit from it.

Two years after the 9/11 attack, I was in Chicago getting a master's degree in construction engineering and management. Until 2006, the construction industry was rising in the US and my initial professional career years passed working in the US and thereafter in Türkiye in the construction and real estate businesses. There were many ongoing construction projects, the housing industry was booming, and the home-ownership rate in the US had hit 69.2%, the largest rate of all time in 2004. At that time, I was working for a company that bid for the finishing works (but couldn't win) of the Trump Tower Chicago Project. Ironically, after a few years, the largest financial crisis in history was triggered by the collapse of the mortgage system which was financing the housing industry in the US. There certainly was something wrong with the system. The economy was warming up, making a peak, and then cooling down, and a crisis was following thereafter. This financial system which is built on a boom-and-bust cycle was evaluated by Alrifai (2015) as the reason for the frequent financial crises because these crises were designed by the system itself by nature, so the structural design needed to be reviewed and replaced.

When the global financial crisis hit the markets in 2008, I was back in Türkiye working for a company that was developing a mixed-use real estate project. A German real estate fund was going to purchase the shopping mall at the end of the completion of the construction with the condition that the rate of the lease would reach 85% of the total leasable area. Due to the domino effect of the crisis, we could not reach the 85% occupancy rate at the long-stop date, and the fund decided not to purchase the mall by using its right in the contract. The company that I used to work for got negatively affected because the construction was financed by a bank loan and the whole amount of the loan was going to be repaid at once when the asset was handed over to the fund. In the middle of the global financial crisis, we had a shopping mall with an occupancy rate below 85% and a big debt problem which was needed to be re-financed soon. The debt was a global problem that is still growing day by day. The 2008 Global Financial Crisis exhibited that the world is over-indebted, and an urgent solution should have been developed against this debt, but on contrary, the capital flows, which started toward the emerging economies due to monetary expansion policies of central banks, put these developing countries into a larger debt spiral like developed economies and the total debt of the world reached from its USD 174 trillion value in 2008 to USD 303 trillion at the end of 2021 according to International Institute of Finance (IIF), (2022).

In addition to the rising global debt which puts the global economy at risk of a potential financial crisis, another main cause and consequence of the financial crises are considered the increasing inequality between societies, genders, and nations (Akgiray, 2019; Piketty, 2013; Stiglitz, 2010). According to Oxfam's 2020 report, the total wealth of 2153 people in the world is more than the total wealth of 4.6 billion people and all the women in Africa have less wealth than the 22 richest men in the world. While 66% of the world's population lives in countries where inequality has grown, income inequality is usually larger in cities compared to rural areas. Promoting equal access to opportunities, developing macroeconomic policies, and fighting against discrimination and prejudice are considered the main points to reducing inequality (World Social Report, 2020).

While the world was struggling with high debt and income inequality problems, an unexpected disease, coronavirus (COVID-19), initiated in Wuhan, China, and rapidly spread all around the world, shifted the focus of the world to a serious health problem that, in a short while, was transformed into a pandemic, affecting the world in sociological, economic, and psychological aspects. The COVID-19 pandemic shut the borders down, stopped international transportation, broke the global supply chain, slowed down international trade, and triggered a global economic crisis due to the "sudden stance" experienced by many economies. The COVID-19 pandemic exhibited that the income level and the wealth of the people did not help them to protect themselves in such a global health crisis environment. Indeed, the firms and households generally were not well prepared to withstand such a shock. For instance, studies before the crisis had exhibited that more than 50% of households in developing and advanced economies were unable to sustain their main consumption for more than three months in the event of income losses, yet income losses caused by the pandemic had more severe impacts on emerging economies due to their preexisting economic fragilities. Similarly, the companies had only 55 days of cash reserve to sustain their operations (Badarinza et al., 2019, Worldbank, 2022). This situation increased the size of the debts which was hit the historically top record and already not sustainable.

Many states applied curfews to decrease the speed of the spreading rate of the infection but were unsuccessful to provide basic protection tools to all their citizens. The difficulties reaching these tools such as masks and disinfectants, the insufficient capacities of intensive care units of the hospitals, the inadequateness of respirators and other medical equipment, the urgent need for medicines or vaccines, and the insufficient capacity of the states matching the basic needs of their citizens regarding their health made people question the current economic systems, especially the dominant capitalism, as well as the meaning and the future of their lives.

It is argued that the effects of the COVID-19-based global economic crisis will be deeper compared to the consequences of the 1929 Great Depression and the 2008 Global Financial Crisis (ECB, 2020).

Roubini (2020) claimed that the crisis that COVID-19 created in the global economy would last a decade. He underlined that an increase in health expenditures may grow the debts, and debts may initiate bankruptcies. He also mentioned that the currencies would lose value and the countries would experience stagflation. According to him, digitalization would speed up and that could increase the unemployment rates. As a consequence of the pandemic, protectionism would increase, popularism would rise, the conflicts between the US and China would increase, and cyber-attacks and wars would take place.

We experienced the post-COVID-19 period with a rise in inflation, a growth in debts, and an increase in inequality. We also witnessed a war started between Russia and Ukraine which led the food and energy prices to rise sharply globally. COVID-19 was also considered a biological war as Bill Gates had warned the world at Munich Security Conference in 2017 by stating that a genetically engineered virus was easy to make and could kill more people than nuclear weapons (KFF.org, 2022).

Another consequence of COVID-19 was the dramatic increase in poverty and inequality among people. While the income of 99% of the world population fell, the fortune of the top ten richest men doubled from 700 billion USD to 1.5 trillion USD in pandemic years. Four people have died in a poorer nation against one death in a wealthy country. The Gini coefficient increased during the COVID-19 period and the employment-to-population ratio decreased (IMF, 2021; Oxfam, 2022).

In addition to the bad experience that we had in the 2008 global financial crisis, I also witnessed several local economic crises in Türkiye. 1994 currency crisis, the 2001 banking crisis, and the 2018 and 2021 currency crises had negative impacts on the Turkish economy in the last few decades. During almost all financial crises, the wealth of the people was melting down, the stock markets were crashing, and it was taking a long time to get recovered. In countries like Türkiye, one of the major challenges of the such economy is fighting against high inflation rates (nowadays that is the problem of almost all developed and emerging economies), and it is hard to find hedging instruments against inflation due to the high volatility of the stocks and limited capital market instruments.

Under high inflation, the main response of people is to find an investment area to at least protect their wealth. Also, people save money and direct their savings to different investment instruments such as purchasing real estate, investing in stock markets, buying gold, or enrolling in pension systems. When I used to work in Chicago, we had a 401 k pension plan in the benefits package. While the history of the pension system started in the 1900s, the private voluntary pension concept in Türkiye goes back only to 2003. Within ten years after the pension system started, the number of enrollments and the size of the pension funds remained very limited. In 2013, the Turkish government issued a new regulation regarding the voluntary pension system, and they offered a 25% (nowadays 30%) state contribution in addition to the deposits of the pension fund account holders (Pension Monitoring Center, 2022). That was a revolution in the Turkish pension system because since then both the size of the pension funds and the number of enrollments grew exponentially, but there still was a problem. The contributions accumulated in pension funds were mostly directed to treasury bills and corporate bonds. In other words, the pension funds were providing an indirect debt to the government and companies. Debt was also an issue in the pension system. The stocks were getting only 12% of the total savings. Another issue about the Turkish pension system was the saving rates. Despite the fast-growing size of the pension funds, the saving rate in Türkiye was around 2.5% of the total GDP, which was far behind the OECD average rate, 50% (OECD Pension Market in Focus, 2021).

On the other hand, in the last few decades, the Turkish economy was structured on the development of construction and infrastructure projects, and these investment projects were financed either by debt or by the public–private partnership (PPP) model. The PPP model, which was originally initiated and used by the UK, was used to finance many projects including highways, tunnels, airports, and hospitals, but the model was criticized due to the financial guarantees given to the contractors who finance and operate the project for a 25-year grace period. Although the government was explaining all these investment projects are being constructed without spending from the government budget, those who oppose the model were claiming that as the years pass, those guarantees would bring additional risks and burdens to the treasury. An alternative financing model would help end such discussions.

During my professional career, while working in several top management positions for different companies, I had the chance to give lectures at different universities. The problems I see in the global economy and the financial system and the lectures I gave at universities made me write academic and non-academic articles on finding solutions to these problems by developing new models. I ultimately wrote a Ph.D. thesis in real estate finance and brought a new perspective to project financing by involving people directly and indirectly in the economy and suggesting alternative investment areas for pension funds. With the new investment and financing ecosystem l developed, I integrated the pension system with the real estate capital market instruments. The main idea behind this model was to include the savings of people in the real economy through capital market instruments. There was no bank loan needed to finance the investment projects, and no financial guarantees were given to the contractors; instead, people were the financers and at the same time the shareholders of the investment projects through the money they saved in their pension accounts. Creditors or other financial institutions were also integrated into the model by replacing their role from being loan providers to shareholders of the fund. That was bringing a new perspective to the pension system as well as the project financing mechanism.

The global financial crisis was triggered by the default of mortgage loans in the US. The high dependency of the financing of the housing industry to bank loans exhibited a need for alternative sustainable financing models. I developed an alternative home financing model which I recommended to establish a Housing Fund, a form of a real estate investment fund, which purchases the housing units and rents them to the person who is willing to purchase that unit. Instead of using a mortgage loan, the potential homebuyer becomes an investor in the housing fund directly or indirectly through the pension funds by directing his savings to the housing fund which will first purchase the housing unit and rent it to the homebuyer. The housing fund participant (homebuyer) starts investing in the fund by making a down payment and then pays the remaining sales price of the unit to the fund in monthly installments directly or through his savings in his pension account. The homebuyer and the fund jointly own the housing unit, and the housing fund rents the unit to the housing fund participant until the total sales price of the unit is paid to the housing fund. The rent of the units constructs the financing cost while each year the ownership rates and the portion of the rent that the participant pays yearly are updated based on the sales price and the rents of the units which are determined by independent valuation companies. The model does not need any bank loan, it is structured on an interest-free financing principle, integrates the diminishing partnership approach of Islamic finance, and brings a new sustainable and alternative solution to home financing by focusing on sharing and saving economy perspectives.

Another new approach that I brought to the business industry was the SME Partnership Fund that I suggested during COVID-19, while many small and middle enterprises (SMEs) were struggling to survive under the sudden stance of economies. I proposed establishing a new fund where again the pension funds may also be one of the main investors of it to strengthen the capital structures of these SMEs instead of providing them new loans which eventually would put them in more trouble. In traditional finance, individual or institutional investors put their money into bank accounts and banks use this money to provide loans to companies or people in need. Under this new approach, people directly or indirectly (again through pension funds) invest in this SME Partnership Fund which directs the investments in the company that needs financing by becoming its shareholder. This approach also decreases the dependency of the private sector on bank loans and emphasizes the partnership economy.

All the models that I developed were putting humans in the center and where the economic and financial system serves them in justice to meet their needs. People need shelter to protect themselves from threats, people want their homes to be warm in winter and cool in summer, people need assurance for their health and their retirement years, people need a good education, and people want to get socialized, so they need entertainment; indeed, people seek peace and want to be happy in their lives. An economic model shall be capable enough to respond to these basic needs of people, and a financial system should regulate such an economic model.

Thus, I combined the solutions I brought for different industries into one single model and applied them to all industries including housing, insurance, energy, tourism, healthcare, infrastructure, and so on. The main structure of the model was making people feel that they work not just to get paid at the end of the month, but more than that, they feel comfortable while spending or saving this money for their benefits as well as by helping others. Thus, involving people in the economic system directly through their money in banks or indirectly through their savings such as in their pension accounts or other investment tools would help many companies in different industries grow, many projects get financed, many people purchase their houses, and the returns of these projects/firms are shared with them. In that context, saving and sharing were designed as the two important pillars of the new model I developed.

We know that humankind always aims to develop itself and get a better life condition, and life itself is built on a balance no matter what we do, how we do, or why we do it, we must follow a balance, such as work and social life balance, or a balance between consuming and saving. Thus, in addition to saving and sharing, developing and balancing constituted the other two important pillars of my new economy approach.

Under these 4 main pillars briefly described here, this book suggests a mindset shift, proposes a paradigm change in the current economic and financial system, and presents an alternative sustainable economic and financial ecosystem. Before going into details of the new approach, it will be useful to overview the history of the economic and global financial systems.

References

Akgiray, V. (2019). *Good finance: Why we need a new concept of finance*. Bristol University Press. 978-1-5292-0000-3

Alrifai, T. (2015). *Islamic finance and the new financial system: An ethical approach to preventing future financial crises*. Wiley. 978–1–118–99063–6.

Amadeo, K. (2020). *Why the US Dollar is the global currency*. https://www.thebalancemoney.com/world-currency-3305931. Last Accessed on January 10, 2023.

Badarinza, C., Balasubramaniam, V., & Ramadorai, T. (2019). The household finance landscape in emerging economies. *Annual Review of Financial Economics, 11*(1), 109–129.

Bastiat, M.F. (1850). *That which is seen and that which is not seen: The unintended consequences of government spending*. https://commonsenseeconomics.com/wp-content/uploads/Bastiat_SeenUnseen_CSE.pdf. Last Accessed on January 09, 2023.

Boissoneault, L. (2017). *The true story of the Reichstag fire and the Nazi rise to power*. https://www.smithsonianmag.com/history/true-story-reichstag-fire-and-nazis-rise-power-180962240/. Last Accessed on January 09, 2023.

Bureau of Economics Analysis. (2022). *GDP product fourth quarter 2001*. https://www.bea.gov/news/2002/gross-domestic-product-fourth-quarter-2001-preliminary-estimate. Last Accessed on January 09, 2023.

European Central Bank (ECB). (2020). *Our response to the coronavirus pandemic*. https://www.ecb.europa.eu/home/search/coronavirus/html/index.en.html. Last Accessed on March 20, 2022.

Ghizoni, S. K. (2013). *Creation of the Bretton Woods system*. https://www.federalreservehistory.org/essays/bretton-woods-created. Last Accessed on January 10, 2023.

History.com. (2022). *9/11 Attacks*. https://www.history.com/topics/21st-century/9-11-attacks. Last Accessed on January 09, 2023.

Honigsbaum, M. (2020). *The pandemic century: A history of global contagion from the Spanish Flu to Covid-19*. WH Allen Publishing.

Huld, A. (2022). *China launches digital Yuan app—All you need to know*. https://www.china-briefing.com/news/china-launches-digital-yuan-app-what-you-need-to-know/. Last Accessed on January 10, 2023.

Institute of Economics and Peace. (2015). *Economic consequences of war on the U.S. Economy*. https://www.economicsandpeace.org/wp-content/uploads/2015/06/The-Economic-Consequences-of-War-on-US-Economy_0.pdf. Last Accessed on January 10, 2023.

Institute of International Finance. (2022). *Global debt monitor*. https://www.iif.com/Research/Capital-Flows-and-Debt/Global-Debt-Monitor. Last Accessed on January 10, 2023.

International Monetary Fund (IMF). (2021). *The IMF and COVID-19*. https://www.imf.org/en/Topics/imf-and-covid19. Last Accessed on March 20, 2022.

Investing.com. (2022). *Down to zero: Terra Luna Crash and its impact on crypto adoption*. https://www.investing.com/news/cryptocurrency-news/down-to-zero-terra-luna-crash-and-its-impact-on-crypto-adoption-2841016. Last Accessed on January 10, 2023.

KFF.org. (2022). *Bill Gates, other panel members at Munich Security Conference warn of potential for global pandemic, urge preparedness*. https://www.kff.org/news-summary/bill-gates-other-panel-members-at-munich-security-conference-warn-of-potential-for-global-pandemic-urge-preparedness/. Last Accessed on January 10, 2023.

Liu, Z. Z., & Pappa, M. (2022). Can BRICS de-dollarize the global financial system?. *Elements in the Economics of Emerging Markets*. https://doi.org/10.1017/9781009029544. 9781009029544. Cambridge University Press.

Lynas, M. (2020). *COVID: Top 10 current conspiracy theories*. https://allianceforscience.org/blog/2020/04/covid-top-10-current-conspiracy-theories/. Last Accessed on January 09, 2023.

OECD.org. (2021). *Pension markets in focus*. https://www.oecd.org/daf/fin/private-pensions/Pension-Markets-in-Focus-2021.pdf. Last Accessed on March 20, 2022.

Oxfam International. (2022). *Inequality*. https://www.oxfam.org/en/tags/inequality. Last Accessed on March 20, 2022.

Pension Monitoring Center. (2022). *IPS summary data*. https://www.egm.org.tr/homepage. Last Accessed on January 14, 2023.

Piketty, T. (2013). *Capital in the twenty-first century*. Harvard University Press.

Roubini. (2020). *Coronavirus: Leading economist warns of 10 years of depression and debt*. https://www.bbc.com/news/business-52752172. Last Accessed on January 10, 2023.

Russia-Briefing.com. (2022). *Russia and Türkiye agree to trade in rubles and dump US Dollar*. https://www.russia-briefing.com/news/russia-and-turkiye-agree-to-trade-in-rubles-and-dump-us-dollar.html/. Last Accessed on January 10, 2023.

Safrany, B. (2013). 9/11 Conspiracy theories. *Hungarian Journal of English and American Studies (HJEAS), 19*(1), 11–30.

Stiglitz, J. E. (2010). *The Stiglitz report: Reforming the international monetary and financial systems in the wake of the global crisis*. The New Press. 978–1595585202.

Willmott, H. P. (2003). *World war I*. Dorling Kindersley Publishing Inc.

Worldbank. (2022). *The economic impacts of the COVID-19 crisis*. https://www.worldbank.org/en/publication/wdr2022/brief/chapter-1-introduction-the-economic-impacts-of-the-covid-19-crisis. Last Accessed on January 10, 2023.

World Social Report. (2020). *Inequality in a Rapidly Changing World*, United Nations publication ISBN 978-92-1-130392-6, eISBN 978-92-1-004367-0, https://www.un.org/development/desa/dspd/wpcontent/uploads/sites/22/2020/02/World-Social-Report2020-FullReport.pdf. Last Accessed on March 01, 2023.

CHAPTER 2

A Brief History of Economic and Global Financial Systems

The world economy has been experiencing tough days. All economic systems as well as the current global financial system are being questioned nowadays. The post-COVID-19 recession, high inflation, political conflicts, trade wars, energy security, food prices, trade barriers, sanctions, ongoing wars, refugee problems, inequality, high debt, housing prices, pollution, and many other social, political, environmental, and economic related issues are waiting to be resolved. There is no state which can claim that its economic system is strong and stable enough to overcome all these problems with its efforts and resources. Many governments are seeking a direction to exit this turbulence. While some states are shifting their views from globalization to localization, others are governed more conservatively and stricter from an economic perspective.

No matter which economic system the states are applying, the nearing of a new possible global financial crisis is undeniable. It seems like the current economic systems, at least the way they are currently implemented, are unable to provide sustainable solutions and avoid any upcoming crisis. In that context, developing alternative sustainable models to replace the current systems or at least repair their flaws, if possible, is essential.

Before describing the details of the proposed alternative approach, it is useful to remember the reasons for the existence of the states, the pros and cons of the economic systems used within history, the structure of the

L. Sümer, *The World Economy and Financial System*,
https://doi.org/10.1007/978-3-031-27530-2_2

global financial system, the reasons for the past economic and financial crisis and the current problems, and the risks of the global economic and financial system. These will help us to see the big picture and to outline the pillars of the model proposed.

Brief History of Economic Systems

An economic system is defined as the organization and distribution of the available resources, services, and goods by societies or governments. Land, capital, labor, and physical resources are controlled and regulated by economic systems. Agencies, institutions, and entities are important actors in economic systems. The state exists with its power and makes decisions about the distribution such as money, products, security, and innovation in society in a fair way. The rules about how the markets work and how societies achieve their goals in global economics are made by state policymakers. Any decision made needs to follow the fair distribution of resources among individuals, groups, and nation-states.

As Balaam and Dillman (2014) state, a market is a place where people do not just purchase or exchange something with the producer, but also it is a major force that shapes human behavior. Social and transnational groups play main roles in shaping the global economy as we all know that the state and market do not exist in a social vacuum, and the policymakers need to find an intersection point of attitudes, opinions, benefits, and beliefs held by members of a group or society. In that context, depending on the conjuncture, during history, many different economic systems were created and used for the benefit of societies.

While traditional economies mainly were relying on people and are based on predominantly farming, in command economies which is common in communist societies, the governments are dominant centralized authorities. On the other hand, in market economies, the markets are free, there is very little government interference, and the regulations are made by people based on the relationship between supply and demand. Finally, mixed economies are a balanced combination of both command and market economies where the government controls public services, but most industries are private. The link between various agencies, organizations, and institutions, the information flow among them, and the social relations within the system are important aspects of economic systems. In that context, socialism and capitalism are accepted as the representatives of the market and planned economies (Rosser & Barkley, 2003).

An economic system is considered a part of the social system, and there exists a strong relationship between political systems and certain ideologies. Feudalism, which was the dominant system of the Medieval European political, economic, and social system from the ninth to fifteenth century was defined as getting the right to live in a land and receive protection for the military service provided in the war for the Crown (Ganshof, 1952). Feudalism declined after the political change in England after Magna Carta Libertatum was signed in 1215, the Black Death Pandemic in the fourteenth century and the 100-year war between England and France which lasted until 1453 expedited this decline. Then, feudalism was replaced by mercantilism.

Although from some aspects, feudalism was considered the earliest form of capitalism as the farmers were working for a small group of lords, mercantilism was regarded as the primitive predecessor of capitalism and was based on accumulating the largest possible share of that wealth such as gold and silver by maximizing the exports and by limiting the imports via tariffs. Mercantilism was the dominant economic system of trade between the sixteenth and eighteenth centuries in Western Europe. Under mercantilism, to protect the local markets and supply sources, the nations engaged their military powers which encouraged imperialism and colonialism, and that is why mercantilism was criticized as it was based on a zero-sum-game, where the advantage of one state was the loss of the other one. Under mercantilism, the economy was under the control of the state. In the nineteenth century, there was a transition from colonialism to imperialism as Said (1993) distinguishes the difference between both controlling and ruling by settling versus controlling and ruling without possessing.

Adam Smith (1876), who is accepted as the father of the modern economy, in his book Wealth of Nations demonstrated that free trade benefits both parties, and efficiency and growth are improved by specialization in production. The markets shall be free (laissez-faire), and this free economy policy is for the benefit of the general population. Smith defends that the benefits of the individuals are for the utility of society. 1974 Nobel Laureate Hayek (1944) also underlying the importance of individualism and was defending that economic decisions shall not be independent of individuals, their values, and goals.

The capitalist system which is considered the most dominant economic system in the world economy in the last century was structured under these free market, individualism, and liberal ideas. Capitalism has different definitions depending on how it is approached. While it is considered a destructive system based on profit maximization, the defenders define capitalism as liberty that enables the free market and free enterprise where profit is the main motive although many firms go bankrupt and lose in the hard competition (Delanty, 2019; Marx, 1867). The private ownership and market economy for coordination are accepted as the core features of capitalism by its defenders. The term capitalism is considered a political consequence of imperial ambitions (Gronow, 2016) remembering that Lenin (1916) had defined imperialism, in which the economic relations of capitalism are transformed into pure relations of power, as the highest stage of capitalism.

Starting from the first industrial revolution, the use of child labor, extended working hours in poor working conditions, and discrimination among genders, ethnicity, and nations increased the inequality among societies. Together with the benefits of industrialization that improved living standards, the world heavily experienced the negative consequences of industrialization brought such as weaponization. Marx (1867) defended the replacement of private ownership with collective ownership, first under socialism and then under communism. According to him, social classes and class struggle would no longer exist in the final stage of human development. Although it was believed communism would start in England where the first industrial revolution started, instead it influenced counties like the Soviet Union, China, and Cuba. Despite its negative effects, the industrial revolution did not stop. As a result of imperial ambitions to get more, own more, and possess more, humankind suffered great destruction in the last century with two great World Wars and many long-lasting local wars. Millions of innocent people were killed in these catastrophes.

The consequences of World War I, the Great Depression in 1929, and World War II forced economists to rethink the global economic systems. Despite Smith's (1876) completely liberal, "invisible hand" and free market idea, Keynes (1936) defended the government intervention in economic crisis periods and suggested expansionary monetary policies and decreasing interest rates. According to Keynesian economics, supply is driven by demand and expenditures are more than savings in healthy economies. During recession periods, government spending even if it means going into debt is encouraged to create jobs and increase the purchasing power of the consumers. Those ideas are still valid but also debatable in terms of side effects such as creating high inflation rates.

Based on the link between the political and economic systems, there is a discussion about the supportive or contradictive relations of capitalism and democracy, which are believed the two most successful economic and political systems. While it is claimed that there is no developed democracy without capitalism, on the other hand, there are different states which have capitalist economic systems while they are ruled by different political systems other than democracy. 1976 Nobel Laureate Friedman (1962) describes capitalism as a prerequisite for political freedom.

After World War II, the world became two-polar: one side was represented by the Soviet Union and the other side by the US. Until the end of the 1980s, communism and socialism were dominant in the East-Bloc countries mainly represented by the Soviet Union. After the fall of the Berlin Wall in 1989 and the collapse of the Soviet Union in 1991, the states which were ruled under communism and socialism started following capitalist economic systems by adapting them to their own culture and perspectives. This situation created new forms of capitalism. In that context, Russian or in some respects the US type of oligarchic capitalism, the Chinese type of state capitalism, the Anglo-Saxon neoliberal aspect of capitalism, the Scandinavian welfare state approach, the East Asian type of capitalism, and Islamic capitalism taken place in the history of capitalist economic systems (Gramm, 1980; Merkel, 2014).

The word "oligarchy" was used by the Greek philosopher Aristotle to describe the ruling by a privileged few, in contrast to the aristocracy. Oligarchic capitalism is defined as maximizing short-term profit for small groups regardless of how much harm is done to people and the planet (Goerner, 2019). Hathaway (2015) mentions oligarchic capitalism as the root cause of the war in the Middle East and suggests replacing it with democratic socialism. Despite the long history of barons in the US, Russia is the first country that comes to mind when discussing oligarchic capitalism. In Russia, it started rising in the early periods of Gorbachev when state control of the economy was weakened. This created opportunities for people to become entrepreneurs, bankers, contractors, corporation owners, and even politicians. Compared to the barons of the US who have been playing important roles in money inflow to the US, the Russian oligarchs are observed to be transferring their wealth abroad (Hoffman, 2002). Rosser (2013) defines the Indonesian economic system as oligarchic capitalism based on the destructive interests of powerful politico-business families although it was developed by a combination of market-based policies and institutions, and direct forms of state involvement. Varma et al. (2016) also describe the economic system applied in India as oligarchic or crony capitalism.

Chomsky (1991) brings a different perspective to capitalism and defines every industrial society as one form of state capitalism. The term state capitalism was first used by Lenin in the 1920s to describe the New Economic Policy which suggests the combination of state-owned companies operated together with private businesses within a market economy supervised by the Communist Party. This constitutes the basic characteristics of China's state capitalism by replacing the Communist Party with an authoritarian and interventionist government (Kennedy & Blanchette, 2021). In the last decade, after applying authoritarian neoliberalism and crony capitalism, there is a debate about the positioning of the Turkish economic system under the state capitalism category after its strong political link with Russia and China.

The Anglo-Saxon model was defined as a capitalist model that emerged in the 1970s based on the Chicago school of economics structured based on the rules of Adam Smith. Low levels of regulation and taxation, the minimal intervention of the government on services, strong private property rights, and ease of doing business with low barriers to free trade are the main characteristics of Anglo-Saxon capitalism (Dore, 2000). The US, the UK, Canada, Australia, Ireland, and New Zealand are considered the main English-speaking countries which adopt the Anglo-Saxon type of capitalism model.

On the other hand, the Scandinavian welfare approach is defined as the combination of a market economy and economic efficiency which provides social benefits including state pensions and income distribution. It can be said that this approach is a combination of capitalism and socialism. In this model, the citizens trust the government, but the tax rates which fund the social services including education, childcare, and other services associated with human capital are high compared to the Anglo-Saxon model. The citizens of Sweden, Norway, Finland, Denmark, and Iceland, collectively known as the Nordic countries, have high living standards and low-income inequality by merging a free market approach with a generous welfare system (McWhinney, 2022). East Asian countries including Japan, South Korea, and Taiwan have a capitalist economic system where investments in certain industries are made by the government to stimulate the growth of specific sectors in the private sector. With its high rate of savings and investments, high educational standards, and export-oriented policy, it is more similar to the Scandinavian approach than the Anglo-Saxon economic model.

With its points of protection of private property and individual rights and commercial honesty, Islamic concepts of capitalism are defined differently from Western capitalism. While profit or private ownership is considered the main motive in Western secular capitalism, human equality, liberty, social and economic justice, and social welfare construct the main pillars of the Islamic form of capitalism (Elshurafa, 2012). On the other hand, the lifestyles of some wealthy Muslims' extravagance and extreme luxury are completely against Islamic moral values which emphasize the idea of "not going to sleep when your neighbor is hungry". While countries especially in the Middle East and North Africa, particularly the wealthy Gulf countries, have implemented Islamic capitalist systems, the concept of Islamic capitalism and its compatibility with Islamic rules is arguable and questionable, yet the term "Islamic capitalism" in that context is more likely to be defined as "Muslim Capitalism" as many scholars do not put the word "capitalism" and "Islam" together because of their different conceptual approach (Costagliola, 2021; Tripp, 2007).

There is a never-ending debate about which economic system is better, but no matter what model is used, the dominance of capitalism in the last century is indisputable. In that context, analyzing the link between the capitalist economic system and its application areas in the global finance industry is crucial.

To refresh our memories, we can briefly discuss the history of finance, the financial system, and the unique and common reasons for past financial crises which may give us important insights to know more about the flaws of the system and allow us to suggest an alternative one.

History of the Global Financial System

A financial system is defined as a set of institutions including banks, insurance companies, and stock exchanges which exist on firm, regional, and global levels. Funds are exchanged by borrowers, lenders, and investors to finance projects, either for consumption or for productive investments. The policymakers are focusing on maintaining global financial stability; on the other hand, the investors are seeking a return on their financial assets. The financial system plays an important role in economic growth, but it is also considered the source of instability, especially during crisis periods.

The first known financial system which was based on customs, social interactions, and hierarchy in the society dates to 9000 BC. Animals, grains, salt, and seashells were the first known forms of money which were later on replaced by precious metals. The first known form of currency, the Mesopotamian shekel, emerged nearly five thousand years ago. Then, silver and gold coins were used by Lydians and Ionians to pay armies. The use of gold and silver as monetary exchange dates to 3000 BC when gold specifically was used in Mesopotamia and ancient Egypt. The first gold coins were minted in Lydia (now Türkiye) during the Grecian age around the year 700 BC. Trade began as barter between individuals and households and developed into an organized form gradually. Egypt, China, India, and Rome were the main ancient civilizations where evidence of local and international trade was found. Shreni in ancient India was an early organization where the firms could independently enter contracts or own property (Alrifai, 2015).

The first paper money was used in China in the seventh century under Tang Dynasty. The banknotes were aimed to avoid the difficulties of transporting coins for large commercial transactions by the merchants. The banknotes and coins were used together until the notice of the central government of the economic advantages of printing banknotes and holding the only right over their issuance. At the same time, banknotes started to appear in China, and another form of paper currency appeared in the Islamic world during the same period banknotes appeared in China. This paper money was called the sakk (plural sukuk), also known as the promissory note which is similar to a cheque seen during the rise of the Islamic Umayyad Caliphate from the year 661 to 750. A sakk was defined as a document representing a contract or transfer of rights, obligations, or monies done in conformity with the Shariah (Islamic) rules. In the thirteenth century, paper money reached Europe through travelers such as Marco Polo. Promissory notes, which were considered the predecessor of the banknotes used today, were used by money traders of medieval Italy to reduce the risk and difficulties of transporting a large amount of money over long distances. The first European banknotes were issued in Sweden, Europe, by the Bank of Sweden in 1661. Trade bills of exchange which allowed the buyer to receive the goods from the seller by making the payment on a determined date in the future were also another method the merchants used in Europe in the Middle Ages. That bill could be redeemed in money at a discount before its due date. The buyers' reputations in that transaction were important, so this system was enlarged to be used in other towns through a network of merchant bankers (Alrifai, 2015).

Around 1633, goldsmith banking, which was brought over from Amsterdam, started being used as a new form of banking in England. Goldsmiths were providing gold storage and issued receipts that started to be used as a means of exchange. Some goldsmiths made deals in foreign and domestic coins, and that became the first step in the goldsmith's evolution toward modern banking. The history of banking dates to the Roman Empire around 1800 BC. Loans were offered and deposits were accepted in these banks, but with the collapse of the empire, these entities disappeared. Banks become reputable organizations within communities by the nineteenth century. The fact that the individuals didn't withdraw all their money at once taught banks to provide more loans than they had. The Bank of the United States, the first bank of the US, was established in 1791 and the Federal Reserve Bank in 1913. At first, many private commercial banks were allowed to issue banknotes, but later, the national governments were the only authorities that issued and controlled the banknotes (Kim, 2011; St.Louisfed.org, 2022).

In history, we see that the stronger empires had the power of trade and currency use. There was not a well-integrated global financial system until the nineteenth century. In the eighteenth century, gold, silver, and rarely copper was used, but after the UK suffered a silver shortage due to the Napoleonic War in 1815, they dropped the standard of silver, and in 1816, they established the gold standard. According to this new system, the banknotes were allowed to be redeemed for gold at the Bank of England at the rate of GBP 4.24 for one ounce of gold. This system allowed the bank to print only a limited number of banknotes and brought stability and trust to trade which helped to increase global trade. Global trade, together with the industrial revolution, increased the mobility of goods and people, but at the same time, protectionism also started in response to globalization. The capital flow kept moving fast, and in addition to London and Paris, the rise in capital flows created new finance centers such as New York and Berlin (Cassis & Bussiere, 2005). World War I started in the Middle of Europe and was widespread all around the world. Except for the US, the war affected the global economy negatively. During the war, a sharp fall in Gross Domestic Product (GDP), a rise in inflation, and food shortage changed the political system and power in Europe and Russia. Gold export was also affected by the war, and trade embargoes applied on gold export by many countries dropped the gold standard which resulted in floating currencies (Lozada, 2005).

When the war broke out in Europe in the summer of 1914, the New York Stock Exchange was closed for more than three months. The US did not enter the war during the first two and a half years of the combat, and they increased their export from USD 2.4 billion to USD 6.2 billion in 1917 by selling cotton, wheat, rubber, machinery, and raw materials mainly to Great Britain, France, and Russia. The unemployment rate of the US also dropped from 16.4% in 1914 to 6.3% in 1916 and the US economy grew 44 months in line and opened the path to becoming the new economic power of the world (Jefferson, 1917).

On the other hand, Great Britain was negatively affected by the war. During the war, they spent more than GBP 3 billion, and soon after the war ended, they increased the taxes to 25% and had to get loans from the US (Crafts, 2014). The war resulted in the replacement of the UK with the US in terms of world economic power.

After World War I, in addition to Great Britain, many countries, especially Germany, suffered from hyperinflation and returned to the gold standard, but this return did not last long. The stock market crash in October 1929 in the US triggered the Great Depression and the devaluation of gold in the 1930s due to the Great Depression ended the gold standard period. US President Herbert Hoover signed the Smoot–Hawley Tariff Act in 1930 and raised import tariffs on goods. Soon after the Smoot-Hawley Tariff Act, the same tariffs were applied on US goods by the US trading partners which affected global trade negatively. High-interest rates and tightening money supply due to the gold reserves were also considered the major negative impacts of the Great Depression which lasted a decade and resulted in World War II (Duignan, 2023).

World War II was a bigger disaster with a loss of more than 60 million people, compared to World War I. Before the war ended, a conference was held in Bretton Woods, New Hampshire, in the US to design a new financial system. Under the new system, countries would fix their exchange rates to the US Dollar and the US Dollar would be convertible to gold at USD 35 per ounce with a 1% fluctuation range. The US Dollar became the reserve currency of the world, and any country wishing to receive gold would first convert its currency to US Dollar. In order to support the Bretton Woods system by providing cooperation among members and support them in emergency cases, International Monetary Fund (IMF) and to help rebuild Europe and Japan World Bank (the former name was

International Bank for Reconstruction and Development (IBRD)) was founded in 1944. Soon after the war ended with great destruction, the United Nations was established in 1945 (FED History, 1944).

All the attempts to create a strong financial system somehow resulted in many local and financial crises. To understand the current problems of the system and develop a sustainable system, it is critical to analyze the reasons for the past financial crisis, how the governments and central banks reacted, and what their consequences were. Chapter 3 focuses on these main issues.

References

Alrifai, T. (2015). *Islamic finance and the new financial system: An ethical approach to preventing future financial crises*. Wiley. ISBN: 978-1-118-99063-6.

Balaam, D. N., & Dillman, B. (2014). *Introduction to international political economy* (5th ed.). Pearson.

Cassis, Y., & Bussiere, E. (2005). *London and Paris as international financial centres in the twentieth century*. Oxford University Press. ISBN 9780191533471

Chomsky, N. (1991). *On capitalism, Noam Chomsky interviewed by David Finkel The Detroit Metro Times*. https://chomsky.info/1991_02/. Last Accessed on March 20, 2022.

Costagliola, A. (2021). *Moral contradictions? The rich kids of Islamic capitalism*. https://blogs.lse.ac.uk/mec/2021/04/15/moral-contradictions-the-rich-kids-of-islamic-capitalism/. Last Accessed on January 12, 2023.

Crafts, N. (2014). *Walking wounded: The British economy in the aftermath of World War I*. https://cepr.org/voxeu/columns/walking-wounded-british-economy-aftermath-world-war-i. Last Accessed on January 12, 2023.

Delanty, G. (2019). The future of capitalism: Trends, scenarios and prospects for the future. *Journal of Classical Sociology, 19*(1), 10–26.

Dore, R. (2000). *Stock market capitalism: Welfare capitalism: Japan and Germany versus the Anglo-Saxons*. Oxford University Press.

Duignan, B. (2023). *Smoot-Hawley tariff act 1930*. https://www.britannica.com/topic/Smoot-Hawley-Tariff-Act. Last Accessed on January 12, 2023.

Elshurafa, D. (2012). Islamic capitalism—An imminent reality or a hopeful possibility for Islamic finance? *Arab Law Quarterly, 26*(3), 339–360.

Federalreservehistory.com. (1944). *Creation of the Bretton Woods system*. https://www.federalreservehistory.org/essays/bretton-woods-created. Last Accessed on January 12, 2023.

Friedman, M. (1962). *Capitalism and freedom*. University of Chicago Press.

Ganshof, F. L. (1952). Feudalism. Longmans, Green.
Goerner, S. J. (2019). The collapse of oligarchic capitalism and the rise of regenerative learning: How the science of energy systems clarifies what's happening today and what comes next. *World Futures, 75*(3), 135–162. doi:https://doi.org/10.1080/02604027.2019.1586452
Gramm, W. S. (1980). Oligarchic capitalism: Arguable reality, thinkable future? *Journal of Economic Issues, 14*(2), 411–432. https://doi.org/10.1080/00213624.1980.11503753
Gronow, J. (2016). *On the formation of marxism: Karl Kautsky's theory of capitalism, the marxism of the second international and Karl Marx's critique of political economy*. Brill.
Hathaway, W. T. (2015). *The root cause of war is oligarchic capitalism*. https://www.middleeasteye.net/opinion/root-cause-war-oligarchic-capitalism. Last Accessed on January 10, 2023.
Hayek, F. (1944). *The road to serfdom*. Routledge Press. ISBN 0-226-32061-8
Hoffman, D. E. (2002). The oligarchs: Wealth and power in the new Russia. *Public Affairs*, 9781586482022. ISBN10: 1586482025.
Jefferson, M. (1917). Our trade in the great war. *Geographical Review, 3*(6), 474–480. https://doi.org/10.2307/207691
Kennedy, S., & Blanchette, J. (2021). *Chinese state capitalism: Diagnosis and prognosis. A report of the CSIS trustee chair in Chinese business and economics and Freeman Chair in China studies*. https://www.csis.org/events/chinese-state-capitalism-diagnosis-and-prognosis-report-launch. Last Accessed on January 10, 2023.
Keynes, J. M. (1936). *The general theory of employment, interest, and money*. Palgrave Macmillan.
Kim, J. (2011). How modern bank originated: The London goldsmith-bankers' institutionalization of trust Young Gee Fitinane. *Business History. Social Science Research Network, 53*, 939–959. https://doi.org/10.1080/00076791.2011.578132
Lenin, V. (1916). Imperialism, the highest stage of capitalism. *Lenin's Selected Works, Progress Publishers, 1*, 667–766.
Lozada, C. (2005). *The economics of world war I*. National Bureau of Economic Research. https://www.nber.org/digest/jan05/economics-world-war-i#:~:text=Rockoff%20estimates%20the%20total%20cost,20%20percent%20in%20money%20creation. Last Accessed on January 12, 2023.
Marx, K. (1867). *Das capital*. Progress Publishers, USSR.
McWhinney. J. (2022). *The Nordic model: Pros and cons*. https://www.investopedia.com/articles/investing/100714/nordic-model-pros-and-cons.asp. Last Accessed on January 12, 2023.
Merkel, W. (2014). Is capitalism compatible with democracy? *Zeitschrift Für Vergleichende Politikwissenschaft, 8*(2), 109–128.

Rosser, A. (2013). The politics of economic liberalization in Indonesia. *Routledge*. https://doi.org/10.4324/9781315028927

Rosser, M. V., & Barkley, J., Jr. (2003). *Comparative economics in a transforming world economy*. MIT Press. ISBN 978-0262182348.

Said, E. W. (1993). *Culture and imperialism*. Knopf. ISBN 0-679-7504-1.

Smith, A. (1876). *The wealth of nations*. Bibliomania.com Ltd.

St.Louisfed.org. (2022). *History and purpose of the federal reserve*. https://www.stlouisfed.org/in-plain-english/history-and-purpose-of-the-fed#:~:text=What%20led%20to%20the%20creation,to%20address%20these%20banking%20panics. Last Accessed on January 12, 2023.

Tripp, C. (2007). *Islam and the moral economy: The challenge of capitalism* (1st ed.). Cambridge University Press.

Varma, A., Hu, B., & Bloomquist, L. (2016). Family oligarchies and crony capitalism in India. In N. Khatri & A. K. Ojha (Eds.), *Crony capitalism in India. Palgrave studies in Indian management*. Palgrave Macmillan. doi:https://doi.org/10.1007/978-1-137-58287-4_8.

CHAPTER 3

Financial Crises: From 1929 Great Depression to 2020 Great Lockdown

The world has experienced many financial and economic crises in the last century. Both terms are confused very often. While the decline in the values of financial assets which affects the investment and financial markets is the cause of a financial crisis, in the economic crisis which covers a financial crisis, the economy slumps overall and entire economic activities are affected negatively. Considerable changes in volumes of national credit and asset prices, serious balance sheet problems, problems in financial intermediary activities, and large-scale government support on liquidation and recapitalization are the signs of a financial crisis that may lead to an unsustainable economy. The financial crises are categorized as quantitative (currency crisis and sudden stop crisis) and qualitative (foreign debt crisis and banking crisis) crises (Claessens & Köse, 2013; Reinhart & Rogoff, 2009).

Currency crises occur because of the diminution of the foreign currency reserves of the central bank, caused by a sudden shift of the demands of the market stakeholders from local currency assets to assets in foreign currency. A currency crisis also occurs when a speculative attack on a country's currency results in a devaluation or severe depreciation, or when the central bank is forced to protect the currency by selling large amounts of reserves or raising interest rates significantly. A sudden stop crisis, also named as capital account or balance-of-payments crisis, is defined as a large and unexpected decrease in international capital inflows

L. Sümer, *The World Economy and Financial System*,
https://doi.org/10.1007/978-3-031-27530-2_3

or a sudden reversal in sum capital flows to a country together with a sharp rise in its credit increases.

On the other hand, in a debt crisis, a country is unable to pay its public and/or private external debts. Countries postpone their liabilities or restructure their debts when they face difficulties in rolling over foreign debts and finding new foreign loans. Debt crises occur when borrowers fail to pay their debts, or when lenders try to repay existing loans and fail to make new loans because they think there is a possibility of default. Debt crises can be caused by private or public debt. Risk perceptions that the public sector will not be able to meet its repayment obligations may lead to a sharp decline in private capital inflows and a currency crisis.

A banking crisis refers to a situation in which commercial banks fall into liquidity problems and subsequently go bankrupt, as the maturity of their debts cannot be extended, or they cannot meet a sudden demand for money withdrawal. General macroeconomic disorders, microeconomic disruptions, and regional crises in public-dominated systems are considered the three main signs of a banking crisis. The failure of a single bank may not always shake the entire banking system; however, in proportion to the size of the share of the bank in the system, a bank crisis may likely affect the entire financial system and economy and turn into a systemic crisis.

From the 1929 Great Depression to the 2020 COVID-19 pandemic-based economic crisis also named as Great Lockdown, the world has experienced financial and economic crises more often. Sometimes financial crisis reminds us of past episodes of previous crises in some respects, and sometimes an extension such as a decision or a move creates a new one.

1929 Great Depression

It was October 24, 1929, when the stock market crashed in the US which triggered a global economic crisis, the Great Depression. World War I resulted in considerable wealth for the US and Western Europe. The capital accumulated in the US was invested in real estate and land purchases. In the Roaring Twenties, a rising economy built an era of mass consumerism in the US (Soule, 1947). The gross national product of the US grew at an average annual rate of 4.7% between 1922 and 1929, and the unemployment rate dropped from 6.7% to 3.2% which resulted in a doubling of the total wealth mostly experienced by the richest Americans. The investors invested in lands, but after the speculative rises, the land prices declined, and the capital was directed to the New York Stock Exchange. Investing in the stock markets by individual Americans started. From 1922 to 1929, the stock market values increased by 218% at a rate of 20% a year (Srinivas, 2018).

An increase in consumption more than affording, overproduction of the companies to keep up with the demand, and the rise in speculation in the stock market including the creation of subsidiaries offering their securities or even selling own stocks by brokers due to weak regulations kept the stock markets climbing until it crashed on October 24 (Field & Kim, 2022). The extreme rise of stock prices and the rupture from reality caused the Federal Reserve to raise interest rates from 7 to 15% in the summer of 1929 to stem the speculative increase. Even before the great crash, a smaller stock crash occurred on March 25, 1929, which was recovered. Volatile markets in September had also resulted in a large sell-off of stocks in mid-October, and on October 24, named as Black Thursday, the American stock market crashed 11% at the opening bell, 12% on October 28 (Black Monday), and another 11% on October 29 (Black Tuesday) when the market saw another 11% drop. Despite a partial recovery on Wednesday and thereafter until April 17, 1930, billions of dollars had been gone and thousands of investors were ruined. From April 17, 1930, until July 8, 1932, the market lost 89% of its value and as shown in Fig. 3.1, it was November 1954 when the Dow Jones index could return to its pre-crash value (Richardson, 2022).

The collapse of the stock market was followed by the collapse of the banks. 744 US banks failed during the first 10 months of 1930. By 1933, 15 million Americans lost their jobs, and 20,000 companies went bankrupt. The enactment of the Glass–Steagall Act of 1933 separated commercial and investment banking activities to avoid a repeat of 1929 by separating the risks of bank types (Alrifai, 2015; Srinivas, 2018).

Within three years after the first stock market shock, the global GDP fell by around 15%. Although recovery started in some economies by the mid-1930s, the negative consequences of the Great Depression including the decline in income, prices, tax revenues, and profits continued until the beginning of World War II (Garraty, 1986). While the unemployment rate in the US rose to 23%, international trade fell by more than 50% (Frank & Bernanke, 2007). Industrial production fell by 46% in the US and 41% in Germany, respectively. While France was the leading country where the

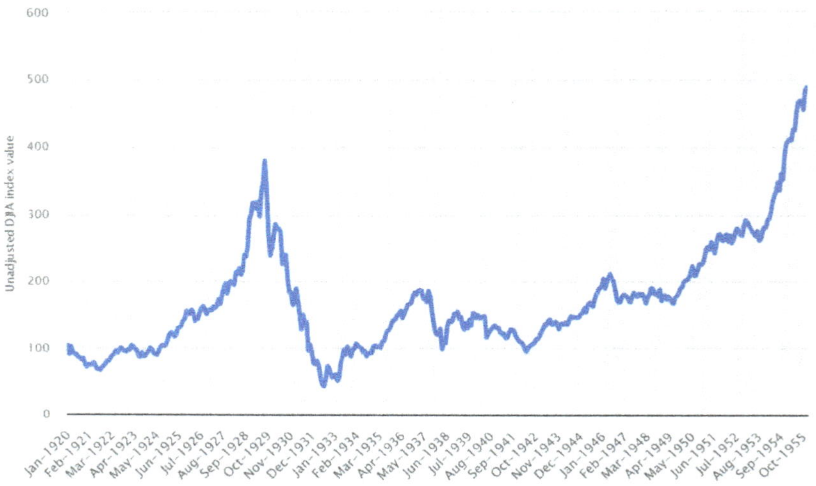

Fig. 3.1 Monthly value of the Dow Jones Industrial Average (DJIA) from January 1920 to December 1955 (Statista, 2022a)

wholesale prices fell by 34%, the UK, the US, and Germany had 33%, 32%, and 29% decline in wholesale prices between 1929 and 1932 (Blum et al., 1970).

On June 17, 1930, the Smoot–Hawley Tariff Act, which is considered the most disastrous act of congress, was passed in the US. Although it was aimed to protect the American economy from the negative consequences of an economic crisis, it extremely failed. While some economists consider the Act as the reason for the Depression, some others think, at least, it worsened the consequences due to the sharp decline in international trade and economic activities after the Act passed in congress (Eichengreen, 1992). Europe responded to this Act by declaring a trade war, and within three years, US exports dropped by 60% (Alrifai, 2015).

Starting with the UK in September 1931 and followed by Japan and Scandinavian countries, the gold standard was left by 35 countries during the Great Depression. While Italy and the US left the standard in 1932, France, Poland, Belgium, and Switzerland kept the standard until 1936. The countries which left the standard earlier had a faster recovery compared to the ones which left later. On the other hand, China, which had a silver standard, was not affected by the depression (Bernanke, 2004).

In summary, due to the excess consumption trend, speculative boom in the 1920s, the stock markets crash in 1929, oversupply and overproduction problems, decrease in demand and increase in unemployment, wrong decisions of Federal Reserve such as increasing the interest rates, limited governmental response, and decrease in trade due to the ill-tariffs, the Great Depression lasted a decade and ended with the start of the World War II where the unemployment rates fell due to the employment in the military industry.

The Oil Crisis 1973 and 1979

The oil crisis is an important example of the impact of politics on the economy. As shown in Fig. 3.2, oil prices have always been very sensitive to political movements (Statista, 2022b). Also known as the 1973 energy crisis and oil shock, the 1973 oil crisis increased energy prices around 4 times and resulted in fuel shortages in the US within 6 months. In a post-Bretton-Woods period, where inflation was rising in the US, the main reason for the crisis is accepted as the embargo applied by Arab oil-producing countries, known as the Organization of the Petroleum Exporting Countries (OPEC), in response to US support of Israel during the 1973 Yom Kippur War (Smith, 2006). Canada, Japan, the Netherlands, the UK, and the US were the countries embargo applied. Although the embargo was lifted in March 1974, its global economic consequences including high inflation, stagnation, recession, and stagflation thereafter were very long-lasting. The effect of oil shock was combined with the negative impacts of the post-Vietnam war, and the unemployment rate in the US rose to 9.1% and industrial production fell by 15%. The UK experienced a banking crisis, and within two years, the Dow Jones Industrial Average (DIJA), Hong Kong's Hang Seng Index, and London Stock Exchange's FT30 Index lost their values by 45%, 83%, and 73%, respectively (Hayes, 2022).

The second oil crisis was initiated by the Iranian revolution after a 7% decline in global oil production within the last quarter of 1978 and the beginning of 1979 which resulted in an increase in oil prices from USD 13 per barrel to USD 34 per barrel in mid-1980. Crude oil buyers panicked in the US due to the loss of production and increased demand

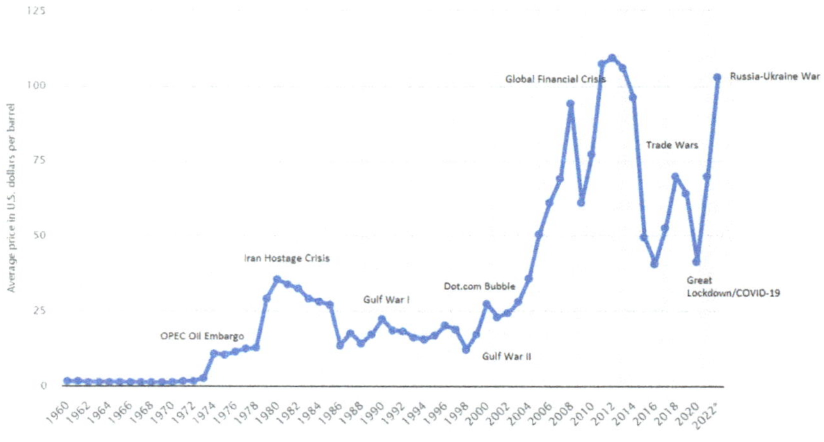

Fig. 3.2 Oil prices since 1960 (Statista, 2022b)

to cover their current and future needs. This situation raised the prices to USD 50 per barrel in the spot market.

The oil crisis of the 1970s resulted in the exploration and production of new oil reserves to decrease the dependency of countries on existing producers. The North Sea, Alaska, and Mexico were already discovered in the 1960s, but the construction of the pipelines was rushed after the first oil crisis in 1973. Additional reserves were discovered in Mexico Gulf which helped to increase the production. While production was increasing, a global recession in the early 1980s decreased the demand and the prices went down to USD 12 per barrel in 1986 (Gross, 2019). The effect of the oil crises lasted more than a decade with high inflation and unemployment rates until the FED's decision to increase the interest rates by 20% which resulted in a decrease in inflation rates in 1983 (Alrifai, 2015; Mishkin & White, 2002). It was 1987 when the FT30 got recovered from the crash just before Black Monday on Wall Street. On the other hand, the DJIA did not get recovered until 1993. Figure 3.2 shows the oil prices since 1960 (Statista, 2022b).

1980 Latin American Debt Crisis

Life is full of dilemmas. Saudi Arabia and the US had an agreement in 1945 and USD was set as the standard currency used to pay for oil globally, which was also accepted by other oil-exporting countries. Excess accumulated dollars gained from the oil sales that were not spendable were called as petrodollars which came into existence following the elimination of the gold standard in 1971 (Amadeo, 2022). After the 1973 oil crisis, OPEC countries deposited their petrodollars in US banks for protection and spending later. The US banks had more money than they could invest. This money was borrowed by Latin American countries including Argentina, Brazil, and Mexico to grow their economies and to be invested in infrastructure projects. These investments increased the outstanding debt of these countries rapidly. In the early 1970s, after the collapse of the Bretton Woods agreement, global economic policies shifted to loosen monetary policies which created an inflation problem globally. From 1970 to 1978, the total outstanding debt rose from USD 29 billion to USD 159 billion and reached USD 327 billion in 1982 (Federal Deposit Insurance Corporation, FDIC, 2022). After Paul Volcker's presidency of FED, the US increased the interest rates severely and 27 countries including Mexico went into default. This situation created a collapse risk for many US banks including Citibank. The Latin American debt crisis is also known as "the Ladecada Perdita - Lost Decade".

At the end of the 1980s, Brady Plan was implemented for highly indebted emerging economies. Several restructuring and recovery plans attempted by IMF and World Bank failed due to strict conditions applied. The new Secretary of the Treasury of the US, Nicholas Brady, announced that the only way to deal with the sovereign debt crisis was to support the banks to participate in "voluntary" debt-reduction programs. According to the Brady Plan, some portions of debt would be erased to ensure the rest of the debt to be paid on schedule. 18 countries accepted the Brady Plan and one-third of (USD 61 billion) outstanding debt was forgiven which also saved many US banks (Alrifai, 2015; Ertürk & Yilmaz, 2014; FDIC, 2022; Statista, 2022b; Vasquez, 1996).

1987 Black Monday

From August 1982 to August 1987, the Dow Jones Industrial Average (DJIA) rose from 776 to 2,722 to its peak value. The indices of the nineteen largest markets in the world rose to 296% on average during the same period. On Monday, October 19, 1987, the global stock markets including 23 major world markets suddenly, unexpectedly, and severely crashed by more than 20%, and in some countries such as Hong Kong, Australia, and Singapore more than 40% with an estimated loss of USD 1.71 trillion worldwide. This crisis is named as Black Monday or Black Tuesday (for Australia and New Zealand because of their time zone) (Bates, 1991; Roll, 1988). The Black Monday crisis shows similarities to Great Depression in terms of the rapid rise of the stock markets. Greed and fraud were also additional factors behind the crash as the Securities and Exchange Commission (SEC) and other agencies investigated many individual traders and companies. FED kept offering liquidity to the market and which is believed brought confidence to the market and helped the recovery within the following two years. After Black Monday, circuit breakers and trade-clearing protocols were developed by the regulators to avoid panic selling (Bernhardt & Eckblad, 2013).

The US Savings and Loans Crisis (1989–1991)

Debt, inflation, and interest rate relations have always been important discussions among economists. In the last quarter of 1979, FED increased the interest rates from 9.5% to 12% to reduce inflation. A cooperative venture established in the UK as a "building society" which is named S&L or "thrift" in the US was a financial institution that accepts saving deposits of individual members and makes mortgage, car, and other personal loans to them. The increased interest rate exceeded the fixed interest rates applied for the loans that S&Ls had issued which resulted in a decrease in the capital flow of the deposits and savings accounts members. As a result of the imbalance between the borrowing and lending rates, an asset-liability mismatch problem arose, and one-third of S&Ls became insolvent. The laws enacted in the early 1980s by the congress that enabled the S&Ls to extend their products including adjustable-rate mortgages grew the S&Ls with a 56% growth rate (more than the growth rate of banks which was 24%) between 1982 and 1985, but beginning from 1986 until 1995, 1,043 out of 3,234 S&L in the US failed and the newly established Resolution Trust Corporation (RTC) took up their responsibilities (Black, 2005).

Fraud was also one of the reasons for the savings and loans crisis. Instead of closing insolvent S&Ls, the regulators allowed them to survive by supporting them and some S&Ls operated Ponzi schemes and millions of dollars were invested in junk bonds (Alrifai, 2015). The crisis ended when the RTC was officially closed at the end of 1995. The total worth of the S&Ls closed was USD 407 billion and the crisis cost taxpayers more than USD 124 billion (Curry & Shibut, 2000). Once again, the S&L crisis exhibited the destroying impacts of rising debt-interest rates-inflation rates spiral on the economy.

1992 Collapse of Japanese Asset Price Bubble

Real estate and construction industries have always been important sectors for economies. The 2008 Global Financial Crisis, which will also be discussed later in this chapter, was triggered by the defaults of mortgage loans. Japan experienced a real estate and stock market bubble from 1986 to 1991 which resulted in stagnation in Japan in early 1992. The rapid rise of asset prices and overheated economic activity and uncontrolled money supply and credit expansion due to the monetary easing policy were the main reasons for such stagnation (Okina et al., 2001). By 1991, the commercial, residential, and industrial land prices increased 302.9%, 180.5%, and 162%, respectively. The total value of real estate reached 4 times the total real estate value of the US (Alrifai, 2015). After the 5th decision of the monetary tightening of the Bank of Japan, the asset prices began to fall, but the decline of the economy which lasted more than a decade resulted in a rapid rise of non-performing loans. Equity values fell 60% from late 1989 to August 1992, while land values declined 70% by 2001. In contrast to its 1980s performance which grew at an average annual growth rate of 3.89%, from 1991 to 2003, the Japanese economy grew only 1.14% annually, far behind many industrialized nations (Nielsen, 2022). Similar to the Latin American debt crisis, the Japanese asset price bubble is also named "the Lost Decade for Japan".

1994 Mexican Peso Crisis

After facing a serious economic crisis during the 1980s, the Mexican economy was in a recovery period in the early 1990s. Foreign investors were attracted after the Mexican treasury issued short-term debt instruments in local currency with a guarantee of repayment in USD. In 1994, the North American Free Trade Agreement (NAFTA) took effect among the US, Mexico, and Canada to ease trade, increase the trade volume, and improve investment relations among them. 1994 was also a year of political instability for Mexico which put pressure on the Mexican economy. An increase in the value of the peso against the USD due to the Mexican central bank intervention to maintain the Mexican peso's peg to the USD resulted in a trade deficit. The overvalued peso started a capital outflow from Mexico to the US. Instead of rising the interest rates, the Mexican Central Bank purchased its treasury securities to maintain the money supply and the dollar reserves of the central bank declined. On December 20, 1994, the Mexican government devaluated Mexican Peso against the USD and the capital flight from Mexico started (Eun & Resnick, 2011).

The central bank raised interest rates, but the cost of borrowing increased and the Mexican economy faced a default. The free float decision did not stop the depreciation of the peso and the inflation rose to 52%. The mutual funds liquidated their Mexican and other developing market assets which turned out the crisis into a global issue. In coordination with IMF and together with the support of G7 and the Bank for International Settlements, a USD 50 billion recovery aid was organized by the US in January 1995. The Mexican economy started getting recovered in 1996 and growing again, but a serious recession, increase in poverty and unemployment, and collapse of several of Mexico's banks along with extensive mortgage defaults were experienced in the aftermath of the crisis (Alrifai, 2015).

1997 Asian Financial Crisis

Another global crisis sparked by a capital outflow was recorded in the financial crisis history as the 1997 Asian Financial crisis, as it hit many East and Southeast Asian economies. On July 2, 1997, the Thai baht collapsed and due to the inadequacy of the foreign currency, the Thai government had to leave the baht on a free float, which also resulted in a capital flight, as well as a burden of foreign debt in Thailand. In the late 1980s and early

1990s, Thailand, Malaysia, Indonesia, Singapore, and South Korea experienced 8% to 12% GDP growth rates. Before the crisis, Southeast Asian economies were maintaining high-interest rates and fixed exchange rates which were attracting a capital inflow and increasing asset prices. The crisis had a contagion effect and the currencies of most of Southeast Asia and later South Korea and Japan depreciated, the stock markets crashed, and private debt increased (Yamazawa, 1998). The economies started getting recovered after the IMF's USD 40 billion programs to stabilize the currencies of the economies affected (Worldbank, 2022). However, the crisis had political consequences. For instance, Indonesian President Suharto resigned after ruling the country for 30 years. An overextension of credit and too much debt accumulation had caused another financial crisis. The crisis also had a negative impact in terms of creating hesitation about investing in emerging economies and economies slowed down. Toward the end of 1998, oil prices fell to as low as USD 11 per barrel which was considered one of the reasons for the 1998 Russian ruble crisis (Zhang, 2013).

1998 Russian Ruble Crisis

As an extension of the Asian financial crisis, the oil price shock affected many oil exporters including Russia which was struggling with internal political and economic problems including the ongoing war in Chechnya, debate about the internal politics regarding the dismissal of the prime minister by President Boris Yeltsin, the decrease in foreign currency reserves, and the impact of the coal miner's strike due to unpaid wages on internal politics (Alrifai, 2015; Pain, 2021). Before the crisis, the central bank policy about the Russian Ruble was semi-floating (floating peg) which means the fluctuation of the ruble against the USD was let free within an accepted range, and in the case, there was a risk of dropping out of the band, and the central bank would spend foreign reserves to keep the ruble stable. Indeed, the Russian economy was in the process of transformation after continuing decline resulting in a cumulative drop of GDP by more than 40% between 1989 and 1996. The country also faced high inflation in this period, and the 1995 IMF support program which focused on strict monetary control had a positive impact on the exchange rate stability but negatively affected the economic activity. The privatization program between 1992 and 1994 resulted in capital accumulation by smaller groups that were not invested in for the use of the economy but rather parked in safe havens, luxury goods, or real estate.

The inadequacy of legal frameworks such as the enforcement of contracts, transparency, or insufficient regulations was the main risk to the sustainable economy in Russia (Akyüz & Rayment, 1998). In addition to the drawbacks of the fiscal system of the country, the interest and exchange rate policies were the main points that initiated the Russian financial crisis in the summer of 1998. On August 17, 1998, the ruble was devaluated by the Russian government, defaulted on domestic debt, and declared a 90-day moratorium for foreign debt (Chiodo & Obyang, 2002). On September 2, 1998, the "floating peg" policy was abandoned, the ruble started floating freely and lost two-thirds of its value, and the value of one USD reached 21 rubles. The inflation in Russia reached 84% and many banks were shut because of the crisis. The oil prices increased during 1999 and 2000 sharply, and that helped the Russian economy get recovered very fast by running a trade surplus (Stiglitz, 2003).

2000 Dot-Com Bubble

Technological developments created web browsers in 1993. This development increased the number of entrepreneurs in the technology area. World Wide Web (www) was a platform for new start-ups to reach and attract new customers. Low-interest rates in 1998–1999 accelerated the establishment of start-up companies. By the late 1990s, these new companies were making their first initial public offerings (IPOs) and experiencing a sharp rise in their stock prices. As shown in Fig. 3.3, from 1995 until its peak in March 2000, the Nasdaq Composite stock market index rose 400%. In 2000, the dot-com bubble burst, and many dot-com start-ups went out of business. The Nasdaq Composite stock market index fell 78% from its peak by October 2002, gave up all its gains during the bubble and USD 5 trillion market capitalization evaporated (Alrifai, 2015).

Pets.com, Webvan, Boo.com, Worldcom, NorthPoint Communications, Global Crossing, and many other online shopping and communication companies failed and shut down. Amazon was one of the companies which were able to survive but lost large portions of its market capitalization, and Cisco Systems lost 80% of its stock value (Powell, 2021). Meanwhile, FED raised interest rates various times which was criticized as the cause of the dot-com bubble crash. On the other hand, Krugman

Fig. 3.3 NASDAQ Composite Index from 1995 to 2004 (Macrotrends, 2023)

(2009) thought that the reason for rising the interest rates was because of the cleaning up of the mess afterward of the crisis. This crisis was equity-based, and as banks were not providing loans to start-ups, little debt was involved. The start-up companies were mostly funded by venture capital companies and individuals buying shares in the stock market. Although it took many years for Nasdaq to reach its peak in 2000, by 2003, the economy was recovered.

2001 September 11 Attacks

On September 11, 2001, four airplanes were hijacked by terrorists in the US and two of them crashed into the Twin Towers of the World Trade Center in New York City, and the third plane into the Pentagon (the headquarters of the US military) in Arlington County, Virginia. The fourth plane was planned to hit a federal government building in Washington, D.C., but passengers in the airplane prevented it and crashed in a field. 2,976 people were killed in the terrorist attack which resulted in at least USD 10 billion in infrastructure and property damage as well as serious harm to the New York City economy and global markets. The US economy was in a transition period when the attack occurred. The unemployment rate hit 4.9% in August 2001 from a low of 3.9% late in 2000, and there was a possibility of a recession risk (Makinen, 2002). After the attack, the stock exchanges did not open until September 17. On the reopening day, the Dow Jones Industrial Average (DJIA) fell 7.1% (Barnhart, 2001). By the end of the week, the DJIA had fallen 14.3%, at the time its greatest one-week point decline in history. In the last quarter of 2021, 430,000 job-months were lost in New York City, and the government provided USD 11.2 billion in immediate assistance to New York City in 2021 and USD 10.5 billion in the first quarter of 2002 (Dolfman & Wasser, 2004). The attack had political consequences, and the US declared war on Iraq and Afghanistan, increased the spending on homeland security, and spent at least USD 5 trillion (Klein, 2011).

2008 Global Financial Crisis

Global financial crisis (GFC) was noted as one of the most severe economic crises of the early twenty-first century and the most devastating one since the 1929 Great Depression. The GFC was triggered by the collapse of the mortgage system in the US which turned out to be one of the most serious financial crises in history. The collapse of the mortgage-backed securities (MBS), as well as derivatives linked to the MBS, was the sparking of the failure of many financial institutions including the bankruptcy of Lehman Brothers in 2008, the initiation of the great recession worldwide, and the rapid increase in unemployment rates in the US (Williams, 2010). According to the report of the National Commission on the Causes of the Financial and Economic Crisis in the US published in 2011, damaged stability of the nation's financial markets due to the extensive failures in financial regulation and supervision, dramatic failures of corporate governance and risk management at many systemically important financial institutions, a combination of extreme borrowing, risky investments, and lack of transparency, insufficient preparation and the inconsistent response of the government which increased uncertainty and panic in the financial markets, a systemic failure in accountability and ethics, collapsing mortgage-lending standards and the mortgage securitization, over-the-counter derivatives, and the failures of credit rating agencies were listed as the main causes of the crisis and the report adds that the crisis was avoidable.

The story of the crisis backs to the decision of the FED about decreasing the interest rates in 2001. Before the dot-com bubble, FED had started raising interest rates in 1998 to cool down the rapid increase in stock markets, but as a result, the economy slowed down and faced a recession risk. In 2001, the FED began decreasing its discount rate, as low as 1.75% in December 2001. The 9/11 attack was also another reason for that decision to prevent any risk of recession. As exhibited in Fig. 3.4, the rates fell to 1% in July 2003. Beginning in 2000, the decline in interest rates dropped the mortgage rates and increased the size of the home refinancing volume from USD 460 billion to USD 2.8 trillion within 3 years. In parallel, home prices started increasing and in some areas such as Sacramento skyrocketed two and a half times within 5 years. Housing starts also increased, and homeownership hit a record of 69.2% in 2004. The purchasers aimed to invest in housing instead of living in it and they were selling the units as they get a higher price. In 2004, FED observed the overheating in the housing market and started increasing the interest rates until 2006 when the housing prices peaked in. The economy was growing, and the unemployment rate was at its lower level, 4.4% in October 2006.

Banks and specialized mortgage companies were providing loans, and once a mortgage was issued, it would be deposited to one of the government-backed agencies or sold to a Wall Street company. One of the

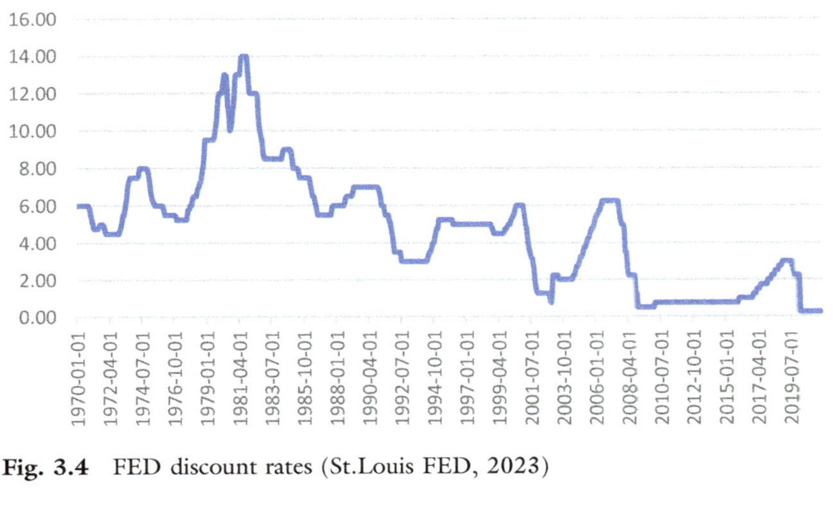

Fig. 3.4 FED discount rates (St.Louis FED, 2023)

critical issues about mortgage applications was the non-use of credit scores and income verification which means many buyers who normally won't qualify for a mortgage were getting a loan easily. Additionally, adjustable-rate mortgages (ARMs) which were issued with lower rates fixed from one to seven years and then rise to the market rates after the expiry date was also increasing the risk of buying a more expensive house due to the low rates offered. "Subprime mortgages", which were designed for individuals who do not have a regular income or no credit history, were not requiring borrowers to prove their income and very few documents were asked to approve such mortgages. The rate of the subprime mortgage over the total outstanding mortgages was 23.5%. Federal National Mortgage Association (Fannie Mae) and the Federal Home Loan Mortgage Corporation (Freddie Mac), which were buying mortgages in the secondary market, pooling, and selling them as a mortgage-backed security to investors on the open market, were increasing the supply of money available for mortgage lending by providing repayment guarantees.

In 2007, the rules of the game started changing. The announcement of Freddie Mac about stopping buying subprime mortgages, the bankruptcy of New Century Financial, a subprime mortgage lender, the liquidation of two hedge funds that invested in subprime mortgages by Bear Stearns, and the bankruptcy of American Home Mortgage Investment which specialized in adjustable-rate mortgages (ARMs) were the strong signs of the crisis in 2007. The number of borrowers who were unable to pay their mortgages started a decline in housing prices. Losses started in government-sponsored enterprises (GSEs) including Fannie Mae and Freddie Mac which had financed the US housing market with USD 6 trillion, half of the size of the total mortgage financing. After the yearly decline in the shares of Fannie Mae and Freddie Mac by 90% in August 2008, on September 7, the government nationalized the GSEs, and the Lehman Brothers failed a week after and triggered a chain failure in the markets (Alrifai, 2015). A collateralized debt obligation (CDO) which is a form of asset-backed security was designed for Wall Street banks to sell poor-quality mortgages to investors. Additionally, they also created the credit default swap (CDS) as an assignable financial derivative product to provide insurance to the buyer against default or loss from an investment. Alrifai (2015) defines the CDS game as the largest casino in the world as investors and hedge funds were purchasing and selling CDSs on different types of investments regardless of whether they had an interest in the underlying performance of the loan or asset. According to him, the actual reason for the global financial crisis was the total losses from CDOs, CDSs, and other derivatives which reached more than USD 6 trillion, while the total losses from subprime mortgages were less than USD 300 million. The global financial crisis resulted in millions of unemployed workers and the unemployment rate rose to 10% and did not drop for many years. Thousands of families lost their homes every month, the values of property fell, and financial markets collapsed.

In 2010, the Dodd–Frank Wall Street Reform and Consumer Protection Act was enacted in the US as a response to the crisis to regulate the financial system. The US Treasury provided a rescue package of USD 200 billion for 734 financial institutions. From January 2008 to April 2014, 495 commercial banks including Washington Mutual and IndyMac failed in the US (Alrifai, 2015). Investment banks were saved from failure, due to the idea of being "too big to fail" which Stiglitz (2010) criticized. All the developing economies were in recession in 2009. The economy of Iceland collapsed and many EU countries including Portugal, Ireland, Italy, Greece, and Spain experienced a sovereign debt crisis in 2010.

European Debt Crisis

It is very interesting that while we are thinking that the global economy got recovered from a crisis, another crisis starts thereafter as the case of the European debt crisis was initiated by the Global Financial Crisis in 2009 and lasted until 2019. Several EU member states including Greece, Italy, Portugal, Ireland, Spain, and South Cyprus Part defaulted, and except for Spain, these countries had to refinance their government debt under the assistance of the European Central Bank (ECB) and the International Monetary Fund (IMF). A sudden stop of foreign capital in countries caused a balance-of-payments crisis. Additionally, since these countries were using a shared currency, Euro, they could not protect their national currency against devaluation. The low-interest rates policy applied by the ECB that provided a money flow from North part of the EU to the South part increased a budget deficit in the Southern countries (Copelovitch et al., 2016; Frieden & Walter, 2017). The collapse of the Greek economy triggered the crisis in Ireland, Spain, Portugal, Italy, and others. Due to the crisis, the unemployment rates in Greece, Italy, and Spain reached 27% and had an overall negative impact on the growth of the EU economy as well as serious political effects including power shifts almost in all the countries that the crisis hit. While most countries such as Spain, Portugal, and Slovakia decided for early elections, and as a result, the ruling parties changed, some other governments lost in general elections. Starting in 2010, the EU member started to develop recovery plans. First, on May 9, 2010, the European Financial Stability Facility (EFSF) which can issue bonds or other debt instruments on the market with the support of the German Debt Management Office was issued. The EFSF could raise the funds required to support Eurozone countries in financial trouble by providing loans, recapitalizing banks, or buying sovereign debt (Thesing, 2011). Then, on January 5, 2011, the European Financial Stabilization Mechanism (EFSM), an emergency funding program was created to raise Euros 60 billion for EU member states in economic difficulty. In the last quarter of 2011, on 26 October, 50% of Greek sovereign debt held by banks was decided to be written off by 17 Eurozone members, increased the bail-out funds held under the European Financial Stability Facility up to Euros 1 trillion, and increased the mandatory level of bank capitalization within the EU to 9% which was criticized by Richard Koo (2011), an expert on banking crisis underlying that raising bank capitals may lead longer periods of recession. Finally, a permanent rescue funding program, the European Stability Mechanism (ESM) was established in July 2012. The Eurozone debt crisis also heated the discussion about the function and the future of the Euro. Although former German Chancellor Angela Merkel and former French President Nicolas Sarkozy defended the integration of the Eurozone, the debate on this issue is still ongoing.

2020 COVID-19 Recession (Great Lockdown)

On January 20, 2020, IMF updated the global growth projection as 3.3% in 2020, a downward revision of 0.1% percentage point for 2020 due to the negative effects of a few emerging market economies, particularly India. Weaker growth rates of emerging countries compared to the projections, trade policy uncertainty, geopolitical tensions, idiosyncratic stress, rising social unrest, and weather-related disasters were listed in the 2020 January outlook of IMF as the main risks of the global economy (IMF, 2020a).

On March 11, 2020, the World Health Organization (WHO) declared the coronavirus disease (COVID-19) a pandemic. In April, three months after the first update of January, IMF (2020b) projected to contraction of the global economy as negative 3% in 2020, considered to be worse than the recession of the 2008–2009 global financial crisis. Soon after the pandemic was declared, global economic activities almost stopped, borders were shut down, and curfews were applied in many countries. During the COVID-19 lockdowns, due to the sudden stance of the global economy, the business in the service sector declined, stock markets crashed, the global supply chain broke down, and thereafter, because of the expansionary monetary policies of many states and the political conflicts arose, inflation rates surged, unemployment rates increased, and global chip storage crisis, global energy crisis, and food crisis began. According to the International Labor Organization, an equivalent of 400 million full-time jobs was lost across the world in the first three months of the pandemic (Pandey, 2020). In the first quarter of 2020, the GDP of the EU and the US fell more than 11% and 9%, respectively. Disposable income per capita, especially for the low-income group, decreased sharply in the second quarter of 2020. Transportation, arts, entertainment, tourism, and hospitality sectors were the industries impacted worst by the lockdown.

China reported the first 27 COVID-19 cases on January 1, 2020. The effects of COVID-19 on the stock markets started on February 20, 2020, after the World Health Organization declared the COVID-19 outbreak to be a Public Health Emergency of International Concern on January 30, 2020, four weeks after the first cases in China. Even before the pandemic, a recession risk was in debate for the US, and the global growing instabilities especially in emerging economies were carried from 2019.

Although the stock market crash began on 20 February, selling deepened during the first half of March to mid-March. The first sharp drop was on March 9, named as Black Monday I, with a 7.79% decline in Dow Jones Index (DJI) (Bayly, 2020). That was followed by a 9.99% decline on March 12, named as Black Thursday, and a 12.93% decrease on March 16, named as Black Monday II, respectively. The crash had a short-term effect, and the markets re-entered a bull market in April 2020, yet the US market indices got recovered in November 2020 (Bloomberg, 2020). Together with other economic indices, the crash in global stock markets sparked the global recession. Governments initiated economic recovery programs and fiscal responses to diminish the impacts of COVID-19. For instance, the interest rates were decreased by FED; Fannie Mae and Freddie Mac provided mortgage forbearance for 12 months, waived associated late fees, and offered loan modification possibilities. Several coronavirus relief plans including the USD 1.84 trillion American Rescue Plan on March 11, 2021, were approved (IMF, 2022). The global economic impact of the pandemic is still ongoing, and with the combined effects of the political conflicts and contractionary monetary policies, it is expected that the global economy will struggle for many years to get recovered if the system is not replaced by an alternative one.

References

Akyüz, Y., & Rayment, P. (1998). *The Russian crisis*. https://unctad.org/system/files/official-document/poirrsd002.en.pdf. Last Accessed on January 12, 2023.

Alrifai, T. (2015). *Islamic finance and the new financial system: An ethical approach to preventing future financial crises*. Wiley. ISBN: 978-1-118-99063-6

Amadeo, K. (2022). *What is the petrodollar?* https://www.thebalancemoney.com/what-is-a-petrodollar-3306358. Last Accessed on January 12, 2023.

Barnhart B. (2001). *Markets reopen, plunge*. https://www.chicagotribune.com/business/chi-010917marketsstory.html. Last Accessed on March 01, 2023.

Bates, D. S. (1991). The crash of '87: Was it expected? The evidence from options markets. *The Journal of Finance, 46*(3), 1009–1044. https://doi.org/10.1111/j.1540-6261.1991.tb03775.x

Bayly, L. (2020). *Dow closes with decline of 2,000 points, almost ending 11-year bull market*. https://www.nbcnews.com/business/markets/dow-set-open-decline-1-300-points-oil-war-adds-n1152941. Last Accessed on January 12, 2023.

Bernanke, B. (2004). *Remarks by Governor Ben S. Bernanke: Money, gold and the Great Depression*. At the H. Parker Willis Lecture in Economic Policy, Washington and Lee University, Lexington, Virginia. https://www.federalreserve.gov/boarddocs/speeches/2004/200403022/default.htm. Last Accessed on January 12, 2023.

Bernhardt, D., & Eckblad, M. (2013). *Black Monday: The stock market crash of 1987*. Federal Reserve History. https://www.federalreservehistory.org/essays/stock-market-crash-of-1987. Last Accessed on January 12, 2023.

Black, W. K. (2005). *The best way to rob a bank is to own one*. University of Texas Press. ISBN 0-292-70638-3.

Bloomberg. (2020). *Down Jones Industrial Average*. https://www.bloomberg.com/quote/INDU:IND?leadSource=uverify%20wall. Last Accessed on January 12, 2023.

Blum, J., Cameron, R., & Barnes, T. G. (1970). *The European world: A history* (2nd ed.). Little Brown.

Chiodo, A. J., & Obyang, M. T. (2002). *A case study of a currency crisis: The Russian default of 1998*. https://files.stlouisfed.org/files/htdocs/publications/review/02/11/ChiodoOwyang.pdf. Last Accessed on January 12, 2023.

Claessens, S., & Köse, M. A. (2013). Financial crisis: Review and evidence. *Central Bank Review, 13*, 1–23. ISSN 1303-0701.

Copelovitch, M., Frieden, J., & Walter, S. (2016). The political economy of the Euro crisis. *Comparative Political Studies, 49*(7), 811–840. https://doi.org/10.1177/0010414016633227

Curry, T., & Shibut, L. (2000). The cost of the savings and loan crisis: Truth and consequences. *FDIC Banking Review, 13*(2), 26–35.

Dolfman, M. L., & Wasser S. F. (2004). *9/11 and the New York City economy*. Monthly Labor Review. https://www.bls.gov/opub/mlr/2004/06/art1full.pdf. Last Accessed on January 12, 2023.

Eichengreen, B. (1992). *Golden Fetters: The gold standard and the Great Depression, 1919–1939*. Oxford University Press. ISBN 0-19-506431-3.

Ertürk, E., & Yilmaz, D. (2014). The Latin American debt crisis and lessons for Europe. *Anadolu Üniversitesi Sosyal Bilimler Dergisi, 14*(1), 159–173. https://doi.org/10.18037/ausbd.25494

Eun, C. S., & Resnick B. G. (2011). *International financial management* (6th ed.). McGraw-Hill/Irwin. ISBN 978-0-07-803465-7.

Fdic.org. (2022). *LDC debt crisis*. https://www.fdic.gov/bank/historical/history/191_210.pdf. Last Accessed on January 12, 2023.

Field, A., & Kim, P. (2022). *7 causes of the Great Depression, and how the road to recovery transformed the US economy*. https://www.businessinsider.com/personal-finance/what-caused-the-great-depression. Last Accessed on January 12, 2023.

Frank, R. H., & Bernanke, B. S. (2007). *Principles of macroeconomics* (3rd ed.). McGraw-Hill/Irwin. ISBN 978-0-07-319397-7.

Frieden, J., & Walter, S. (2017). Understanding the political economy of the Eurozone crisis. *Annual Review of Political Science, 20*(1), 371–390. https://doi.org/10.1146/annurev-polisci-051215-023101

Garraty, J. A. (1986). *The great depression*. Harcourt.

Gross, S. (2019). *What Iran's 1979 revolution meant for US and global oil markets*. https://www.brookings.edu/blog/order-from-chaos/2019/03/05/what-irans-1979-revolution-meant-for-us-and-global-oil-markets/. Last Accessed on January 12, 2023.

Hayes, A. (2022). *1973 energy crisis*. https://www.investopedia.com/1973-energy-crisis-definition-5222090. Last Accessed on January 12, 2023.

IMF. (2020a). *IMF World Economic Outlook*. https://www.imf.org/en/Publications/WEO/Issues/2020a/01/20/weo-update-january2020a. Last Accessed on January 12, 2023.

IMF. (2020b). *IMF World Economic Outlook*. https://www.imf.org/en/Publications/WEO/Issues/2020b/04/14/weo-april-2020b. Last Accessed on January 12, 2023.

IMF. (2022). *Policy responses to COVID-19*. https://www.imf.org/en/Topics/imf-and-covid19/Policy-Responses-to-COVID-19. Last Accessed on January 12, 2023.

Klein, E. (2011). *Bin Laden's war against the U.S. economy*. https://www.washingtonpost.com/blogs/ezra-klein/post/bin-ladens-war-against-the-us-economy/2011/04/27/AFDOPjfF_blog.html. Last Accessed on January 12, 2023.

Koo, R. (2011). *The world in balance sheet recession: Causes, cure, and politics* (Real-World Economics Review, Issue No. 58). Nomura Research Institute. http://www.paecon.net/PAEReview/issue58/Koo58.pdf. Last Accessed on January 12, 2023.

Krugman, P. (2009). *The return of depression economics and the crisis of 2008* (p. 142). W.W. Norton. ISBN 978-0-393-33780-8.

Macrotrends. (2023). *NASDAQ composite—45 year historical chart*. https://www.macrotrends.net/1320/nasdaq-historical-chart. Last Accessed on January 20, 2023.

Makinen, G. (2002). *The economic effects of 9/11: A retrospective assessment*. Congressional Research Service, The Library of Congress. https://irp.fas.org/crs/RL31617.pdf. Last Accessed on January 12, 2023.

Mishkin, F. S., & White, E. N. (2002). *U.S. stock market crashes and their aftermath: Implications for monetary policy*. National Bureau of Economic Research, Working Paper. https://doi.org/10.3386/w8992, https://www.nber.org/papers/w8992. Last Accessed on March 01, 2023.

Nielsen, B. (2022). *The lost decade: Lessons from Japan's real estate crisis*. https://www.investopedia.com/articles/economics/08/japan-1990s-credit-crunch-liquidity-trap.asp. Last Accessed on January 12, 2023.

Okina, K., Shirakawa, M., & Shiratsuka, S. (2001). The asset price bubble and monetary policy: Japan's experience in the late 1980s and the lessons: Background paper. *Monetary and Economic Studies, 19*(S1), 395–450. Institute for Monetary and Economic Studies, Bank of Japan.

Pain, E. (2021). From the first Chechen war towards the second. *The Brown Journal of World Affairs, 8*(1), 7–19.

Pandey, K. (2020). *COVID-19: 400 mln jobs lost in Q2 2020, says ILO*. https://www.downtoearth.org.in/news/economy/covid-19-400-mln-jobs-lost-in-q2-2020-says-international-labour-organization-72086. Last Accessed on January 12, 2023.

Powell, J. (2021). Investors should not dismiss Cisco's dot com collapse as a historical anomaly. *Financial Times*. https://www.ft.com/content/81a03045-86f7-4e57-afbd-5ff83679615f. Last Accessed on March 01, 2023.

Reinhart, C. M., & Rogoff, K. S. (2009). The aftermath of financial crises. *American Economic Review, 99*(2), 466–472. https://doi.org/10.1257/aer.99.2.466

Richardson, G. (2022). *The great depression*. https://www.federalreservehistory.org/essays/great-depression. Last Accessed on December 12, 2022.

Roll, R. (1988). The international crash of October 1987. *Financial Analysts Journal, 44*(5), 19–35. https://doi.org/10.2469/faj.v44.n5.19

Smith, C. D. (2006). *Palestine and the Arab-Israeli conflict*. Bedford.

Soule, G. H. (1947). *Prosperity decade: From war to depression: 1917–1929*. Routledge 1977.

Srinivas, V. (2018). *Major financial crisis—From great depression to great recession*. https://taxboard.rajasthan.gov.in/images/MAJOR_FINANCIAL_CRISIS_2OTH_CENTURY.pdf. Last Accessed on January 12, 2023.

Statista. (2022a). *Monthly value of the Dow Jones Industrial Average (DJIA) from January 1920 to December 1955*. https://www.statista.com/statistics/1249670/monthly-change-value-dow-jones-depression/. Last Accessed on December 17, 2022.

Statista. (2022b). *Average annual OPEC crude oil price from 1960 to 2022*. https://www.statista.com/statistics/262858/change-in-opec-crude-oil-prices-since-1960/. Last Accessed on January 20, 2023.

Stiglitz, J. (2003). *The ruin of Russia*. https://www.theguardian.com/world/2003/apr/09/russia.artsandhumanities. Last Accessed on January 12, 2023.

Stiglitz, J. E. (2010). *The Stiglitz Report: Reforming the international monetary and financial systems in the wake of the global crisis*. The New Press. ISBN 978-1595585202.

St.Louis FED. (2023). *Interest rates, discount rate for United States*. https://fred.stlouisfed.org/series/INTDSRUSM193N. Last Accessed on January 20, 2023.

The greatest defunct Web sites and dotcom disasters. https://www.cnet.com/tech/computing/the-greatest-defunct-web-sites-and-dotcom-disasters/. Last Accessed on January 12, 2023.

Thesing, G. (2011). *European rescue fund may buy bonds, recapitalize banks, ECB's stark says*. https://web.archive.org/web/20110124054857/http://www.bloomberg.com/news/2011-01-22/ecb-s-stark-says-rescue-fund-may-buy-bonds-recapitalize-banks.html. Last Accessed on January 12, 2023.

Vasquez, I. (1996). The Brady plan and market-based solutions to debt crises. *Cato Journal, 16*(2), 233–243.

Visualvapitalist.com. (2023). *Visualizing $65 trillion in hidden dollar debt*. https://www.visualcapitalist.com/visualizing-65-trillion-in-hidden-dollar-debt/. Last Accessed on January 15, 2023.

WHO. (2020). *WHO Director-General's opening remarks at the media briefing on COVID-19–11 March 2020*. https://www.who.int/director-general/speeches/detail/who-director-general-s-opening-remarks-at-the-media-briefing-on-covid-19---11-march-2020. Last Accessed on January 12, 2023.

Williams, M. (2010). *Uncontrolled risk: Lessons of Lehman Brothers and how systemic risk can still bring down the world financial system*. McGraw Hill.

Worldbank.org. (2022). *Global waves of debt: Causes and consequences*. https://www.worldbank.org/en/research/publication/waves-of-debt. Last Accessed on January 12, 2023.

Yamazawa, I. (1998). The Asian economic crisis and Japan. *The Developing Economies, 36*(3), 332–351. https://doi.org/10.1111/j.1746-1049.1998.tb00222.x

Zhang, Y. (2013). The links between the price of oil and the value of US dollar. *International Journal of Energy Economics and Policy, 3*(4), 341–351. ISSN: 2146-4553.

CHAPTER 4

The Global Risks and Problems of the Economic and Financial Systems

Ernest Hemingway (1935) defines inflation and war as the first two panaceas for a mismanaged nation which both bring temporary prosperity but eventually a permanent ruin that the political and economic opportunists refuge in. The world economy has been struggling with many challenges for a long time. The recession that occurred due to the coronavirus disease (COVID-19) pandemic experienced in the last two years ended up with high inflation rates globally. The political conflicts, especially the ongoing war between Russia and Ukraine, increased global economic risks. The rise in the inflation rates put many states in a difficult situation as the welfare and purchasing powers of people sharply decreased. In that sense, the central banks were in a dilemma and were not sure about fighting against inflation by increasing the interest rates because of the stagflation risks that they may face or focusing more on growth and encouraging production but with the risk of uncontrollable inflation rates.

Beyond the negative impacts of the pandemic or the effects of the latest political conflicts, the risks to the world economy have been increasing in the last few decades due to the flawed structure of the world economy and financial system. This structure is being questioned by many scholars including Stiglitz (2010), Piketty (2013) and Akgiray (2019) due to the increased frequency and the heavy consequences of the latest financial crises. While Stiglitz (2010) criticizes the policies which protected the

L. Sümer, *The World Economy and Financial System*,
https://doi.org/10.1007/978-3-031-27530-2_4

banks from failing in the global financial crisis because they were considered too big to fail, Piketty (2013) underlines the problems caused by the inequalities among nations and societies. In addition, Akgiray (2019) warns us about the potential consequences of the never-ending increase in global debt.

Global Debt

Despite more often global recessions experienced in the last half-century, the global economy keeps growing. Gross domestic product (GDP), which was developed in the US by an American economist and statistician and Nobel Prize Laureate Simon Kuznets in the 1930s, is the most used tool for measuring economic growth. Combining the financial value of individuals, companies, and the government is the main idea of assessing the size of an economy. As shown in Fig. 4.1, despite a decline in 2020 due to the recession during COVID-19, as of the end of 2021, the global GDP reached USD 96.1 trillion. With its USD 23 trillion size, the US is the leading country in the global economy, and it is followed by China, Japan, and Germany. China's GDP is expected to increase to USD 31.73 trillion, and China will become the leading country in terms of GDP value by 2030 (Worldbank, 2022).

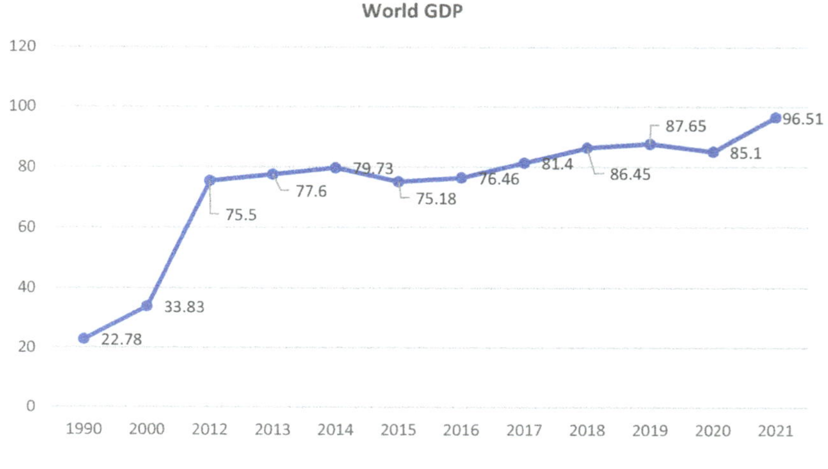

Fig. 4.1 Size of the global GDP (*Source* World Bank [2022])

On the other hand, the size of the global debt is growing much faster than the growth rate of the global GDP. The total size of the global GDP was USD 33.65 trillion in 2000. Within the last two decades, the size of the global economy grew 2,52 times, but the total global debt grew 4,39 times within the same period and reached USD 303 trillion USD, corresponding to %355 of the total GDP of the world. Figure 4.2 exhibits the increase in global debt since 2015. Comparing the sizes of the global debt in 2000 (USD 69 trillion) and 2008 (USD 174 trillion), this new historically record high debt volume is uncoubtedly increasing the risks to the global economy (Akgiray, 2019, IIF. 2022). The rise in off-balance sheet debt to USD 65 trillion also puts additional risks on the global financial system (Neufeld & Lam, 2023).

Among USD 303 trillion, non-financial companies had USD 88.8 trillion in debt, while public debt reached USD 88.1 trillion. These figures were followed by USD 69.8 trillion in financial sector debt and USD 56.9 trillion in household debt, respectively. The states, companies, and people have been spending the money they do not have. This situation made the

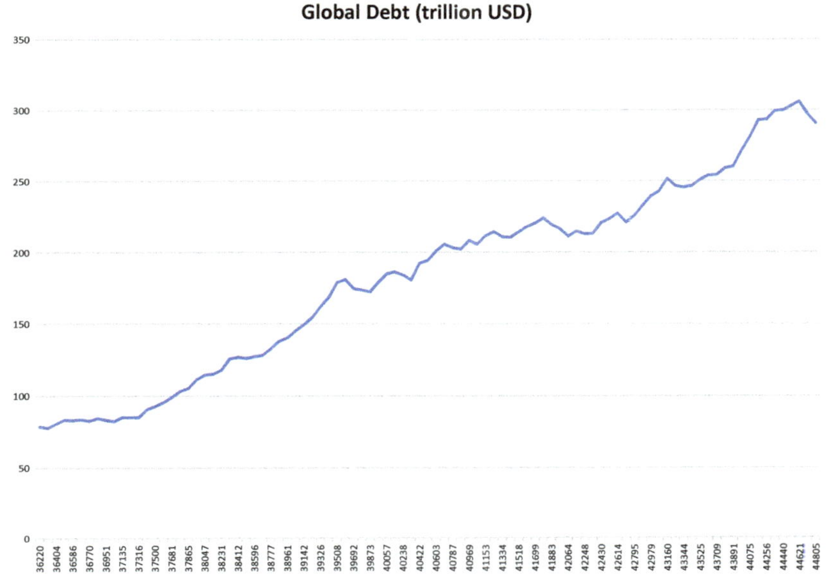

Fig. 4.2 Total global debt (*Source* IIF [2022])

financial systems more dependent on large financial institutions, states, or organizations which have the rule and control over the global money flow.

IIF also reports that 80% of the new debt burden came from emerging markets where total debt is nearing USD 100 trillion. When combined with the interest rate-increasing policy of the FED, it seems that new challenges are waiting for emerging economies in 2023. The debt of China reached USD 60 trillion, almost 20% of the total global debt and 60% of the debts of emerging markets, so what will happen next if there is a default on repayment of such debts? The recent Evergrande case, the real estate giant of China and the most indebted property development in the world with USD 300 billion debt, gave an initial serious signal about the future of the world economy in such debt default problems (NYTimes, 2021). According to OECD 2023 report, the government debt-to-GDP ratio in the US rose from 108.8%, its level in 2019, to 137% as of the end of 2021. Japan still is the most indebted country with its 268% debt-to-GDP ratio, and while the Euro area countries have an average 96% ratio, emerging countries such as Türkiye, China, Mexico, Russia, and Indonesia have a relatively low debt-to-GDP ratios. Despite these low ratios, within 2 years, the debt-to-GDP ratio of Türkiye, Indonesia, and China rose 10, 12, and 10%, respectively. The government debt over GDP ratio of selected OECD countries is shown in Fig. 4.3.

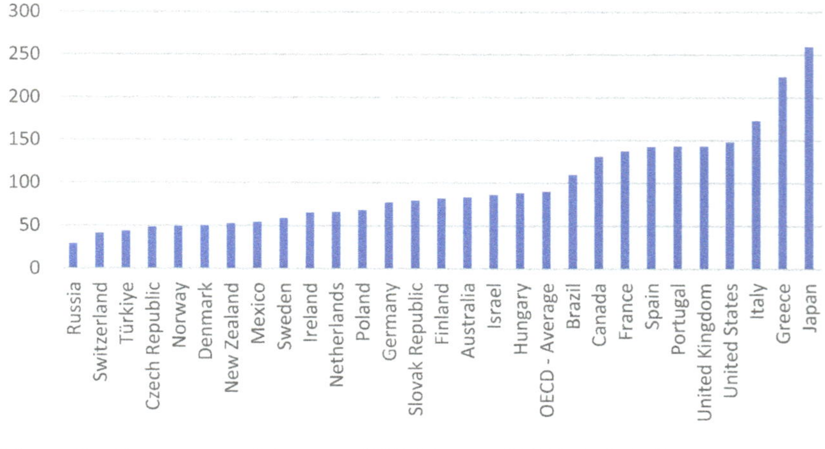

Fig. 4.3 Government debt over GDP (*Source* OECD [2023a])

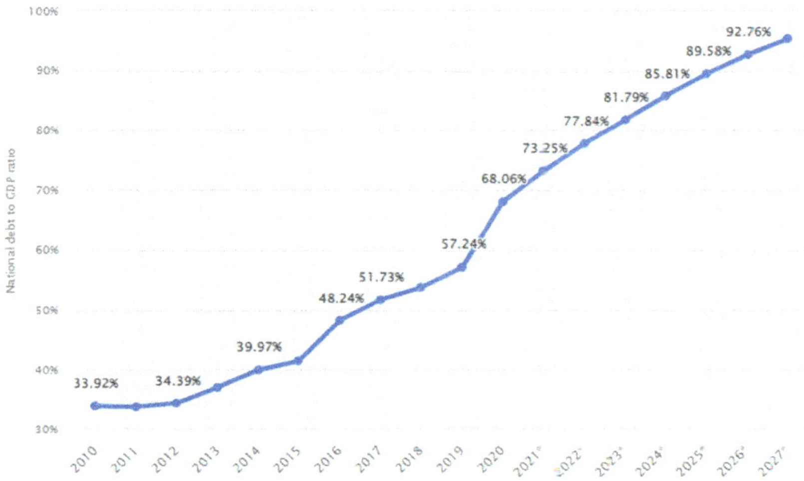

Fig. 4.4 China debt-to-GDP ratio (*Source* Statista [2022c])

Within 10 years, China's total debt-to-GDP ratio doubled and it is expected that it will reach 93% by 2027 (Statista, 2022c). Considering the Chinese economy, which is projected to be the largest in 2030, this rapid increase put additional risks to the global economy. Figure 4.4 shows the rapid rise in the debt-to-GDP ratio of China.

Another indicator of the debt ratio is household debt over net disposable income. The citizens of the Nordic countries which have a higher GDP per capita income than the average of G20 countries are the most indebted populations in the world with a more than 200% debt ratio. While the US stands in the middle of the graph with a 101% debt-to-net disposable income ratio, most of the Eurozone countries, the UK, Australia, Canada, New Zealand, Switzerland, and South Korea, have a higher debt-to-income ratio than the US. Emerging countries like Russia, Mexico, and Brazil, together with former Soviet countries and South American states, have relatively less debt-to-income ratios compared to other emerging economies (OECD, 2023b). Figure 4.5 shows the debt to the net disposable income of OECD countries.

Outstanding mortgage rates are also important indicators for analyzing debt. As shown in Fig. 4.6, in 2008, the outstanding mortgage debt was

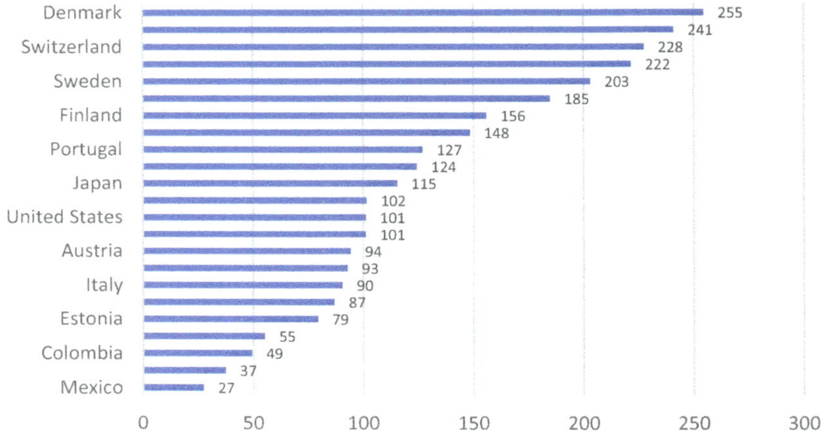

Fig. 4.5 Debt to net disposable income (*Source* OECD [2023b])

around USD 15 trillion, and this amount increased to USD 16.8 trillion in 2020 and USD 18 trillion at the end of 2021 due to the increase in home sales and prices in the US (Statista, 2022b).

Despite the increase in debt-to-GDP and debt-to-net disposable income ratios and the size of mortgage loans, the non-performing loan (NPL) rate in the US stands at 0.9%. Compared to the 5% NPL rate in the aftermath of the global financial crisis, this level is a positive indicator. The intervention of the government by providing fiscal responses to COVID-19 was successful in the short term and helped the households and firms not put in default, but it is critical to follow any potential increase in the case a recession occurs in the US and compare these rates with the pre-2008 global financial crisis. Figure 4.7 shows the NPL rates of the US after the great recession in 2008 (Statista, 2022e).

As of March 2022, mortgage loans reached 5.06 trillion Euros in the Eurozone. While Germany with the least homeownership rate (49,5%) after Switzerland in Europe has the most mortgage loans with Euros 1.8 trillion, France and Sweden follow Germany with Euros 1.2 trillion and Euros 498 billion, respectively. Similar to the US, the NPL ratio is in decline in the Euro area which is a good indicator of the potential risks of debt default, but the interest policy of central banks to fight against

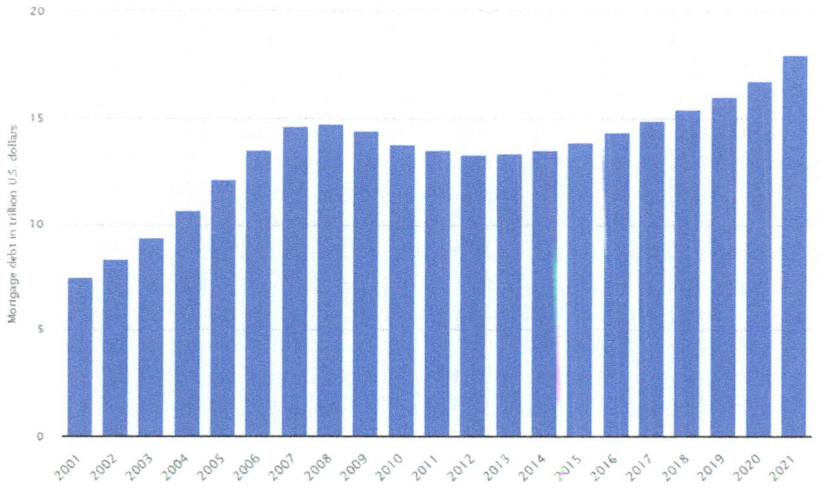

Fig. 4.6 US outstanding mortgage loans (*Source* Statista [2022d])

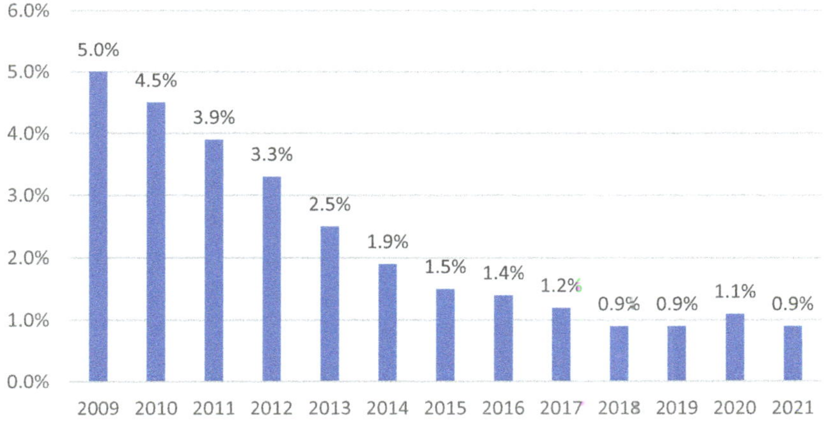

Fig. 4.7 NPL rates in the US (*Source* Statista [2022e])

inflation may result in a recession which may increase the NPL rates and create new financial risk.

On the other hand, the outstanding housing mortgages in China rose from Yuan 40 trillion to Yuan 46 trillion (USD 6.39 trillion) within the first quarter of 2022. Although as of the second quarter of 2022 the NPL rate of all loans in China is 1.7%, any potential default in the mortgage loans combined with the recession in the US carries the potential to trigger a new financial crisis. The rise in outstanding home loans in Türkiye is also remarkable. Before the COVID-19 pandemic started, the size of the outstanding mortgage loan was TL 200 billion in December 2019. This figure rose to TL 354 billion as of September 2022 (GYODER, 2022). The share of 3 public banks in these loans also rose from 56.5% to 65.7% within the same period which shows that the housing industry in Türkiye is financed mainly by public banks. The global housing industry is also highly dependent on bank loans. As of August 2022, the NPL rate in Türkiye is around 2.4% in total loans and 0.3% in mortgage loans, which is a good indicator, but the size of the loans provided in foreign currencies which is TL 2.5 trillion (USD 134 billion) corresponds to 31% of the total loan puts the banking industry in risk considering the interest rate policy of the central bank of Türkiye Republic, and the rapid devaluation of TL against USD in the last year (GYODER, 2022). Unlike most of the central bank policies including FED and ECB, the low-interest rate policy of Türkiye under high inflation is criticized by many local and international economists.

Post-COVID-19 Debate: Inflation vs. Unemployment/Recession (From Keynesian Policies to Friedman Approach)

Keynesians view expansionary monetary policy helps the economy through lower interest rates, and the consumers and businesses increase their expenditures. According to Keynesians, fighting against unemployment is more important than fighting against inflation. When the pandemic was declared in March 2020, the unemployment rates in the world, especially in the US, rose sharply. As demonstrated in Fig. 4.8, the unemployment rate hit 14% at its peak in the US and increased from 3.67% to 8.05%, with a 4.38% increase compared to 2019 (Statista, 2022c). The peak rate recorded in 2020 was higher than the peak rate of the 2008 Global Financial Crisis. Many central banks followed Keynesian policies during the COVID-19 period which resulted in high

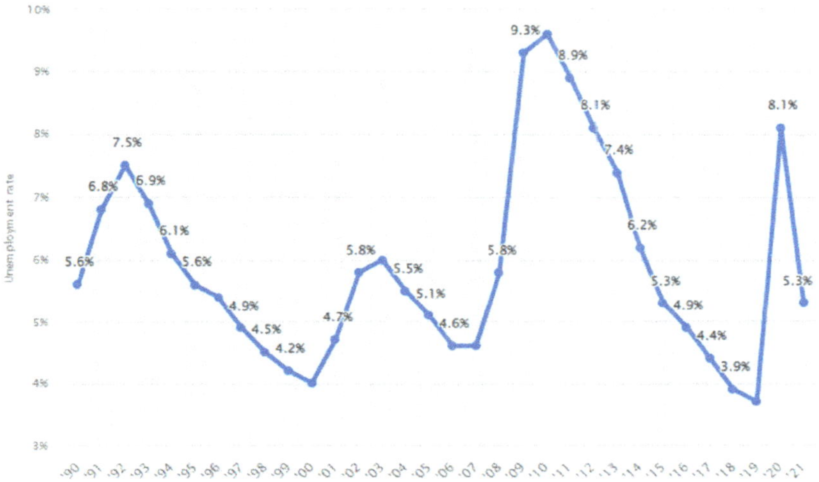

Fig. 4.8 US unemployment rates (1990–2021) (*Source* Statista [2022f])

inflation and a sharp increase in global debt. On the other hand, Nobel Laureate Milton Friedman defines inflation as a form of taxation to use for government expenses. Friedman (1962) argues that the monetary expansion policies of the central banks only create inflation which puts the economies in trouble. If the central banks press more money, people will spend more and vice versa. Despite the Keynesian approach which argues that the politicians shall control the economy through fiscal policies, Friedmann puts the central banks in the middle of the control of the economy by using the interest rates.

Until the last quarter of 2021, both Jerome Powell, the President of the Federal Reserve (FED) and Christine Lagarde, the President of the European Central Bank (ECB), were claiming the rise in inflation rates caused by COVID-19 as "temporary" (Pfaffenbach, 2021; Saphir, 2021). The International Monetary Fund (IMF) Chief Kristalina Georgieva was supporting this idea and was hoping for a decline in the inflation rates with the help of the increase in vaccination against COVID-19 (Lanman, 2021). Maybe their optimism was likely to occur if the war between Russia and Ukraine did not start in the first quarter of 2022, but the recent rise in energy and food prices kept increasing the inflation rates in

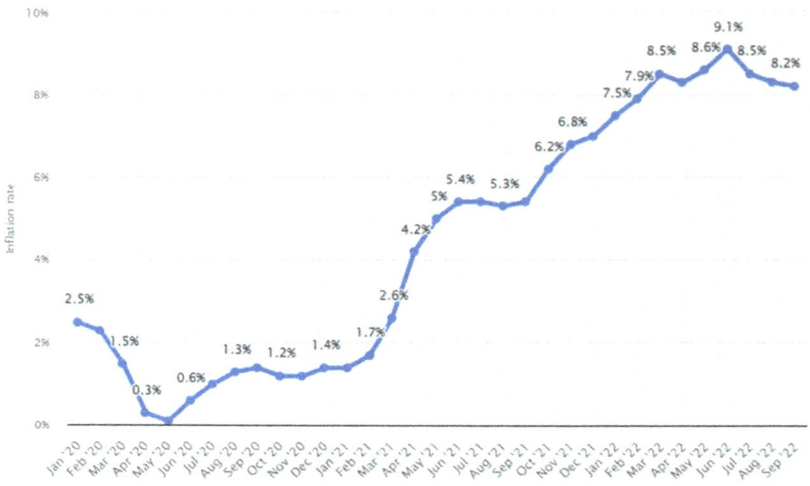

Fig. 4.9 Inflation rate in the US (2020–2022) (*Source* Statista [2022g])

both developed and emerging markets. The inflation rate in the US was 0.1% in May 2020. Within a year and a half, the inflation rate rose to its 9.3% peak value in July 2022. Figure 4.9 shows the rapid rise in the inflation rate in the US covering the COVID-19 period and Fig. 4.10 shows how FED responded to this increase (Statista, 2022d, 2022e). After the decision to increase interest rates, inflation started declining in the US. The inflation rate in the UK reached 9.9% in September 2022 mostly caused by the increase in food prices. Eurozone inflation also hit two-digit inflation with a 10% rate, a 6.6% increase within one year, due to the rapid rise in energy prices.

Nowadays, Powell says that the inflation rates would not rise that much if we had not experienced the COVID-19 pandemic. He may be right of course, there would not be any economic crisis if everything went smoothly in the world, but is it right to blame the pandemic itself for the problems, or shall we rethink about the decisions given or not given, the timings of the decisions, and the potential consequences of them? For instance, FED printed USD 3.38 trillion in 2020 and USD 13 trillion in 2021 which corresponds to 50% of the total USD printed in history (Surz, 2021). Didn't we know that would create inflation while the money

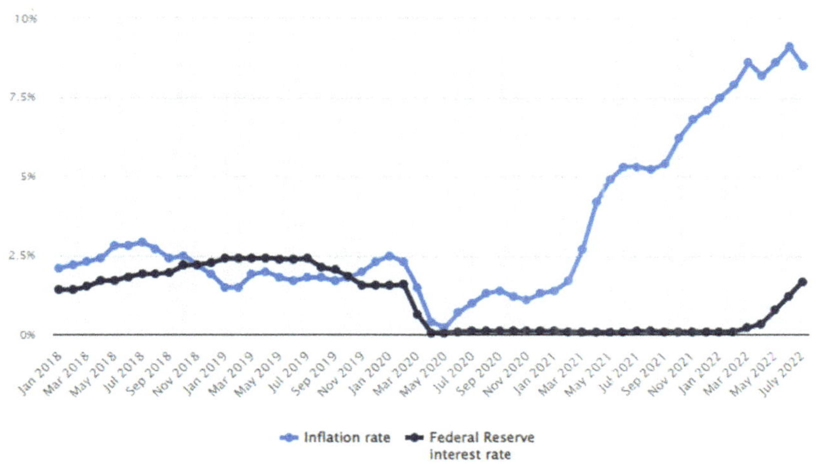

Fig. 4.10 US inflation rates vs. FED interest rates (*Source* Statista [2022h])

started flowing to stocks and cryptocurrencies? The expansionary monetary and quantitative easing policy of the FED is very criticized in that sense. Could FED print money as much as it can? In fact, after the collapse of the Bretton Woods agreement in 1971, where the convertibility of USD to gold was suspended, no new and sustainable system or agreement replaced it since then. In the 1980s, some attempts under the name of "a new Bretton Woods" was made by the US and French finance officers, but no road map or goals were articulated in these meetings.

The idea of Bretton Woods II was also discussed by Dooley et al. (2004) which underlined the trade policies and barriers from the current account deficits and surplus perspectives. In this new approach, the global markets were again somehow dependent on the US economy from FED interest rates and inflation rates. In 2019, Stephen Pickford, senior fellow of Chatham House, suggested "a new Bretton Woods agreement" to be drafted to redefine the institutional basis of the IMF and World Bank and focus on new economic development and cooperation models. Lagarde and her successor Georgieva also suggested a new Bretton Woods movement by emphasizing the urgent need to restructure debt and debt transparency, developing policies for people by taking into consideration creating strong health and education systems, expanding technology, decreasing inequality, and focusing on climate change. (IMF, 2020).

Recently, former Federal Reserve and United States Treasury Department official and now Credit Suisse Strategist Zoltan Pozsar (2022) started a new discussion about the falling apart of the world order. According to Pozsar, reverse globalization, the sanctions which cut Russia off from the global financial system, the high energy prices in Europe, and restrictions applied on technology transfer to China are the main signs of the start of a new era. He underlines that access to commodities is more important than access to the dollar and this new situation is challenging the dollar. On the other hand, Perry Mehrling, Professor of Economy at Boston University is standing against this idea. Mehrling acknowledges reverse globalization but also mentions the own problems of China and Russia. He underlines the supply chain problems caused by the pandemic, stresses the disruptions caused by geostrategies, and concludes that we are not at a turning point yet (Regan, 2022). While the economists are discussing the future of the dollar and the possible new Bretton Woods agreement, FED started increasing the interest rates, and the values of the USD and Euro equalized. Soon after the FED decision about rising the interest rates, ECB also increased the interest rates sharply.

These steps can be considered a policy shift from monetary expansion during COVID-19 to monetary tightening to fight against inflation. During COVID-19, like many central banks in the world, as a response to the pandemic, the US federal fund's effective rate was radically lowered from 1.58% to 0.05% within 2 months after the pandemic was declared by the World Health Organization (WHO) in March 2020. By keeping it at its lowest value until April 2022, parallel to the FED contractionary monetary policy, the federal fund's effective rate started increasing in the last few months and reached 2.33% by August 2022. After the negative interest rate policy which lasted 8 years, ECB also increased the interest rates in 2022 July and 2022 September by 0.5% and 0.75%, respectively (ECB, 2022). The new 1.25% interest rate has been recorded as the highest rate in the Euro area since 2011. Soon after the Euro slightly gained value against the USD. These developments brought fear to IMF and United Nations about the possible consequence of the global recession, and recently, these two institutions warned the FED about being cautious regarding its interest rate increase decisions which may have put the US into recession and make a domino effect on the global economy.

Table 4.1 Selected macroeconomic indicators of G20

Countries (%)	*Inflation CPI (%)*	*Interest rates (%)*	*GDP annual growth rates (%)*	*Unemployment rates (%)*	*GDP per capita (USD) (%)*
Türkiye	83.5	10.50	7.3	10.10	13.251*
Argentina	78.5	75.00	6.9	6.90	12.391
Netherlands	14.5	1.25	5.1	3.80	48.424
Russia	14.3	7.50	−4.1	3.80	10.127
Euro Area	10.0	1.25	4.1	6.60	36.352
Germany	10.0	1.25	1.7	5.50	42.527
UK	9.9	2.25	4.4	3.60	46.209
Spain	9.0	1.25	6.8	12.48	26.239
Italy	8.9	1.25	4.7	7.80	31.512
Brazil	*8.8*	*13.75*	*3.2*	*8.90*	*8.551*
Mexico	*8.7*	*9.25*	*2.0*	*3.50*	*9.255*
US	8.3	3.25	1.8	3.70	61.280
South Africa	7.6	6.25	0.2	33.90	5.865
Singapore ara>	7.5	2.34	4.4	2.10	66.176
India	7.0	5.90	13.5	6.40	1.961
Canada	7.0	3.25	2.9	5.40	43.946
Australia	6.1	2.60	3.6	3.50	58.780
Indonesia	6.0	4.25	5.4	5.83	3.856
South Korea	5.6	2.50	2.9	2.50	32.645
France	5.6	1.25	4.2	7.40	38.210
Switzerland	3.3	0.50	2.8	2.00	88.224
Japan	3.0	−0.10	1.6	2.50	35.278
Saudi Arabia	*3.0*	*3.75*	*9.9*	*5.80*	*19.018*
China	*2.5*	*3.65*	*0.4*	*5.30*	*11.188*

*GDP per capita of Türkiye was USD 9,661.2 at the end of 2021 according to Worldbank statistics
Source Tradingeconomics (October 2022)

Parallel to FED and ECB policy shifts, many central banks increased the interest rates to fight against inflation, but as shown in Table 4.1, among G20 countries, only Brazil, Mexico, Saudi Arabia, and China have positive effective interest rates. On the other hand, despite its highest inflation rate among G20 countries, the Central Bank of Türkiye Republic, starting from September 2021, decreased the interest rates from 19% to 10.5% within one year as exhibited in Fig. 4.11. This policy has been criticized by many economists since the inflation rate rose from 19.58% to 83.45% within the same period. Although it indirectly affected around a 4%

decrease in the unemployment rate and the economy kept growing within 2021 and the first half of 2022, the Turkish Lira depreciated sharply against many currencies and the purchasing power of people decreased due to the rapid rise in inflation (Tradingeconomics, 2022a).

Russia is another country that has been decreasing its interest rates since April 2022. As shown in Fig. 4.12, when the war started with Ukraine, the interest rate was 9.5% in Russia, but to protect against the devaluation of the Russian Ruble, the Central Bank of Russia increased the interest rates sharply to 20% in February 2022. Then, the rates gradually fell to 7.5% even less than the rates when the war started (Countryeconomy, 2022).

The Russian Ruble is also more valuable now than its value before the war started. Due to the sanctions applied, the Russian economy is in recession now, but the energy policy of Russia is keeping increasing the inflation in the world, mostly in Europe due to the high dependency of most of the European countries on Russian oil. This situation forced the ECB to increase the interest rates to control the rise in inflation but that might create another risk, stagflation in Europe. Combined with the possible recession of the US economy, dark nights seem on the edge of winter 2022 for the global economy.

China's economy which has been the rising star of emerging economies for the last few decades is slowing down. The strict lockdown policy the Chinese government applied to control the spread of COVID-19 among Chinese cities affected economic activities negatively, and the mobility restrictions as part of the zero COVID-19 strategy of Chinese authorities disrupted economic activity severely.

Fig. 4.11 Interest rates vs. inflation in Türkiye (*Source* CBRT [2022])

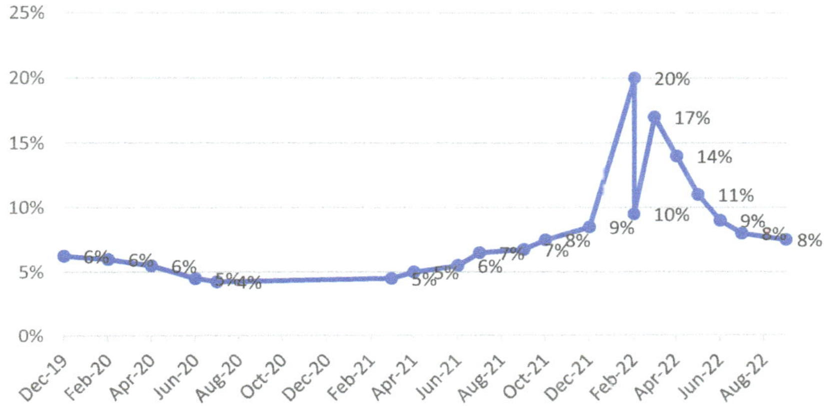

Fig. 4.12 Interest rates in Russia (*Source* Countryeconomy [2022])

Shanghai which is one of the main supply chain hubs entered a strict lockdown in April 2022 and stopped economic activities for about eight weeks. The lockdowns and slowdown of economic activities in China disrupted the global supply chains and declined domestic spending decreasing the demand for Chinese goods and services. The slowdown of the construction and real estate industries also increased the risks to the Chinese economy. In the second quarter of 2022, the Chinese economy grew by only 0.4%, the lowest level since 1992. In contrast to many other G20 countries, China's inflation rate is below the official target ceiling and the central bank of China lowered the interest rates by 0.05% in August 2022 to stimulate economic activities. With its 3.65% value, the interest rate in China is still above the inflation rate which is 2.5% (Tradingeconomics, 2022b).

Inequality in Wealth Distribution

High inflation rates have serious social impacts such as decreasing social welfare, increasing crime rates, and widening the gap between low- and high-income classes where the middle-income-level groups disappear. As exhibited in Fig. 4.13, according to the World Inequality Report, as of the end of 2021, the richest 10% of the global population currently takes 52% of global income. On the other hand, the poorest half of the total

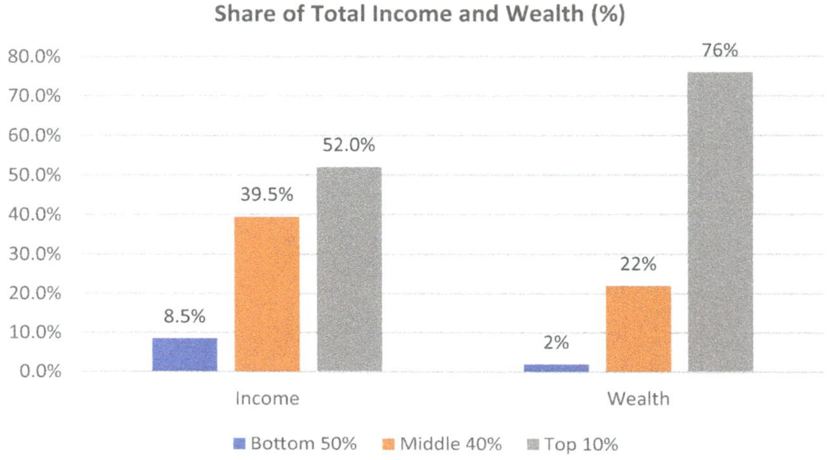

Fig. 4.13 Global income and wealth inequality (*Source* World Inequality Report [2022])

population earns only 8.5% of it. While an individual from the top 10% of the global income distribution earns USD 122.100 per year, an individual from the poorest half of the global income distribution makes USD 3,920 per year on average. The richest 10% of the global population owns 76% of all wealth, whereas the poorest half of the global population possesses only 2% of the total wealth.

As of the end of 2019, 648 million people in the world are living under the poverty line, which is USD 2.15, the World Bank reports (Worldbank Poverty and Shared Responsibility, 2022). 60% of 648 million are living in sub-Saharan Africa and 24% in South Asia.

The Gini index is an important measure of the distribution of income across a population, and the less the coefficient the countries have, the less the inequality among the population they have. During the COVID-19 pandemic, the Gini coefficient increased in many countries (Chen et al., 2021). Adarov (2022) from World Bank underlines the increase in inequalities in emerging markets and developing economies due to weak economic recoveries. The Gini index has some limitations. For instance, the same Gini coefficient does not mean that the countries are at the same economic development level. The US, representing a developed economy, and Türkiye, listed as an emerging economy, have almost the same Gini

Table 4.2 Countries with the lowest & highest income inequalities

Rank	*Lowest income inequality*	*Gini (%)*	*Highest income inequality*	*Gini (%)*
1	Slovakia	23.20	South Africa	63.00
2	Slovenia	24.40	Namibia	59.10
3	Belarus	24.40	Suriname	57.90
4	Armenia	25.20	Zambia	57.10
5	Czech Republic	25.30	Sao Tome and Principe	56.30
6	Ukraine	25.60	Central African Republic	56.20
7	United Arab Emirates	26.00	Eswatini	54.60
8	Moldova	26.00	Colombia	54.20
9	Iceland	26.10	Mozambique	54.00
10	Azerbaijan	26.60	Botswana	53.30

Source World Population Review (2022)

coefficient, 41.5% and 41.9%, respectively. As shown in Table 4.2, except for South Africa which is considered a developing economy, although the least developed African economies have the highest Gini coefficient, there are no developed economies in the top ten list of the countries with the least Gini coefficients, so economic development is not necessary for the equalities of the people living in a country.

Re-Globalization Under the Shadow of Brexit, Trade Wars, COVID-19, and Geopolitical Conflicts

The industrial revolution which started in the eighteenth century changed human life radically. In the last 250 years, more technology was created than in the previous years of known human history, and the industrial revolution brought a significant change in terms of production and efficiency. In the last century, the industrial revolution kept going fast forward and continuously. The rapid advancement of technology, the spread of the internet, and the increasing digitalization together with the mobility brought by the industry 4.0 revolution made our world more interconnected. The mobility of goods, people, data, and knowledge from economic, social, technological, cultural, and political perspectives introduced a new concept called globalization, which was first used as a term back in 1944s. Although the term globalization was used before,

Theodore Levitt (1983), professor at Harvard University, is usually credited with its coining through the article he wrote in 1983 for the Harvard Business Review entitled "Globalization of markets". Globalization is the word used to describe the growing interdependence of the world's economies, cultures, and populations, brought about by cross-border trade in goods and services, technology, and flows of investment, people, and information. The term gained popularity after the Cold War in the early 1990s. Short-term and long-term competitiveness, intellectual property rights, search for innovative human resources, and lower labor costs were the main motivations for the companies going global. On the other hand, Tomohara and Takii (2011) put forward that globalization brings higher wages for local employers as foreign companies are given market access.

In addition to the Western economies, countries like China, Russia, India, and Brazil also play important roles in world trade. Khan and Riskin (2001) point out that China's poverty reduction can be attributed to the opening of its economy. Rogoff (2003) argues that the globalization process helps push down inflation and any reversal of the free flow of production factors that may re-introduce price pressure.

In the last two decades, globalization has come to a halt based on social and political instabilities, insecurities, and volatilities. The neoliberal market economies of the 1990s were protested at World Trade Organization's Conference in 1999 in Seattle by activists focusing on workers' rights, sustainable economies, and environmental and social issues. The developments in the last two decades including the 9/11 transnational terrorist attacks in New York in 2001, the 2008 global financial crisis, the European sovereign debt crisis, the refugee crisis, the rise of national populism, the Brexit decision of the UK to exit from the EU, the trade sanctions applied to different countries by the US and the "Trade Wars" started between the US and China, COVID-19 pandemic, and the ongoing war between Russia and Ukraine which affected the global energy and food prices and increased the inflation, especially in the EU, opened a new discussion of redefining the "globalization". Hillebrand (2010) argues that protectionism may improve income equality in some countries although he still thinks that a retreat from globalization will lead to profoundly negative implications for the global economy.

On the other hand, the argument of Rogoff (2003) is more important than ever considering the sanctions applied to Russia due to its ongoing war with Ukraine. Russia responded to these sanctions by cutting off the gas supplies to Europe which expedited the rise in inflation in Europe. The COVID-19 pandemic had broken the global supply chain in 2020. That chain has not been repaired completely so far, yet the zero COVID-19 policy of China added more risks to the global economy under the shadow of reverse globalization.

The Effects of Brexit

The UK's withdrawal from the EU (Brexit) had many economic consequences such as creating barriers to trade and cross-border exchanges or constraints on immigration which may affect the workforce. The transportation crisis in the Port of Felixstowe exhibited a sample workforce problem in the UK in 2021 (The Guardian, 2021). Labor shortages and strikes also disrupted London, Amsterdam, Paris, Rome, and Frankfurt airports in the spring of 2022, not just only because of Brexit but also the COVID-19 effect. Brexit also had deep impacts on the UK's internal politics. Lis Truss, the former prime minister of the UK, resigned only 45 days after becoming the prime minister. In the first two weeks under her governance, Queen Elizabeth II who was the queen for the last 70 years passed away, and Prince Charles became the new king of the UK (WSJ, 2022). Truss was the fourth prime minister (now the fifth one, Rishi Sunak, the first Indian-origin prime minister) in the UK after Brexit, and the UK had only 5 different prime ministers in 37 years before Brexit (Gov.uk, 2022). There may be several reasons for her resignation such as the negative reflections of the promises of the finance minister (who was immediately taken off-duty) to cut taxes for the highest earners and biggest corporation, devaluation of the British Pound, replacing half of her ministers, and losing support in the community. Beyond the reasons behind her resignation, it is for sure that Brexit had and is still having negative impacts on the economies of both the UK and the EU.

Jean-Pierre Lehmann (2016), a professor at the International Institute for Management Development (IMD) which is an independent academic institution with Swiss roots and global reach, defines Brexit as the reflection of the rising tide of deglobalization. Prof. Lehmann puts the rise in inequality, the perceptions about refugees and immigrants, and the reflection of the populism rising in the world as the main reasons behind the Brexit decision, mostly a result of the "leave vote" of people elder than 65 years old. Considering Weiss and Blockmanns' (2016) arguments about how Brexit would affect the politics in other European countries such as the approaches of the leaders of right-wing anti-immigration parties in the Netherlands or France who express the feeling of becoming freer by not being an EU member, Lehmann states that the European dream has evaporated after the Brexit decision.

Trade Wars

When former President Donald Trump was elected in 2016 in the US, he promised to "make America great again". This slogan was not new and was used before by Ronald Reagan in his 1980 election campaign at the time the US economy was suffering from stagflation (PBS.com, 2022). Bill Clinton also used the slogan in his speeches during the 1992 elections (Margolin, 2016). Beyond the debate of whether this slogan is racist or patriotic, the 4-year presidency of Trump is being remembered mostly for the trade battle he started against many countries including American allies but especially against China.

As shown in Fig. 4.14, according to the US Census Bureau, the trade volume deficit of the US exceeded USD 400 billion in 2018, and Trump was explaining the reason for each war he declared to overcome a national

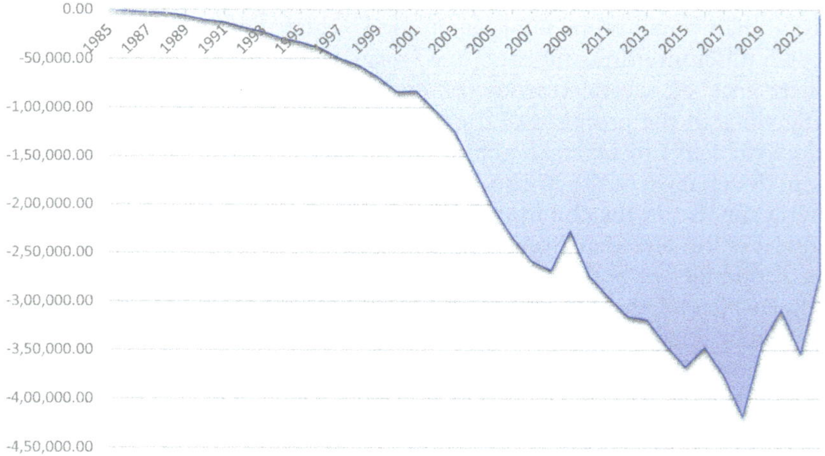

Fig. 4.14 Trade balance of the US with China (*Source* The US Census Bureau [2022])

security threat by imposing tariffs and/or quotas on imports increasing the risks on the global economy. Solar panel and washing machine imports injuring the US industries, imports of aluminum and steel threatening national security, the potential harms of China's laws, policies, practices, or actions on American intellectual property rights, innovation, or technology development, and the impacts of the imports of autos and parts on US employment rates were some of the battles with their reasons that the Trump administration had declared. The trade imbalance between the US and Europe is also increasing. In 2021, the net trade volume deficit of the US with Europe reached USD 218.7 billion.

Some economists think that the trade deficit is the result of macroeconomic factors instead of trade policies (Bekkers & Schroeter, 2020). Thus, the latest figures for 2021 exhibited an upward deficit after a decline in 2020. The Joe Biden administration did not withdraw Trump-era tariffs on Chinese imports, as of October 2022, yet they introduced new restrictions such as export limits and brought new bans for investments of Chinese companies in the US to protect US economic and military interests. In December 2022, in addition to Huawei company, the US Department of Commerce expanded sanctions to additional 36 Chinese companies (USNews, 2022).

The Effects of COVID-19

The COVID-19 pandemic had a shocking impact on the world economy and started the largest global economic crisis in the last century. In January 2020, two months before the World Health Organization (WHO) declared COVID-19 as a pandemic, the global economic growth projection of the International Monetary Fund (IMF) for 2020 was 3.3%, but many countries entered into recession and the global economy fell by about 3.06% in 2020 compared to the previous year due to the negative impacts of the COVID-19 on the global economy (IMF, 2020). As shown in Table 4.3, although some economies such as the US, Netherlands, Poland, Brazil, and India got recovered from the recession in 2021, the recovery of some economies including Germany, the UK, France, Japan, and Canada seems to be extended to upcoming years based on the IMF projections.

Beyond its mid- and long-term effects such as global recession and rise in inflation rates, the pandemic had initial shocking impacts such as the stock market crash. Within two weeks after the declaration of the

Table 4.3 Growth rates and projections

			Projections	
	2020	*2021*	*2022*	*2023*
Argentina	−9.9	10.4	4.0	3.0
Australia	−2.1	4.8	3.8	2.2
Brazil	−3.9	4.6	1.7	1.1
Canada	−5.2	4.5	3.4	1.8
China	2.2	8.1	3.3	4.6
Egypt	3.6	3.3	5.9	4.8
France	−7.9	6.8	2.3	1.0
Germany	−4.6	2.9	1.2	0.8
India	−6.6	8.7	7.4	6.1
Indonesia	−2.1	3.7	5.3	5.2
Iran	1.8	4.0	3.0	2.0
Italy	−9.0	6.6	3.0	0.7
Japan	−4.5	1.7	1.7	1.7
Kazakhstan	−2.6	4.1	2.9	3.9
Korea	−0.7	4.1	2.3	2.1
Malaysia	−5.5	3.1	5.1	4.7
Mexico	−8.1	4.8	2.4	1.2
Netherlands	−3.9	4.9	2.5	1.0
Nigeria	−1.8	3.6	3.4	3.2
Pakistan	−0.9	5.7	6.0	3.5
Philippines	−9.5	5.7	6.7	5.0
Poland	−2.2	5.9	4.5	2.0
Russia	−2.7	4.7	−6.0	−3.5
Saudi Arabia	−4.1	3.2	7.6	3.7
South Africa	−6.3	4.9	2.3	1.4
Spain	−10.8	5.1	4.0	2.0
Thailand	−6.2	1.5	2.8	4.0
Türkiye	1.8	11.0	4.0	3.5
UK	−9.3	7.4	3.2	0.5
US	−3.4	5.7	2.3	1.0

Source IMF (2022b)

pandemic, on March 23, 2020, the S&P 500 index fell to 66% of its peak value it had reached on February 19, 2020. Since then, the market has recovered and exceeded its pre-COVID-19 values, but after reaching its new peak value in December 2021, the index is around 18% below this peak value as exhibited in Fig. 4.15. As also shown in Table 4.4, health care, food, software, and technology companies got positively affected

Fig. 4.15 S&P 500 index (*Source* Investing [2022])

Table 4.4 Industry returns and volatility during the March 2020 stock market crash

Industry	*Return (%)*
Healthcare and medical devices	25.58
Food and grocery distribution	24.55
Software and technology	22.32
Natural Gas	20.95
Crude petroleum and oil services	−76.88
Real estate	−72.05
Hospitality and entertainment	−69.96

Source Mazur et al. (2021)

by the declaration of COVID-19 as a pandemic, but on the other hand, energy, real estate, hospitality, and entertainment services were the top three industries that the pandemic hit the worst with 77, 72, and 70% decline in March 2020, respectively (Mazur et al., 2021). Although the S&P 500 index and some of the industries including information technology, consumer discretionary, and materials sectors got fully recovered one year after the pandemic, real estate and utilities were still behind their peak values in February 2020 (Wen & Arbogast, 2021).

The governments responded to the pandemic very swiftly and embraced many policies including large direct income supports, debt

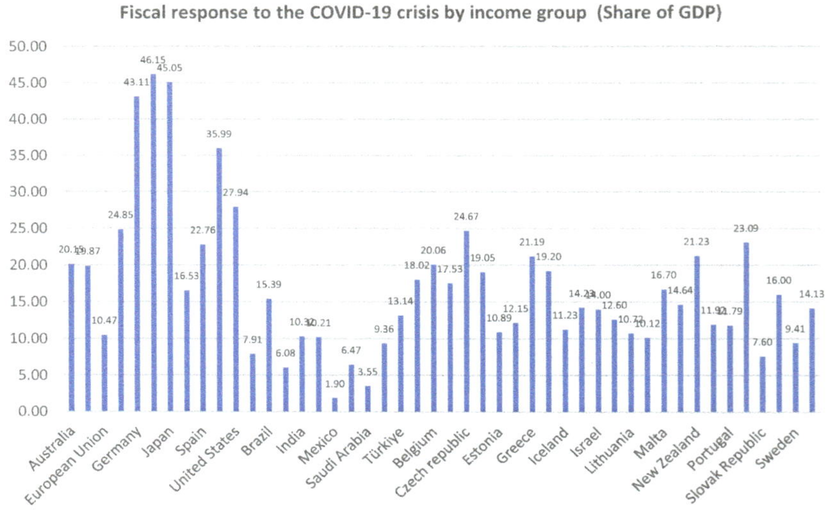

Fig. 4.16 Fiscal response to the COVID-19 crisis by income group (*Source* IMF [2022a, b])

moratoria for households and firms, and asset purchase programs. As exhibited in Fig. 4.16, the size of the fiscal response to the crisis as a share of GDP was larger in high-income countries such as Italy, Japan, the UK, and the US compared to mid-income level countries including Brazil, Türkiye, Chile, Peru, and India. The low-income economies had the least fiscal responses due to their economic conditions (IMF, 2022a, b).

The financial support of states during COVID-19 had an impact on the balance between supply and demand across countries. The fiscal stimulus did not notably have a big impact on production but increased the consumption of goods which resulted in increasing excess demand pressures in good markets. Beyond the negative effect of the war between Russia and Ukraine, it is estimated that the US fiscal stimulus during the pandemic contributed to an increase in inflation of about 2.5% in the US, and the inflation rate rose 0.5% in the UK due to the fiscal policy of the central bank of England. Countries such as Türkiye, which gave large fiscal responses to the pandemic or with high exposure to foreign impacts through international trade, experienced stronger inflation upsurges (IMF, 2022a). In addition to fiscal responses of central banks, restrictions were applied on mobility within the country and across borders; the mandatory use of masks and the curfews applied by many governments were the initial steps to decrease the spread of the virus. On the other hand, people were expecting good and fast news about vaccination studies. Brueck (2020) mentioned that there was no vaccine for an infectious disease produced in less than several years before COVID-19, and yet there was no vaccine existing for preventing the coronavirus infection in humans (Brueck, 2020). Under the urgent need pressure, the physical distancing conditions where the laboratories were closed were making it more difficult to produce the vaccines. This pressure was increasing the potential risks and failures of delivering a safe, effective, and tested vaccine. As of the end of October 2022, 12.89 billion doses have been administered globally and 68% of the world population got vaccinated with at least one dose, but only 23.1% of people in low-income countries have received at least one dose (Our World in Data, 2022). Only 6% of the people living in the poorest 52 countries which host 20% of the world population got vaccinated reported in the Global Risk Report of 2022.

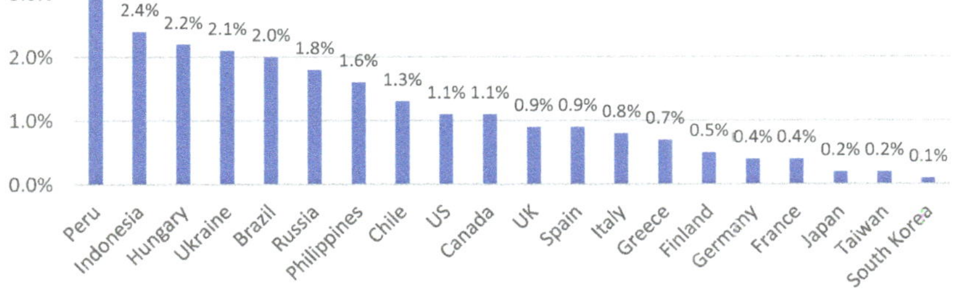

Fig. 4.17 Observed case-fatality ratio (*Source* John Hopkins University Coronavirus Research Center [2022])

Although the rates in low-income countries are still too low, the daily doses fell to 1.87 million globally. Interestingly, despite the low vaccination rates, the number of cases and the case-fatality ratio of African countries remained low due to early lockdown decisions, decreased mobility, warm climate, young population, genetic factor, preexisting immunity, limited testing, and open-air lifestyles of people (Maeda & Nkengasong, 2021). Figure 4.17 shows the countries with the top case-fatality ratios in the world. John Hopkins University Coronavirus Research Center analyzed the number of deaths per 100 confirmed cases (observed case-fatality ratio) of twenty countries COVID-19 currently affected most worldwide. Peru is observed as the leading country which is followed by Indonesia, Hungary, and Ukraine. The US was also listed as the top country with the highest case-fatality ratio among developed economies.

After vaccination rates increased, the governments decided to loosen the restrictions and gradually normalize them. Except for China where the first cases of COVID-19 were identified and which is still applying strict lockdowns in many cities, the daily lives in many countries are now normalized, but as of the end of October 2022, the number of cases exceeded 635 million, and 6.6 million people died (Worldometer, 2022).

Geopolitical Conflicts

Political tension has been rising all around the world. Some of the conflicts have been pending for more than decades, while some of them such as the war between Russia and Ukraine got worsened and changed their form from a conflict to an ongoing war. For the first time in a decade, high-intensity armed conflicts exceeded half of (53%) all conflict cases worldwide (Millian et al., 2022). Regional tensions, illegitimate economic gain, absent state institutions, limited resources worsened by climate change, and failure of the rule of law are considered by the United Nations as the main causes of conflicts (Millian et al., 2022).

Kristiina Rintakoski, the executive director of Crisis Management Initiative launched by Martti Ahtisaari, the former President of Finland and 2008 Nobel Peace Prize winner, underlines the exacerbated poverty and economic inequality caused by the Western economies, difficulties to access energy and food, and technological impacts on inequality as other reasons of conflicts (Mbe, 2009). While some of the conflicts are armed, such as the war between Russia and Ukraine or Civil Wars in Syria, Yemen, or Afghanistan, some of them are socio-politic crises. According

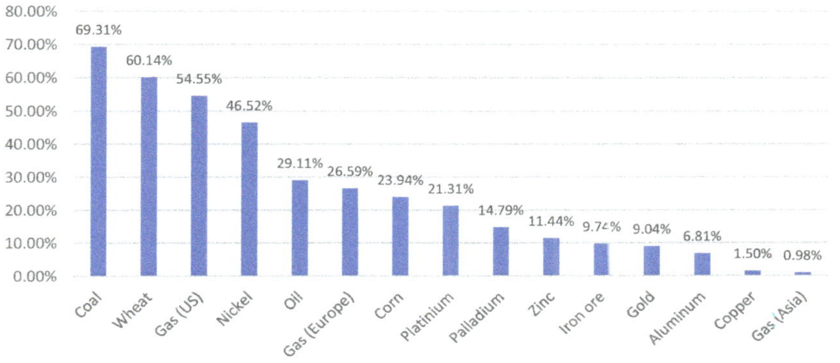

Fig. 4.18 Commodity prices from February 24 to June 1, 2022 (Compared to January 2022) (*Source* Statista [2022i])

to the report on human rights and peacebuilding published by Escola de Cultura de Pau published in 2022, 15 of 32 armed conflicts in 2021 were reported in Africa, Asia with 9 conflicts, and the Middle East with 5 conflicts followed by Africa. Europe and America had two and one conflicts, respectively (Millian et al., 2022).

The ongoing war between Russia and Ukraine which started in February 2022 resulted in a rise in commodity prices and increased inflation rates, especially in Europe. Figure 4.18 shows the impact of the war on the increase in selected commodity prices. As shown in the figure, coal and wheat prices are the most rose commodities with 69,31% and 60,14% increase rates, respectively. On the other hand, in 2020, the COVID-19 pandemic resulted in a decline in oil demand due to lockdowns and travel restrictions.

As exhibited in Fig. 4.19, the problem of storing excess oil exhibited negative prices on April 20 and April 22, 2020. Since then, oil prices started rising. After Russia declared war against Ukraine, the oil prices hit the peak value in March 2022 by exceeding USD 120 per barrel (the highest value since the 2018 global financial crisis), the Brent crude oil, West Texas Intermediate (WTI) oil, and OPEC basket oil prices stood at USD 79.65, USD 74,63, and USD 77.57 per barrel in January 2023, respectively. Potential global recession risk is considered the main reason for the decrease noted since August 2022. The US and European countries had imposed sanctions against Russia since the beginning of the war, but the bad economic conditions made some of the countries step back for instance the Netherlands issued 91 waivers to sanctions against Russia by the end of October 2022.

In summary, the never-ending rise in debt which hit a record in 2022, the increase in inequality and widened gap among people, the residual effects of COVID-19 on global production and trade, the Brexit effect on the future of European and global economy, the impact of trade wars on global trade volume, the effects of the Russia-Ukraine war on the increased energy and food prices, the high inflation rates, the late responses of the central banks to fight against the inflation, the potentially negative social outcomes of high inflation, and the rising interest rates which may result in another global recession are the outstanding risks of the global economy need to bring a sustainable solution.

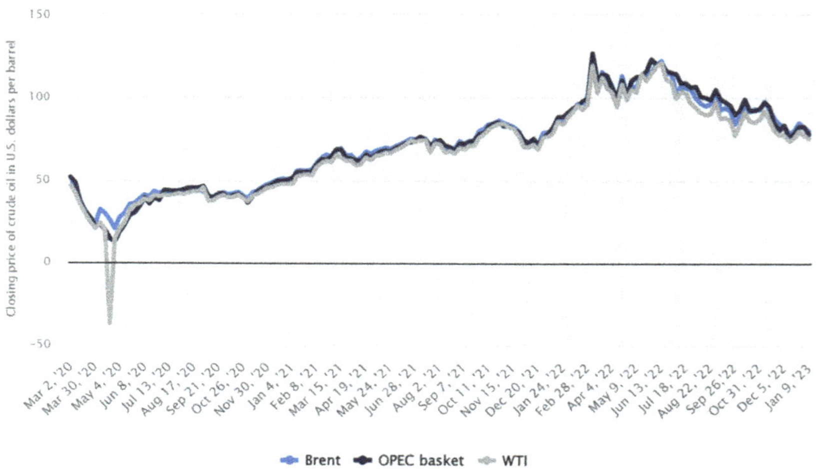

Fig. 4.19 Oil prices since the start of the COVID-19 pandemic (*Source* Statista [2023])

References

Adarov, A. (2022). *Global income inequality and the COVID-19 pandemic in three charts*. https://blogs.worldbank.org/developmenttalk/global-income-inequality-and-covid-19-pandemic-three-charts. Last Accessed on January 13, 2023.

Akgiray, V. (2019). *Good finance: Why we need a new concept of finance*. Bristol University Press. ISBN 978-1-5292-0000-3.

Bekkers, E., & Schroeter, S. (2020). *An economic analysis of the US-China trade conflict* (WTO Staff Working Paper No. ERSD-2020-04). World Trade Organization (WTO), Geneva. https://doi.org/10.30875/5b611474-en

Brueck, H. (2020). *Bill Gates says the pandemic wiped out 25 years of vaccine progress in 25 weeks*. https://www.businessinsider.com/bill-gates-pandemic-wiped-out-25-years-progress-vaccines-2020-9. Last Accessed on March 03, 2023.

CBRT. (2022). *Interest rates*. https://evds2.tcmb.gov.tr/index.php. Last Accessed on March 03, 2023.

Census.gov. (2022). *Trade in goods with China*. https://www.census.gov/foreign-trade/balance/c5700.html. Last Accessed on January 13, 2023.

Chen, T., Gozgor, G., & Koo, C. K. (2021). Pandemics and income inequality: What do the data tell for the globalization era? *Frontiers in Public Health, 9*, 674729. https://doi.org/10.3389/fpubh.2021.674729

Countryeconomy. (2022). *Russian central bank key rates*. https://countryeconomy.com/key-rates/russia. Last Accessed on January 13, 2023.

Dooley, M., Folkerts-Landau, D., & Garber, P. M. (2004). An essay on the revived Bretton Woods system. *International Journal of Finance and Economics*, *9*(4), 307–313.

ECB. (2022). *Monetary policy decisions*. https://www.ecb.europa.eu/press/pr/date/2022/html/ecb.mp221215~f3461d7b6e.en.html. Last Accessed on January 13, 2023.

Friedman, M. (1962). *Capitalism and freedom*. University of Chicago Press.

Gov.uk. (2022). *Past prime ministers*. https://www.gov.uk/government/history/past-prime-ministers. Last Accessed on January 14, 2023.

GYODER. (2022). *Outstanding mortgage rates in Türkiye*. https://www.gyoder.org.tr/files/202212/9ea37fc0-eb43-4262-9cf0-1acc9fda2271.pdf. Last Accessed on January 12, 2023.

Hemingway, E. (1935). *Notes on the next war: A serious topical letter*. https://www.ft.com/content/b498f790-4893-11de-8870-00144feabdc0. Last Accessed on January 12, 2023.

Hillebrand, E. (2010). Deglobalization scenarios: Who wins? who loses? *Global Economy Journal, 10*(2), 1–21.

IIF. (Institute of International Finance). (2022). *Global debt monitor*. https://www.iif.com/Products/Global-Debt-Monitor. Last Accessed on February 06, 2023.

IMF. (2020). *A new Bretton Woods moment*. https://www.imf.org/en/News/Articles/2020/10/15/sp101520-a-new-bretton-woods-moment. Last Accessed on January 13, 2023.

IMF. (2022a). *Fiscal monitor database of country fiscal measures in response to the COVID-19 Pandemic*. https://www.imf.org/en/Topics/imf-and-covid19/Fiscal-Policies-Database-in-Response-to-COVID-19. Last Accessed on January 21, 2023.

IMF. (2022b). *World Economic Outlook*. https://www.imf.org/en/Publications/WEO. Last Accessed on January 14, 2023.

Income Inequality by Country. (2022). *World Population Review*. https://worldpopulationreview.com/country-rankings/income-inequality-by-country. Last Accessed on January 13, 2023.

Investing. (2022). *S&P 500 index*. https://tr.investing.com/indices/us-spx-500. Last Accessed on January 14, 2023.

John Hopkins University of Medicine. (2022). *Coronavirus (COVID-19) vaccinations*. https://ourworldindata.org/covid-vaccinations. Last Accessed on January 14, 2023.

Khan, A., & Riskin, C. (2001). *Inequality and poverty in China in the age of globalization*. RePEc:oxp:obooks:9780195136494.

Kuznets, S. (1937). *GDP definition*. https://foreignpolicy.com/2011/01/03/gdp-a-brief-history/. Last Accessed on January 12, 2023.

Lanman, S. (2021). *IMF chief says more vaccinations can help tame inflation*. https://www.bloomberg.com/news/articles/2021-11-02/imf-chief-says-more-vaccinations-can-help-tame-inflation-spike. Last Accessed on January 12, 2023.

Lehmann, J. P. (2016). *Brexit shows up the failures of globalization*. https://globalnetwork.io/perspectives/2016/06/brexit-shows-failures-globalization. Last Accessed on January 13, 2023.

Levitt, T. (1983). *The globalization of markets*. https://hbr.org/1983/05/the-globalization-of-markets. Last Accessed on January 13, 2023.

Maeda, J. M., & Nkengasong, J. N. (2021). The puzzle of the COVID-19 pandemic in Africa. *Science, 371*(6524), 27–28. https://doi.org/10.1126/science.abf8832. PMID: 33384364.

Margolin, E. (2016). *Make America great again—Who said it first?* https://www.nbcnews.com/politics/2016-election/make-america-great-again-who-said-it-first-n645716. Last Accessed on January 13, 2023.

Mazur, M., Dang, M., & Vega, M. (2021). COVID-19 and the March 2020 stock market crash: Evidence from S&P1500. *Finance Research Letters, 38*, 101690. ISSN 1544-6123, https://doi.org/10.1016/j.frl.2020.101690

Mbe, V. S. (2009). *Global conflict: Causes and solutions for peace*. https://thoughteconomics.com/global-conflict-causes-and-solutions-for-peace/. Last Accessed on January 14, 2023.

Millian, I. N., Aspa, J. P. R., Garcia, J. U., Arestizabal, P. U., Arino, A.V., & Arino, M. V. (2022). *Alert 2022! Report on conflicts, human rights and peacebuilding*. https://reliefweb.int/report/world/alert-2022-report-conflicts-human-rights-and-peacebuilding. Last Accessed on January 14, 2023.

"Mortality in the most affected countries". https://coronavirus.jhu.edu/data/mortality. Last Accessed on January 14, 2023.

Neufeld, D., & Lam, S. (2023). *Visualizing $65 trillion in hidden dollar debt*. https://elements.visualcapitalist.com/visualizing-65-trillion-in-hidden-dollar-debt/. Last Accessed at March 03, 2023.

New York Times. (2021). *China Evergrande defaults on its debt: Now what?* https://www.nytimes.com/2021/12/09/business/china-evergrande-default.html. Last Accessed on January, 12, 2023.

OECD. (2023a). *General government debt*. https://doi.org/10.1787/a0528cc2-en. https://data.oecd.org/gga/general-government-debt.htm. Last Accessed on January 20, 2023.

OECD. (2023b). *Household debt*. https://doi.org/10.1787/f03b6469-en. https://data.oecd.org/hha/household-debt.htm. Last Accessed on January 20, 2023.

PBS.com. (2022). *Acceptance of the republican nomination for president*. Available at http://www.shoppbs.pbs.org/wgbh/amex/reagan/filmmore/reference/primary/acceptance.html. Last Accessed on January 13, 2023.

Pfaffenbach, K. (2021). *Inflation, inflation, inflation still seen as temporary, Lagarde says*. https://www.reuters.com/world/europe/inflation-inflation-inflation-still-seen-temporary-lagarde-says-2021-10-28/. Last Accessed on January 12, 2023.

Pickford, S. (2019). *Renew the Bretton Woods system*. https://www.chathamhouse.org/2019/06/renew-bretton-woods-system. Last Accessed on January 13, 2023.

Piketty, T. (2013). *Capital in the twenty-first century*. Harvard University Press.

Pozsar, Z. (2022). *We are witnessing the birth of a new world monetary order*. https://www.credit-suisse.com/about-us-news/en/articles/news-and-expertise/we-are-witnessing-the-birth-of-a-new-world-monetary-order-202203.html. Last Accessed on January 13, 2023.

Regan, B. (2022). *New world order or continued global economy*? https://www.thestreet.com/retirement-daily/news-commentary/new-world-order-global-economy. Last Accessed on January 13, 2023.

Rogoff, B. (2003). *The cultural nature of human development*. Oxford University Press.

Saphir, A. (2021). *Why Fed's Powell still thinks high inflation is 'temporary'*. https://www.reuters.com/business/why-fed-chair-powell-still-thinks-high-inflation-is-temporary-2021-08-27/. Last Accessed on January 12, 2023.

Statista. (2022a). *Monthly value of the Dow Jones Industrial Average (DJIA) from January 1920 to December 1955*. https://www.statista.com/statistics/1249670/monthly-change-value-dow-jones-depression/. Last Accessed on December 17, 2022.

Statista. (2022b). *Average annual OPEC crude oil price from 1960 to 2022*. https://www.statista.com/statistics/262858/change-in-opec-crude-oil-prices-since-1960/. Last Accessed on January 20, 2023.

Statista. (2022c). *National debt of China in relation to GDP 2010–2027*. https://www.statista.com/statistics/270329/national-debt-of-china-in-relation-to-gross-domestic-product-gdp/. Last Accessed on January 12, 2023.

Statista. (2022d). *Mortgage debt outstanding in the U.S. 2001–2021*. https://www.statista.com/statistics/274636/combined-sum-of-all-holders-of-mortgage-debt-outstanding-in-the-us/. Last Accessed on January 12, 2023.

Statista. (2022e). *Non-performing loans as a share of total gross loans in the United States from 2009 to 2021*. https://www.statista.com/statistics/211047/percentage-of-non-performing-loans-held-by-us-banks/. Last Accessed on January 20, 2023.

Statista. (2022f). *United States: Unemployment rate from 1999 to 2021*. https://www.statista.com/statistics/263710/unemployment-rate-in-the-united-states/. Last Accessed on January 12, 2023.

Statista. (2022g). *Monthly 12-month inflation rate in the United States from January 2020 to September 2022*. https://www.statista.com/statistics/273418/unadjusted-monthly-inflation-rate-in-the-us/. Last Accessed on November 2022.

Statista. (2022h). *Inflation rate and Federal Reserve interest rate monthly in the United States from January 2018 to November 2022*. https://www.statista.com/statistics/1312060/us-inflation-rate-federal-reserve-interest-rate-monthly/. Last Accessed on November 2022.

Statista. (2022i). *Change in average price of selected commodities from February 24 to June 1, 2022*. https://www.statista.com/statistics/1298241/commodity-price-growth-due-to-russia-ukraine-war/. Last Accessed on January 14, 2023.

Statista. (2023). *Closing price of Brent, OPEC basket, and WTI crude oil at the beginning of each week from March 2, 2020 to January 9, 2023*. https://www.statista.com/statistics/326017/weekly-crude-oil-prices/. Last Accessed on January 21, 2023.

Stiglitz, J. E. (2010). *The Stiglitz report: Reforming the international monetary and financial systems in the wake of the global crisis*. The New Press. ISBN 978-1595585202

Surz, R. (2021). *Money printing and inflation: COVID, cryptocurrencies and more*. https://www.nasdaq.com/articles/money-printing-and-inflation%3A-covid-cryptocurrencies-and-more. Last Accessed on January 13, 2023.

The Guardian. (2021). *Felixstowe backlog risks delays in run-up to Christmas for £1.5bn of imports*. https://www.theguardian.com/business/2021/oct/13/felixstowe-backlog-improving-so-shop-normally-for-christmas-says-minister. Last Accessed on January 13, 2023.

Thenationalnews.com. (2023). *Global debt climbs to record $303tn in 2021 amid pandemic-driven uncertainties*. https://www.thenationalnews.com/business/2022/02/23/global-debt-climbs-to-record-303tn-in-2021-amid-pandemic-driven-uncertainties/. Last Accessed on January 21, 2023.

Tomohara, A., & Takii, S. (2011). Does globalization benefit developing countries? Effects of FDI on local wages. *Journal of Policy Modeling, 33*(3), 511–521. https://doi.org/10.1016/j.jpolmod.2010.12.010

Tradingeconomics. (2022a). *Turkey inflation rate*. https://tradingeconomics.com/turkey/inflation-cpi. Last Accessed on January 13, 2023.

Tradingeconomics. (2022b). *China indicators*. https://tradingeconomics.com/china/indicators. Last Accessed on January 13, 2023.

USNews. (2022). *US puts 3 dozen more Chinese companies on trade blacklist*. https://www.usnews.com/news/business/articles/2022-12-16/us-puts-3-dozen-more-chinese-companies-on-trade-blacklist. Last Accessed on January 14, 2023.

Weiss, S., & Blockmann, S. (2016). *The EU deal to avoid Brexit: Take it or leave*. https://www.ceps.eu/ceps-publications/eu-deal-avoid-brexit-take-it-or-leave/. Last Accessed on January 13, 2023.

Wen, Y., & Arbogast, I. (2021). *How COVID-19 has impacted stock performance by industry*. https://www.stlouisfed.org/on-the-economy/2021/march/covid19-impacted-stock-performance-industry. Last Accessed on January 14, 2023.

World Bank Poverty and Shared Prosperity Report. (2022). https://openknowledge.worldbank.org/bitstream/handle/10986/37739/9781464818936.pdf. Last Accessed on January 13, 2023.

World Inequality Report. (2022). https://wir2022.wid.world/www-site/uploads/2021/12/WorldInequalityReport2022_Full_Report.pdf. Last Accessed on January 13, 2023.

Worldbank. (2022). *GDP current USD*. https://databank.worldbank.org/reports.aspx?source=2&type=metadata&series=NY.GDP.MKTP.CD. Last Accessed on January 20, 2023.

Worldometers. (2022). *Coronavirus cases*. https://www.worldometers.info/coronavirus/. Last Accessed on November 1, 2023.

WSJ. (2022). *Prince Charles becomes King: What to know about King Charles III*. https://www.wsj.com/articles/prince-charles-becomes-king-what-to-know-about-britains-new-monarch-11662677405. Last Accessed on January 13, 2023.

CHAPTER 5

A Short Anatomy of the Turkish Economy and the Signs of a New Crisis

Türkiye is one of the emerging economies listed in the G20 countries which faces several crises almost every decade. While some of these crises are the extension or a reflection of a global crisis, some of them are the results of internal political conflicts and wrong economic decisions. The roots of Türkiye back in 1923, the date it was founded as the Turkish Republic, but the history of Turkish states starts before BC 220 when the Great Hunnic Empire was established. Until the foundation of the Turkish Republic, 16 Turkish states took place in the history scene, where each of them represented a star in the Presidential Seal of Türkiye (Demokan, 1973).

Among the past Turkish states established, the Ottoman Empire, the predecessor of the Turkish Republic, is the most well-known one which ruled in three continents, Asia, Europe, and Africa over 600 years. Beyond its military and political success which peaked in the sixteenth century, its monetary, financial, and fiscal policies and institutions were important factors in that long-term successful governing. Flexibility, adaptability, openness to technological innovation, and pragmatism were the main characteristics lying behind the success of the Ottoman Empire. The borrowing system was constructed on Islamic law, and the roles of the foundations (vakf) and moneylenders (sarraf) in the borrowing mechanism, mudaraba, mufawada, and musharaka partnership forms of Islamic finance were also important in business life. Another important strength

L. Sümer, *The World Economy and Financial System*,
https://doi.org/10.1007/978-3-031-27530-2_5

of the Ottomans was their jurisdiction system which was providing confidence to the partners. Gold, silver, and copper were the three main coins of the Ottoman monetary system which were left on a free float in the market. The taxation system under the name of Timar was based on agricultural taxes collected locally and by state employees living in rural areas (Sipahis) who used these revenues to supply and prepare a predetermined number of soldiers for military operations.

The Timar system was successfully used during the years when the state finances were strong, but parallel to the decline of the state power, the taxes were started to be auctioned off at Istanbul. In addition, starting from 1535, some privileges (capitulations) were given to traders of certain European states (later enlarged for many other European countries), such as exemptions from customs duties for the foreign coinage they brought. During the decline years of the Empire, the budget deficit increased, and starting from the seventeenth century, the financial transactions and trade were mainly controlled by non-Muslims including Greeks, Jews, and Armenians. The growing influence of the European institutions of both private and public finance during the eighteenth century replaced the tax farming system with government borrowing with tax revenues as collateral and finally government bonds. European and Ottoman modern banks also took the places of the local financiers, and the Ottoman economy attracted significant amounts of European direct investment until World War I, mostly in infrastructure, railroads, and ports. A stock exchange was opened in Istanbul in 1873. External borrowing of the European financial markets starting in 1854 led to a default in the 1870s and the state finance was partially controlled by European creditors (Pamuk, 2004).

When the Turkish Republic was founded 100 years ago, in 1923, one of the critical issues that the new state needed to resolve was repaying the majority debt of the Ottoman Empire. The total debt and its interest were going to be repaid by 1955 according to Paris Agreement signed in 1928. After the 1929 Great Depression, the Turkish government asked for a re-assessment of the debt due to the global economic crisis, and 80% of the debt was written off which was evaluated as a political success. In 1954, 100 years after the first borrowing, the total debt was repaid. The debt to individuals who held bonds was excluded from the debt agreements. For this reason, the re-payment of such bonds and their interests continued until the end of the 1990s (Eğilmez, 2011; Ozdemir, 2010).

Turkish Economy: From 1923 to 2023

After World War I ended in 1918 with great destruction, despite its victory in many battles, the Ottoman Empire signed the Armistice of Mudros on October 30, 1918 as its allies including Germany lost the war. Soon after the armistice, Istanbul and many other cities were occupied by Allied Countries. The Turks did not accept this occupation and after several battles won against the occupiers and their allies including Greece, Armenia, France, and England, the Armistice of Mudros was over and the Treaty of Lausanne, signed on July 24, 1923, following the Turkish victory in the War of Independence. Under the leadership of Mustafa Kemal Atatürk, the Turkish Republic was founded on October 29, 1923 (Fromkin, 2009).

Even before the foundation of the Republic, the structure of the economic system was discussed in the First İzmir Economy Congress on February 17, 2023. Encouraging domestic production and exports, avoiding luxury imports, allowing foreign capitals to ensure economic development, replacing traditional Ottoman *ashar* taxation with a new system, reorganizing the Agriculture Bank and establishing an industrial bank, and developing transportation infrastructure were some of the main decisions made in the congress. In the early years of the republic, the liberal economic structure was built on these decisions, but then the state aimed to industrialize through private ventures by supporting them under a "mixed-economy model". In the cases that the private sector was not capable to proceed, the state was aiming to lead the investments. This Keynesian approach that helped the global economy to get recovered from the 1929 Great Depression was accepted in Türkiye in that period. Another reason for applying the state-led economic approach was the planned economic success of the Soviet Union after World War I (Durmus & Aydemir, 2016).

During World War I, due to its agriculture-based economy, Türkiye was caught in the crisis on a micro-scale, but the Turkish Lira depreciated rapidly due to the fixed exchange rate regime. The dependence of the economy on agriculture, along with the decrease in the price of agricultural products, led to a decrease in export revenues. Deterioration in the balance of payments started, and deflation occurred due to the continuation of price decreases. The government took many steps to combat the crisis; followed policies to increase exports and imports. Until the end of World War II, the state-led economy aimed to industrialize, increase export, and build the infrastructure of the country. By adopting the principle of statism, industrialization was accelerated by the state. To ensure stability in the Turkish Lira, the Central Bank of the Republic of Türkiye was established, and the Law on the Protection of the Value of the Turkish Currency was enacted.

Although Türkiye was not involved in the war, the Second World War hurt the Turkish economy. The prolonged mandatory military service had affected agriculture due to the inadequate workforce, and the export of agricultural products rose sharply due to the decreased production and contracted global markets due to the war effect. The high intervention of the government in agriculture and trade resulted in a change of the powerholders and with the lead of the Democrat Party, the economy shifted to a more liberal approach. Supporting the farmers, increasing industrialization, investments in infrastructure, incentives to foreign investors, especially to oil companies, UN and NATO membership, involvement in the Marshall Plan, and Korean War were the most important economic and political events of the second half of the 1940s and 1950s. After the recession years of the 1940s, the economy grew 7% on average in the 1950s. Table 5.1 shows the 10-year average growth rates of Türkiye from 1923 to 2021. As shown in Table 5.2, the Turkish economy had an average of more than 5% since its foundation. Under Prime Minister Adnan Menderes's government, this growth brought a rapid increase in GDP per capita which rose from USD 153 at its level in 1949 to USD 584 at the end of 1959. Together with the economic growth, the debt level of the state rapidly increased. In fact, until the mid-1940s, except for the debts provided from the US in 1930, from the Soviet Union in 1934, and from England in 1938, the state did not use debt, in contrast, and had a trade balance surplus (Olcar, 2013). In the post-war years, due to the negative consequences of the war and the liberalization policies, as shown in Table 5.2, starting from 1947, a trade balance deficit occurred. The government decided to use debt to finance the deficit, and the size of the debt increased rapidly which resulted in a foreign exchange shortage. On August 4, 1958, the government declared a moratorium and Türkiye entered an arrangement with IMF for the first time. The Turkish Lira was devaluated, and the value of 1 USD increased from 2.80 TL to 9 TL.

In the 1960s, the economic approach of the country was structured in the opposite direction of the 1950s. The liberal and free economic policies were replaced by state-led economic ones and the import substitution

Table 5.1 Growth rates and GDP per capita (1923–2021)

Period	*Growth rate (%)*	*GDP per capita (End of the period) USD*
1923–1929	9.4	71
1930–1939	6.0	93
1940–1949	−0.9	153
1950–1959	7.0	584
1960–1969	5.7	586
1970–1979	5.9	1.877
1980–1989	4.0	1.959
1990–1999	4.2	4.003
2000–2009	4.0	8.980
2010–2019	5.8	10.925
2020	1.8	8.599
2021	11.0	9.539

Source Eğilmez (2020) and TUIK (2022)

Table 5.2 Trade balance of Türkiye 1945–1960

Years	*Export*	*Import*	*Balance*	*Export/import ratio*
1945	168.2	96.9	71.3	173.6
1946	214.5	118.8	95.7	180.6
1947	223.3	244.6	−21.3	91.3
1948	196.7	275	−78.3	71.5
1949	247.8	290.2	−42.4	85.4
1950	263.4	285.6	−22.2	92.2
1951	314	402	−88	78.1
1952	362.9	555.9	−193	65.3
1953	396	532.5	−136.5	74.4
1954	334.9	478.3	−143.4	70.0
1955	313.3	497.6	−184.3	63.0
1956	304.9	407.3	−102.4	74.9
1957	345.2	397.1	−51.9	86.9
1958	247.2	315	−67.8	78.5
1959	353.7	469.9	−116.2	75.3
1960	320.7	468.1	−147.4	68.5

Source Olcar (2013)

development strategy has been adopted. The foreign exchange bottleneck and foreign debt payment problems experienced by the country in this period, and external debt were needed to finance investment projects. In 1960, State Planning Organization (SPO) was established, and the external debt was limited. The 1960s were also the years that the period of coups started taking place in Türkiye. In May 1960, a coup was conducted by the army and Prime Minister Adnan Menderes was executed on September 17, 1961. Following years, almost every ten years, a coup was attempted in Türkiye. March 12, 1971, September 12, 1980, February 28, 1997, and July 15, 2016 were the ones that affected the politics and socio-economics of the Turkish Republic's history deeply.

In the 1970s, when the global economy was struggling with high inflation after the oil crisis, Türkiye was involved in the Cyprus Peace Operation in 1974. The combined effects of the global economic situation, the Cyprus conflict, the external debt level, the unemployment rates, and high inflation increased during these years. Implementation of the import substitution policies did not result in what was expected, and the balance of payments and the external deficit increased continuously. The second oil crisis in 1980 also increased the prices and unemployment rates. The inflation rates skyrocketed to triple digits. The January 24 Decisions were put into effect in 1980 and Turkish Lira devaluated again. In addition, the fixed exchange rate policy was abandoned, a controlled floating exchange rate regime was adopted, and incentives were made for foreign capital inflows.

The 1980s were the years of liberalization years under Prime Minister Turgut Özal's leadership. The new program enabled Türkiye to overcome the balance-of-payments crisis, helped the country to borrow in international capital markets, and led to renewed economic growth. The trade deficit decreased, the tourism industry started growing, and foreign investments started investing in the country. Pipeline fees from Iraq also added value to growth. Despite the rapid economic growth and regained reputation of the country in the international markets, the inflation and unemployment rates remained a problem. One of the main crises of the 1980s was the banker's crisis. Thousands of people invested their money in bankers to obtain high-interest income. The collapse of the system due to high-interest rates left more than 300,000 people to lose their money and created a social outrage, suicides, killings, and injuries. Terrorism had started in Türkiye in the late 1960s with the Armenian terrorist attacks targeting Turkish diplomats, but the 1980s were also the years the ongoing PKK terrorism started in Türkiye (Ak & Altintas, 2017). Terrorism had a negative impact on Turkish economic stability.

In the 1990s, the economy experienced several economic crises caused by internal and external factors such as the threats of terrorist attacks, internal interest rate policy, or the global financial crisis including the Mexican Peso crisis, the Asia financial crisis, and the Russian ruble crisis. High inflation rates and public deficits were very high in this period. The political instability resulting in frequent elections, out-of-control public deficits, the impacts of the Gulf Crisis, and the budget allocated to fight against terrorism were the main issues that impacted the economy negatively. High-interest rates of the Central Bank were encouraging the money inflow to the country and TL was overvalued which was increasing the trade deficit. The decision of the Central Bank about decreasing the interest rates in 1993 resulted in a devaluation of the Turkish Lira and increased dollarization. On January 26, March 1, and March 17, 1994, the currency devaluated three times and the money outflow started. In the 1994 economic crisis, as a result of the low-interest rate policy, the inflation rates rose to triple digits, the welfare lost, the economy fell into recession, stock markets fell, and thereafter the interest rates were increased. A USD 700 million loan agreement was signed with IMF to get recovered from the crisis (Keyder, 2022).

2001 was a dramatic year for the Turkish economy. A new crisis arose from an internal political conflict between the President and the Prime Minister. The reasons behind this crisis were more on economic conditions, but the political crisis ignited the economic crisis. High debt stocks, emptied banks, the post-1999 great earthquake recession, high inflation, and interest rates, were the main problems that the country's economy was struggling with. On February 21, 2001, when the political crisis took place, the stock market lost 29% in value on the third day of the crisis, and repo rates climbed to 7,500%. USD 7.6 billion foreign exchange outflow from the Central Bank and the economy shrank by 9.5% in 2001. The inflation rate has approached 90%. To fight against the crisis, a new "National Programme" has been put into practice, the fixed exchange rate was abandoned, and the floating exchange rate regime was adopted. The autonomy of the Central Bank was ensured by law, to prevent the burden of duty losses on public banks, the budgetary and extra-budgetary funds were closed, and the public procurement and expropriation laws were amended. As a result of the 2001 banking crisis which cost to Turkish economy USD 20 billion, 24 banks were bankrupted and after the elections in 2002, the government changed in Türkiye (Sungur, 2015).

After the new government came to the power in 2002 under the leadership of Recep Tayyip Erdoğan, who is still ruling the country, the economic decisions taken in 2001 were applied strictly. The new government emphasized EU membership of Türkiye, as well as the specialization program. Before the global financial crisis, there were strong growth rates, 7.5% on average between 2003 and 2007. Parallel to the global economic situation which resulted in a recession in 2009, the economy kept growing but with smaller average rates. The inflation rate fell as low as 6.2% in 2012 (Sungur, 2015). The investments in infrastructure including airports, tunnels, bridges, highways, and railways have surged, and remarkable success was gained. The government also incentivized the construction and real estate industry, and the development of the defense industry was sparked. On the other hand, the trade deficit, and private and public debt were increasing, and the low-interest rate policy of the government was putting pressure on the central bank's monetary decisions.

In the 2000s, there was significant success in fighting terrorism but after 2014, the terrorist attacks increased, political conflicts arose and in 2016 a serious coup attempt was defeated by the brave defense of the public. In addition to the terrorist attacks and the coup attempt, the broken down relations with Israel after the Israeli attack on private Turkish humanitarian aid ships in international waters which caused the death of 10 people in 2010, the abandoned relationship with Egypt after the coup took place in 2013, the suspended relations with Syria after the civil war started in 2011 which resulted in hosting of Türkiye millions of Syrian refugees, the tension with Russia in 2015 after the shot of a Russian attack aircraft, and the broken down of the Türkiye and the US relations due to the reasons including the disagreement on Syrian politics, decisions of Turkish government about purchasing S-400 missile system, the US positioning, and support about the terrorist groups threatening Türkiye, arrestment of Pastor Andrew Brunson who was accused of being an agent in October 2016 and released in 2018 were important political events that affected the Turkish economy negatively in the 2010s. Besides the political risks, the decisions about economic management such as the interest rate policy which caused depreciation in the Turkish Lira and resulted in high inflation, the decrease in foreign exchange reserves of the

Central Bank, the increase in debt, and the COVID-19 effect increased the pressure on the Turkish economy.

Are There Signs of a New Crisis?

COVID-19 resulted in a global recession in 2020. Thereafter, inflation started rising globally and the ongoing war between Russia and Ukraine increased the pressure on economies. Despite recession risks, many central banks including FED and ECB eventually started increasing the interest rates to fight against the highest inflation rates recorded in the last 30–40 years. In contrast to many central banks, the Central Bank of Türkiye Republic went the opposite direction and decided to decrease the interest rates and keep the economic activities alive. As a result, as shown in Figs. 5.1, 5.2, and 5.3, the interest rates were decreased to as low as 9%, while the inflation rate rose to 85% in December 2022 (declined to 65% due to base effect) and Turkish Lira kept losing value.

In 2021, the government declared a new Economy Model based on increasing the export volume, decreasing the trade deficit, and making Türkiye a trade hub, aiming to replace China in terms of supplying products to Europe and the rest of the world by using its geographical advantage. Although this policy helped to increase the employment rates in the post-COVID-19 era (see Fig. 5.4), the trade deficit kept increasing as the import volume grew faster than the export as shown in Fig. 5.5.

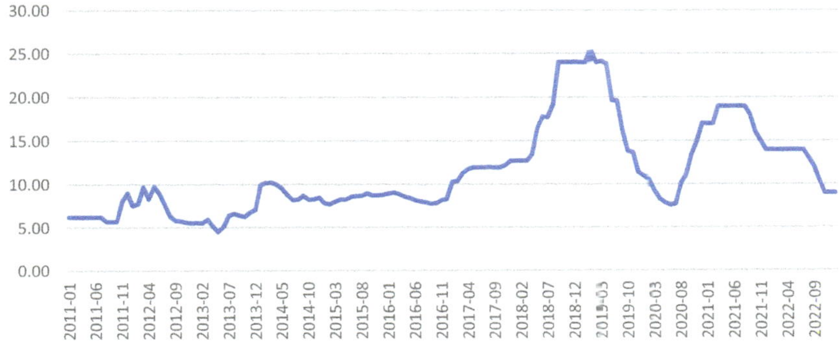

Fig. 5.1 Interest rates in Türkiye (*Source* CBRT [2022])

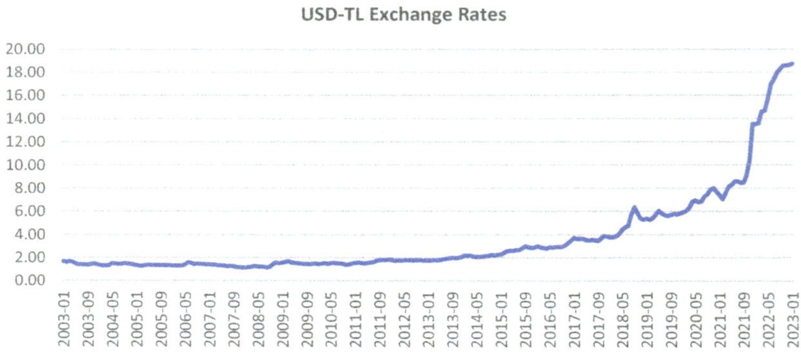

Fig. 5.2 USD-TL (2003–2022) (*Source* CBRT [2022])

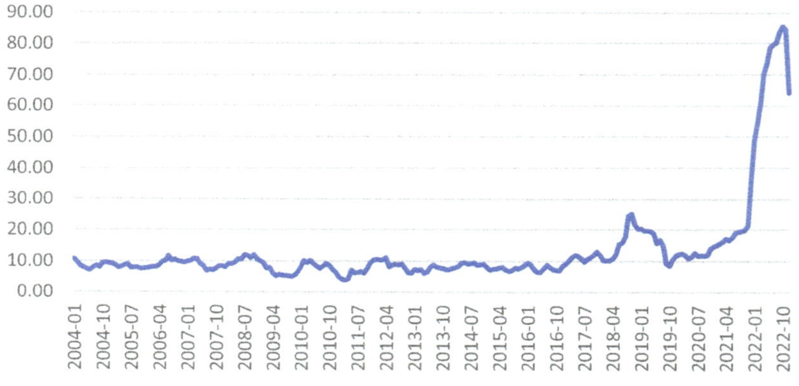

Fig. 5.3 Inflation rates (CPI) in Türkiye (*Source* CBRT [2022])

Since 1974, Türkiye has had a trade deficit that expanded by 53% year on year to USD 10.4 billion in December of 2022, from USD 6.8 billion in the corresponding month of the previous year. Considering the January to December period of 2022, the country's trade deficit surged by 138.4% to USD 110.2 billion, as imports soared 34.3% to USD 364.4 billion while exports increased at a softer 12.9% to USD 254.2 billion (Tradingeconomics, 2023).

As shown in Figs. 5.6 and 5.7, the size of gross external debt and total loans including consumer credits, and private sector credits are

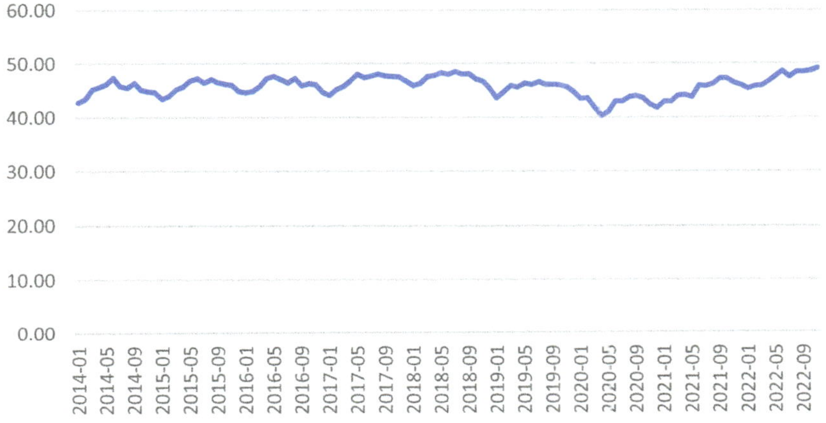

Fig. 5.4 Employment rates in Türkiye (*Source* CBRT [2022])

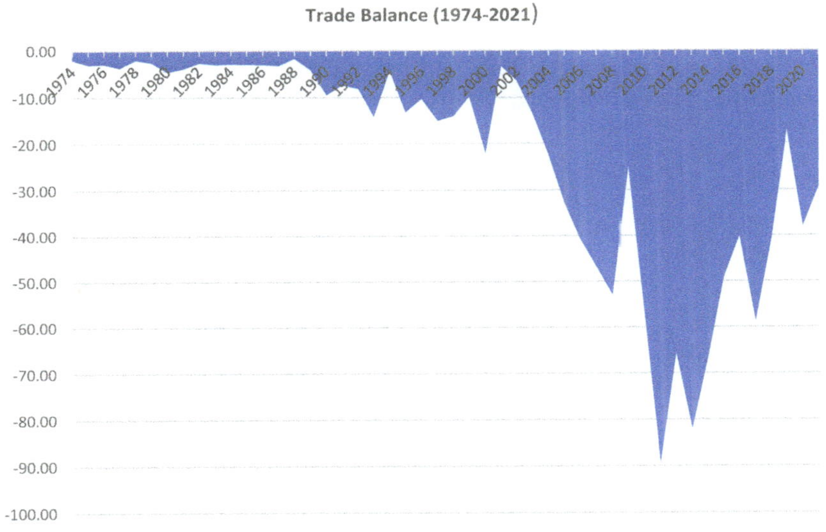

Fig. 5.5 Trade balance of Türkiye (1974–2021) (*Source* Worldbank [2023])

increasing steeply. Despite there is no increase in non-performing loans, the combined potential threats of inflation-interest rates and depreciation of TL on the economy are outstanding. The external debt in Türkiye has been increasing sharply in the last decade. After hitting its record in the first quarter of 2018 with USD 457.31 billion, as of the end of the third quarter of 2022, it stands at USD 442.9 billion, close to its 2018 record (Ministry of Trade, 2023). On the other hand, consumer credit which averaged TL 297,995,600.77 from 2000 until 2022 reached TL 1,512,642,117 in November of 2022. Private sector credit also reached an all-time high of TL 5,524,965,691 in November 2022 (Tradingeconomics, 2023).

The monthly average foreign direct investment in Türkiye is USD 838.10 million from 2003 until 2022. After its USD 46 million records low value in October 2005, it reached its all-time high of USD 6.57 billion in May of 2006. Figure 5.8 shows a significant decline in FDI in the last few years (Ministry of Trade, 2023).

After a decline in the early phase of COVID-19, the Borsa Istanbul 100 index started rising sharply and broke record highs to trade above the 5,600 level in January 2023 as shown in Fig. 5.9. While investors are using equities as a hedge against rising consumer prices, Turkish residents

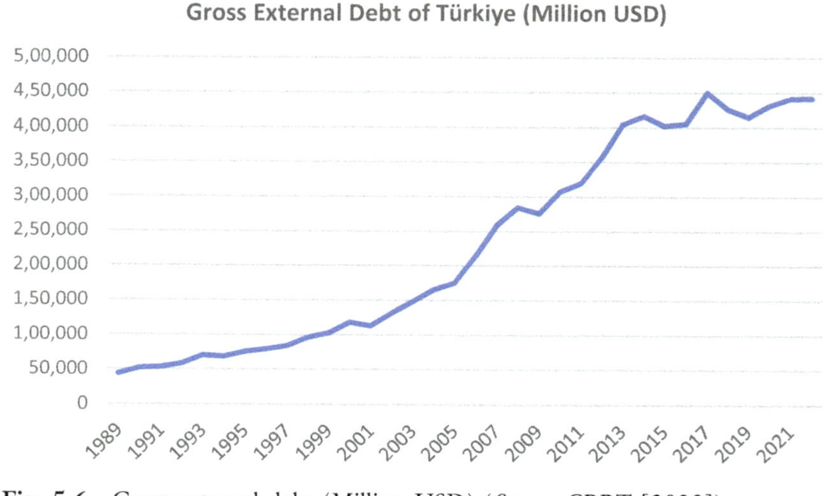

Fig. 5.6 Gross external debt (Million USD) (*Source* CBRT [2023])

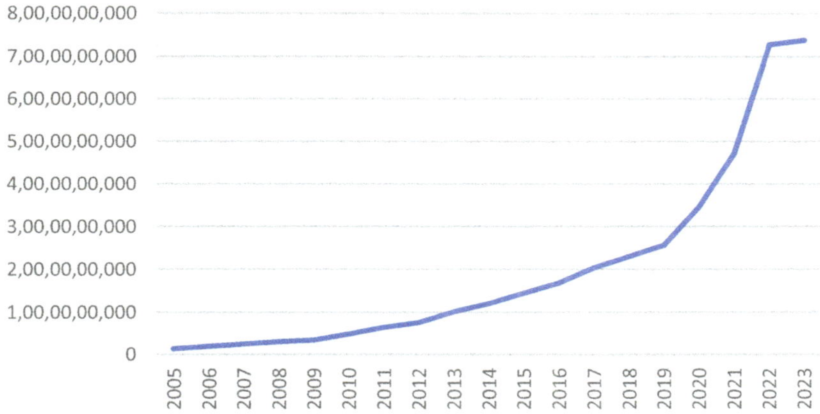

Fig. 5.7 Total loans (Thousands TRY) (*Source* CBRT [2023])

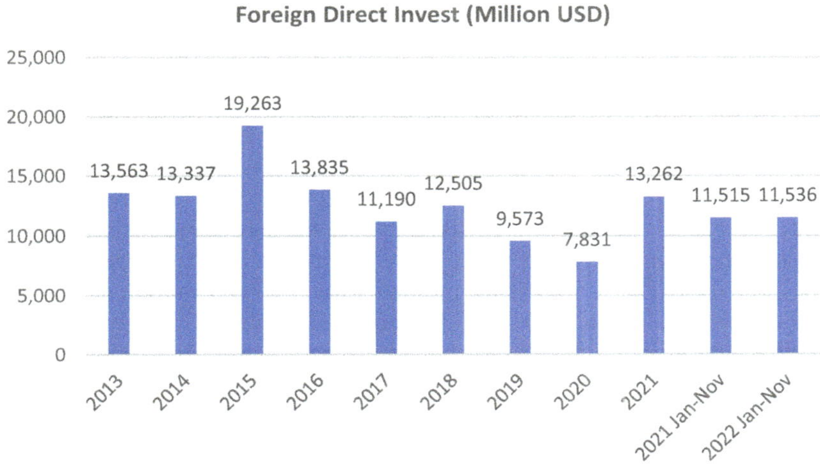

Fig. 5.8 Foreign direct investment (*Source* Ministry of Trade [2023])

seek out assets to store their savings. Meanwhile, the inflation rate fell to 64.3% in December 2022 mainly due to the base effect, the Borsa 100 index was up nearly 200% in 2022. Despite this sharp increase, it is also noteworthy to underline that, as exhibited in Fig. 5.10, the share

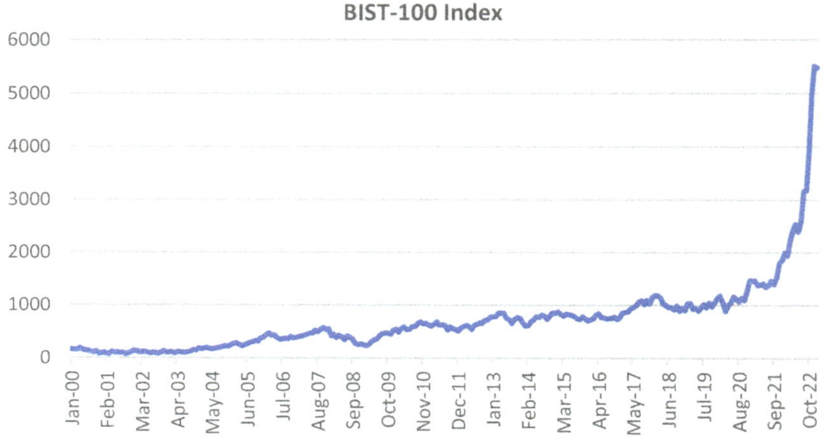

Fig. 5.9 Istanbul Stock Exchange (BIST 100) (*Source* Borsa Istanbul [2023])

of foreign investors in the Borsa İstanbul 100 index fell from 65.6% to 29.8% since January 2019.

The figures above exhibit that the Turkish economy is struggling with high inflation rates and the government is increasing the base wages to keep the purchasing power of the citizens as stable as they can. There is no solid policy of CBRT to decrease the inflation rates, as the trade deficit and the size of the debt in all aspects are increasing while the foreign direct investments and the rate of foreign investors in the stock market are declining. The interest rate policy of the CBRT resulted in a value loss of the Turkish Lira very fast. To protect the value of TL, the government announced a new tool which brought a fixed-interest rate guarantee based on the weighted average cost of the CBRT funding, a guarantee given by the Treasury of Türkiye plus the value increase of USD against TL in the periods where the investors convert their foreign currencies to TL or directly deposit their TL in this new account. Although this new account type (currency-protected account) is evaluated as a hidden increase in interest rates, the potential burden of the Treasury is unknown in the case TL keeps losing its value against USD. On the other hand, a potential policy shift from low-interest rates to higher interest rates to fight against inflation may reduce the stock prices deeply and a stock market collapse is likely to occur. The increase in interest rates may also

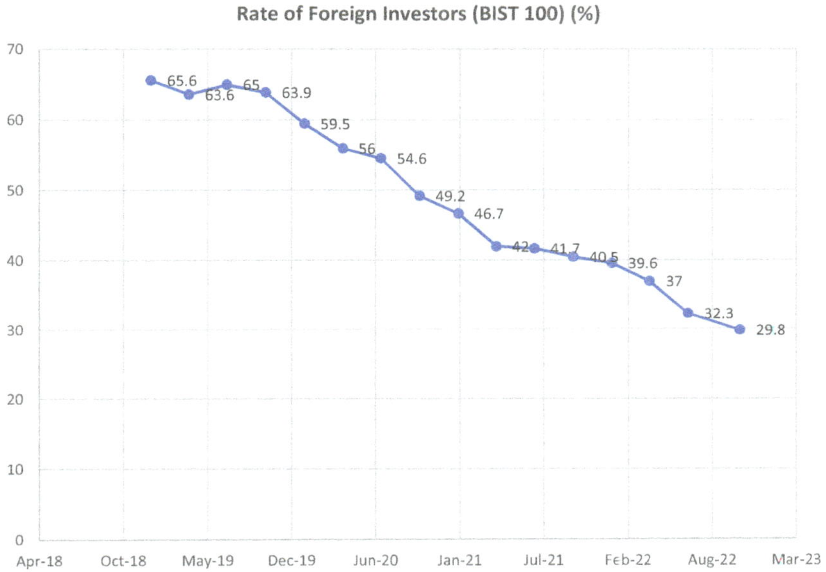

Fig. 5.10 Share of foreign investors (BIST 100) (*Source* Central Securities Depository (MKK) [2022])

put the economy into a recession which may lead to an increase in high unemployment rates, default of loans, and shutdown of many firms. If the interest rate policy of CBRT remains the same, the inflation rates may increase again, and the country may face a three-digit inflation rate in a very short time. This may result in a worse economic situation and put the country into a deep economic crisis. An urgent and sustainable solution is needed for the Turkish economy.

References

Ak, M. Z., & Altıntaş, N. (2017). Türkiye'de Terörizm ile İktisadi Büyüme İlişkisinin Nedensellik Analizi. *Bilgi Sosyal Bilimler Dergisi*, *1*, 20–31.

Borsa Istanbul. (2023). *BIST Stock Indices*. https://www.borsaistanbul.com/en/sayfa/3542/bist-stock-indices. Last Accessed on March 03, 2023.

Central Securities Depository (MKK). (2022). *Türkiye rate of foreign investors at stock market*. https://www.mkk.com.tr/en. Last Accessed on January 14, 2023.

Central Bank Republic of Türkiye (CBRT). (2022). *Türkiye exchange rates*. https://evds2.tcmb.gov.tr/index.php?/evds/serieMarket/#collapse_2. Last Accessed on January 14, 2023.

Central Bank Republic of Türkiye (CBRT). (2023). *Selected statistics*. https://evds2.tcmb.gov.tr/index.php. Last Accessed on January 21, 2023.

Demokan, H. F. (1973). *Contemporary Turkey: Geography, history, economy, art, tourism*. Basın-Yayın Genel Müdürlüğü, Ajans-Türk, Türkiye: Cumhuriyetin 50. Yıl Kitabı, Ajans-Türk Matbaacılık Sanayii.

Durmus, S., & Aydemir, N. K. (2016). Atatürk Dönemi Türkiye Ekonomisi (1923–1938). Kafkas Üniversitesi İktisadi ve İdari Bilimler Fakültesi KAÜİİBFD Cilt, 7, Sayı 12, ISSN: 1309-4289 E—ISSN: 2149-9136.

Eğilmez, M. (2011). *Osmanlı'dan Devraldığımız Borçlar*. https://www.mahfiegilmez.com/2011/12/osmanlidan-devraldigimiz-borclar.html. Last Accessed on January 14, 2023.

Eğilmez, M. (2020). *Türkiye Ekonomisi*. Remzi Kitabevi, İstanbul.

Fromkin, D. (2009). *A peace to end all peace: The Fall of the Ottoman empire and the creation of the modern Middle East* (pp. 360–373). Macmillan. ISBN 978-0-8050-8809-0.

Keyder, N. (2022). Türkiye'nin Kriz Deneyimleri 1994, 2000–2001, 2008–2009 ve 2018–2022 Krizleri. *İktisat ve Toplum Sayı, 141*, 4–13.

Ministry of Trade. (2023). *Monthly Foreign Trade statistics tables—December 2022*. https://www.trade.gov.tr/statistics/foreign-trade-statistics/monthly-foreign-trade-statistics-tables-december-2022. Last Accessed on January 21, 2023.

Olcar, A. (2013). *Türkiye'nin Dış Borç Sorunu ve Kriz Etkileri*. T.C. Hitit Üniversitesi Sosyal Bilimler Enstitüsü, İktisat Anabilim Dalı, Yüksek Lisans Tezi, Çorum.

Ozdemir, B. (2010). *Osmanli Devleti Dis Borclari*. T.C. Maliye Bakanligi, Strateji Gelistirme Baskanligi, 2010/403, 2. Baskı, Ankara.

Pamuk, Ş. (2004). The evolution of financial institutions in the Ottoman Empire, 1600–1914. *Financial History Review, 11*(1), 7–32. https://doi.org/10.1017/S0968565004000022

Sungur, O. (2015). 2000 Sonrası Türkiye Ekonomisi: Büyüme, Enflasyon, İşsizlik, Borçlanma ve Dış Ticarette Gelişmeler. *Tematik Yazılar, Toplum Ve Demokrasi, 9*(19–20), 243–269.

Tradingeconomics. (2023). "Türkiye Trade Balance". https://tradingeconomics.com/turkey/balance-of-trade. Last Accessed on January 14, 2023.

TUIK. (2022). "Gross Domestic Products". https://data.tuik.gov.tr/Kategori/GetKategori?p=ulusal-hesaplar-113&dil=2. Last Accessed on March 01, 2023.

Worldbank. (2023). "Net trade in goods (BoP, current US$)—Turkiye". https://data.worldbank.org/indicator/BN.GSR.MRCH.CD?locations=TR. Last Accessed on March 03, 2023.

CHAPTER 6

Time to Question

The picture taken in this book exhibits that today's conventional economic models, financial system, and the current fiscal and economic policies are seemed to be mostly serving the benefits of small groups instead of the general benefits of society and are incapable of resolving the current economic problems of the world. Remembering the reasons for the existence of states, this situation does not match the social state idea. That is why there is a big gap between the living standards of the citizens of a society and among the citizens of different states. The reason behind this gap is the egocentric and imperialist approach of people, companies, and states.

From a social perspective, the COVID-19 pandemic also rapidly started transforming our lives in many areas including workspaces, vacation habits, accommodation choices, and the business environment. As a result of online shopping, distance work, remote education, virtual meetings, and minimum human interaction, COVID-19 accelerated digitalization, but also made people question the current system. The employees realized that they could also be efficient while working from home, and there was no need to lose hours in traffic during the day and spend the whole week in the office. People also understood the importance of their health and the happiness the work-life balance brought to their lives.

There were also some negative effects of distance working especially for those who decreased their daily mobility. In addition, some employers put

L. Sümer, *The World Economy and Financial System*,
https://doi.org/10.1007/978-3-031-27530-2_6

additional pressure on employees to make them work more by e-mailing them beyond regular working hours, increasing the number of daily meetings one after another, and forcing them to spend more time online. This situation is also evaluated as the negative impact of the current dominant economic system, capitalism. Considering that capitalism did not provide a solution to financial crises that we encounter regularly, a serious threat to our lives brought a new opportunity to discuss the future of capitalism, the system that most of the world is suffering from. Elshurafa (2012) claims that poverty, income inequality, underemployment, and pollution are the natural components of capitalism, and Chomsky (2020) defines COVID-19 as the payment of the logic of capitalism and the crimes of its violent neoliberal form. The role of the states in terms of market creation, correction, intervention, and direction is also arguable in the COVID-19 pandemic days as there are also ideas on the weakness of capitalism exposed in the pandemic (Nelson, 2020; Van Apeldoorn & De Graaf, 2022).

In that sense, although it is a long and difficult journey, COVID-19, a great disaster that affected the whole world, stands as an opportunity to produce a sustainable and fair economic system, a system that embraces all people, and treats them with justice, distributes the resources fairly and in a more balanced way.

The main principles of being a social state are providing the major needs of the citizens including accommodation, food, health, education, and justice equally in all circumstances. There is a famous piece of advice from his teacher, Sheikh Edebali, to Osman Gazi who is the founder of the Ottoman Empire stating that "let the people live so that the state can live". Maybe that was the main and the most important doctrine of the Ottoman Empire which let them rule the world for almost six centuries. The state exists for the happiness of the people living in its territory. The main services provided by the state does not limit the private business venture, yet it provides a framework that regulates the rules of doing business by aiming for the people to live as an individual but by integrating them into society, to enable them to work for themselves by respecting the needs of the society. In that context, we need to discuss the needs of people, the reasons why people work, the meaning of money, the way we become happy, and the ways we can resolve conflicts.

What Are the Main Needs of People?

The main needs of the people include accommodation, subsistence, education, health, justice, peace, security, respect for their beliefs, freedom, and acting freely without disrespecting and trespassing others' rights. A state which is unable to provide these rights and services to its citizens is unsuccessful no matter what kind of economic accomplishment it gains.

Housing

Today, it is estimated that 150 million people are homeless all around the world (Charlton, 2019). Nigeria, Pakistan, and Egypt are listed as the top three countries with 24.4 million, 20 million, and 12 million homeless people, respectively (Worldpopulationreview, 2022a, b). According to an OECD report published in 2021, nearly all countries included in the report had less than 1% homeless rate of their population. According to the Worldpopulationreview report (2022a, b), while developing countries such as Türkiye and Russia have less than a total of 100,000 homeless people, 2.6 million and 1.8 million homeless people are living in China and India, respectively. On the other hand, among developed economies, the US is listed as the top country with 580,466 homeless people living in, and the UK follows the US with 365,535 homeless people recorded. According to Habitat for Habitat.org (2017), 1.6 billion people around the world live in inadequate shelters.

On the other hand, according to the United Nations Refugee Agency report, as of June 2022, there are 103 million forcibly displaced people worldwide. This number rose to 13.7 million people only within 6 months of 2022. The number of people worldwide who were forcibly displaced more than doubled in the last decade. By the end of 2021, there were 32.5 million refugees in the world, and 7.8 million new Ukrainian refugees who had to leave their countries after the war started were added in 2022. Russia, Poland, and Germany are the three countries that host Ukrainian refugees with 2.9 million, 1.4 million, and 1 million refugees, respectively. Among 32.5 million refugees recorded by the end of 2021, Türkiye is the leading country that is hosting 3.8 million refugees officially. Colombia with 1.8 million and Uganda and Pakistan with 1.5 million refugees hosting each follows Türkiye. Beyond the Ukrainian refugees, Syria (6.8 million), Venezuela (4.6 million), and Afghanistan

(2.7 million) are the top three countries where people leave and seek a host country. While an estimated 36.5 million of 89.3 million forcibly displaced people were children who were below 18 years old (41%) as of the end of 2021. Also, 1.5 million children were born as refugees.

There is interesting data about the income levels of the host countries. As demonstrated in Fig. 6.1, 83% of the refugees are hosted in low- and middle-income-level countries, while the rate of the high-income countries which host refugees is only 17%, even below the rate of low-income countries which is 22%. There are also 4.3 million people living in 95 countries who are categorized as stateless.

All these figures show that hundreds of millions of people in the world do not have access to accommodation, the main need of people. The figures for subsistence are even worse than the accommodation. As mentioned before, as of the end of 2019, 648 million people in the world are living under the poverty line, which is USD 2.15, the World Bank reports. 84% of these people are living in Sub-Saharan Africa and South Asia, so access to minimum living earnings is also impossible for millions of people.

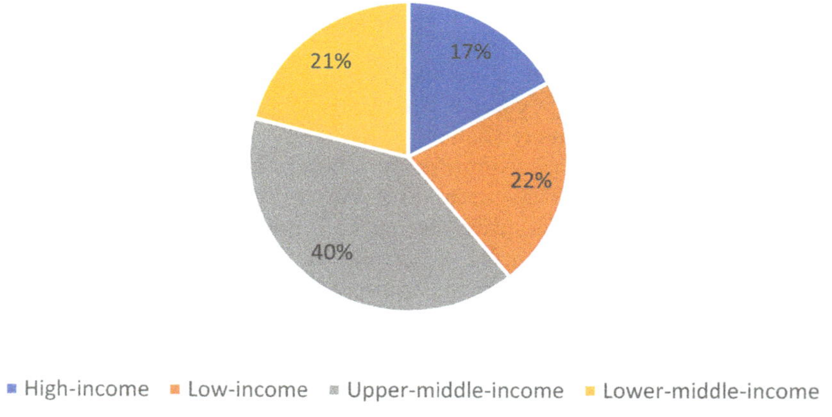

Fig. 6.1 Distribution of the refugee host countries by income level (The UN Refugee Agency, 2022)

Education and Health

The situation for access to education and health is not different compared to other statistics. Although around 90% of the world population had completed primary education in 2020, the rate of completion of secondary education is 66%. UNESCO Institute for Statistics reports that as of 2019, 258 million children, adolescents, and youth are out of school. 58 million children of primary school age which is 8% of 787 million of the total number of kids of primary school age do not go to school. Figure 6.2 shows the global and regional out-of-school rates. Sub-Saharan Africa with its 19%, 37%, and 58% out-of-school rates for primary, lower secondary, and upper secondary ages, respectively, is the least educated region in the world. The out-of-school rate of upper secondary age in Europe and Northern America is only 7%.

Half of all out-of-school children live in conflict-affected countries such as Syria, Yemen, Sudan, and Nigeria. Access to education is also strongly

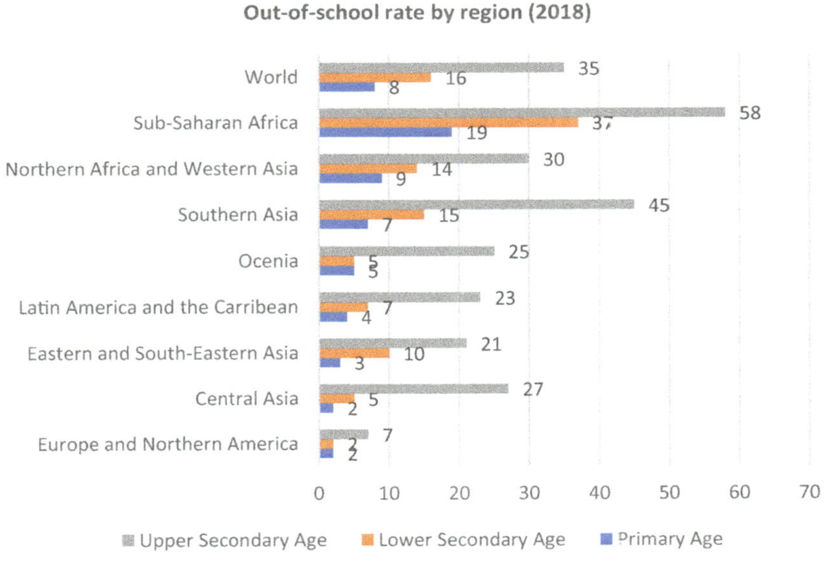

Fig. 6.2 Out-of-school rate by region and age group (UNESCO Institute for Statistics, 2019)

correlated with poverty. Figure 6.3 shows that the government expenditures on education over the total GDP are around 4.3% on average in 2020. Public finances for education in low-income countries are very low compared to the annual spending of high-income countries. For instance, the expenditures in Austria are more than 200 times higher per student than the expenditures of the Democratic Republic of Congo. Poverty also requires children to work which means these kids must leave school early or never enter school.

According to the World Health Organization (WHO), the current health expenditures as of percentage of GDP is 9.83%. WHO also reports that as of 2017, half the world lacks access to essential health services, and health expenses push 100 million people into extreme poverty (WHO, 2022). The fact that only 6% of the people living in the poorest 52 countries got COVID-19 vaccinated also exhibits that access to basic healthcare needs is not fairly met globally. Sub-Saharan Africa and Southern Asia are also listed as regions with inequality in access to health. While 17% of mothers and children in the poorest fifth of households in low- and lower-middle-income countries received at least six of seven basic maternal and child health interventions, this rate is 74% in the wealthiest fifth of households. Figure 6.4 exhibits the global access to healthcare index of the top-performing 20 countries. According to

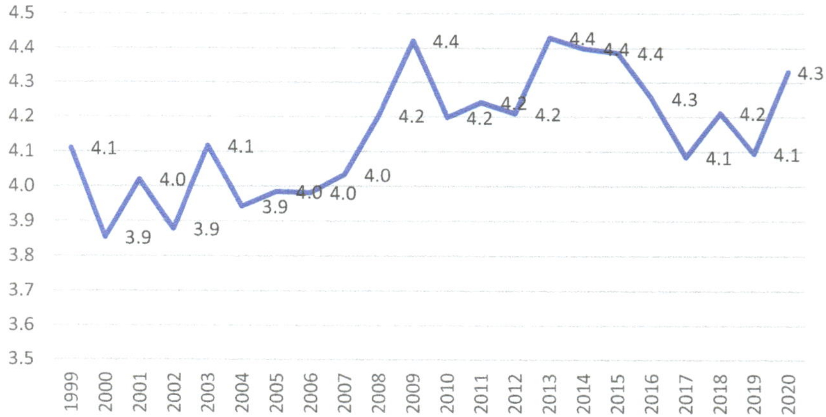

Fig. 6.3 Government expenditure on education, total (% of GDP) (Worldbank, 2022)

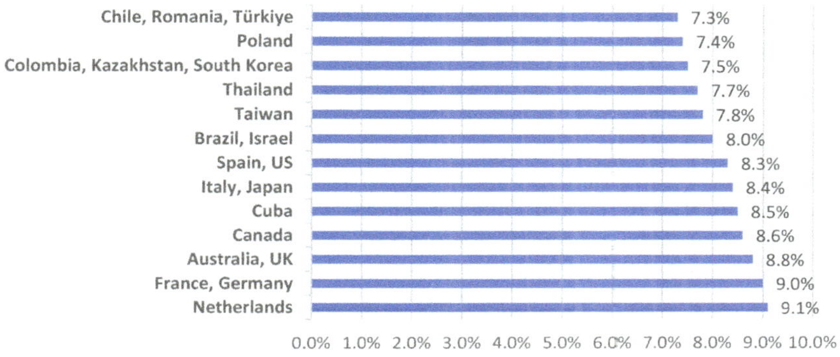

Fig. 6.4 Top-performing countries in the global access to healthcare index (Economist.com, 2017)

the global healthcare report published by Economist Intelligence Unit in 2017, it is important to ease access to health services and create sustainable health systems, and political will and a social compact, public investments, extending universal coverage, access to data, a well-trained and integrated workforce, and good primary care are important for that.

Peace

The Institute for Economics and Peace (IEP) publishes the Global Peace Index (GPI) yearly by ranking 163 independent states and territories according to their level of peacefulness (which corresponds to 99.7% of the world's population) and by including their level of societal safety and security, ongoing domestic and international conflict, and the degree of their militarization (Visionofhumanity, 2022). According to the 16th report published in 2022, the world peace index deteriorated 11th times in the last fourteen years, and the peacefulness declined to the lowest level in 15 years due to the economic uncertainty caused by the COVID-19 and Russia-Ukraine war. Iceland listed as the most peaceful country in the world since 2008, followed by New Zealand, Ireland, Denmark, and Austria. On the other hand, Afghanistan is listed as the least peaceful country in the world for the fifth consecutive year. Yemen, Syria, Russia, and South Sudan were also listed as the ten least peaceful countries for the last three years followed by Afghanistan. The index was constructed on

23 indicators including violent demonstrations and crime, external and internal conflicts, refugees, relations with neighboring countries, political Instability, violent crime, imprisonment rate, weapons imports and exports, political terror, police rate, perceptions of criminality, military expenditure (% GDP), terrorism Impact, homicide rate, nuclear and heavy weapons, and UN peacekeeping funding. The report also underlines the global economic impact of violence which reached USD 16.5 trillion in 2021, equivalent to 10.9% of global GDP, or USD 2,117 per person.

Freedom and Rule of Law

Freedom is one of the main needs of people to live a happy and peaceful life. According to the 2022 Freedom in Report published by Freedom House, like the peace index, the global freedom index which is constructed on political rights and civil liberties is also in decline for the last 16 consecutive years. Based on the Freedomhouse.org (2022), among 195 countries and 15 territories analyzed in the report, 60 countries suffered declines over the past year, while only 25 improved. The decline was in all categories including the electoral process, political pluralism, and participation, functioning of government, freedom of expression and belief, associational and organizational rights, rule of law and personal autonomy, and individual rights. On the other hand, while 38% of the global population lives in "Not Free" countries which is the highest rate since 1997, about 20% of the world population live in "Free" countries.

Another important index, the Rule of Law Index which was developed by The World Justice Project (WJP) as a quantitative tool that measures the rule of law in practice. Rule of law is defined as a system that supports the equality of all citizens and prevents the arbitrary use of power by reducing corruption, fighting against poverty and disease, and protecting people from any type of injustice. The index is constructed on 44 sub-factors under 8 major factors including constraints on government powers, absence of corruption, open government, fundamental rights, order and security, regulatory enforcement, and civil and criminal justice. According to the latest report published in 2022, Nordic countries including Denmark, Norway, Finland, and Sweden were listed as the top countries which adhere to the rule of law, and the Democratic Republic of Congo, Afghanistan, Cambodia, and Venezuela were listed as the worst performing countries in that context. Based on the data collected in 140 countries and jurisdictions, the rule of law fell in 61% of countries in 2021.

Although there was a partial improvement compared to the results of the year 2020 when justice systems were disrupted and civic liberties were curtailed due to COVID-19 shutdowns, the declines were concerning because scores for seven of the Index's eight factors fell in many countries for the last consecutive years (Worldjusticereport, 2022).

The increasing rate of homelessness, a sharp rise in the number of refugees, the low rates of access to education and health, the declines in world peace, freedom, and rule of law indices exhibit that the main needs of people in the world are not satisfactorily met by the current systems.

Why Do People Work?

Working is a requirement for people to survive and have a happy and peaceful life, but eventually working is not an aim in life but simply a tool. From a social perspective, working helps to produce benefits for people by using the individuals' knowledge, skills, efforts, and time. In that context, working can be defined as the total efforts which provide benefits for individuals and societies. An effort that does not make individuals happy and which does not provide benefits to society means nothing but loss of time, energy, and health.

The funny story of the fisherman and the businessman is a very good starting point for us to question the reason we work. Remembering the story, when the businessman was advising the fisherman who was enjoying the warmth of the sun and catching a fish to work harder to catch more fish and then to get bigger nets and then to buy a boat and catch more and more fish and become rich and eventually no need to work and sit on the beach and enjoy the sunset what exactly the fisherman was doing at that moment (Storytellers, 2022).

Of course, life is not that easy to handle, but it is also not that difficult indeed. It depends on which side we look at work: is it the aim of life or a tool to have a better and happier life? Do we work to live or live to work? Shall we postpone doing the things that make us happy until we get retired because we don't find enough time due to our booked business agenda or is it possible to enjoy the social and work lives together? There is an anonymous saying "Find something you love to do, and you'll never have to work a day in your life". I know this is not easy and maybe there are only a limited number of people who are that lucky to work in a job they love, but this is an important point to question our lives from a working perspective.

De Neve and Ward (2017) analyze the relationship between happiness and working lives, and their study exhibits that white-collar and managerial workers are happier than blue-collar workers in general. Their research also reports that being your boss is stressful although it is more rewarding. Like being unemployed, working in an environment where the unemployment rate is high also makes people unhappy. While salary is an important factor for happiness, autonomy and work-life balance are also other important factors that may influence the happiness rate. People who can separate their social lives from work, who learn new things, and who can plan their time during the day are more satisfied with their jobs and feel happier. Job site safety is also an important indicator of happiness while people who work in jobs with high health and safety risks feel worse than those who have safer working conditions.

According to a report conducted by Badenoch and Clark in the UK in 2018, agile/flexible working environments were found the most important factor for workplace happiness (Badenochandclark, 2022). That was followed by benefits, career progression, strong leadership, and additional holidays. While some global companies had started adapting flexible working hours for their employees even before the COVID-19 pandemic, the outbreak expedited the process and changed the workspace environment and working behaviors. During the pandemic, remote work was very common due to the lockdowns and mobility restrictions. After the normalization decision of the governments, some firms started calling back their employees to offices. According to the study by Hopkins and Bardoel (2022), 23% of the employees are now back in the regular weekly offices, and again 23% of them keep working completely remotely. 44% of the employees are working hybrid, where 15% of them are free to be flexible to decide when to go to the office and when to work remotely.

Remote working during the COVID-19 pandemic had also negative impacts on employees. The Great Resignation, a term that started being used in May 2021, describes the highest number of employees leaving their jobs since the beginning of COVID-19. The extended period of working from home with no travel made people question their work-life balance and every one of five-employee planned to resign according to a PwC report published in 2022. According to the report, the reasons for resigning were listed as fair compensation, job fulfillment, and the ability to be one's true self at work (PwC, 2022). The results of the study of the PEW Research Center conducted in the US about the reasons to quit jobs in 2022 were similar to the findings of PwC report. Low pay, no opportunities for advancement, and feeling disrespected at work were found as the main reasons to quit. As of July 2022, while Forbes reports the resignation trend did not slow down, a new trend of silent resignation or quiet quitting has been observed recently. Employees with silent quitting mindsets continue to perform their regular work, but do not contribute beyond their assigned tasks (Forbes, 2022). As long as their tasks are accomplished, this situation does not seem to cause any problem, but in fact, it may harm both the employees in terms of their well-being and professional growth and the employers from efficiency and sustainability perspectives. To avoid silent quitting, Kotz and Bolino (2022) suggest redefining workers' core job tasks, listening to them, investing in them, and creating a sustainable leadership culture where the employees get the opportunity to be involved in areas that make them feel better and comfortable.

What is Money for?

There is an old Turkish song lyric saying: "Money, money, money, its existence is a distress, absence is a hurt". People who do not have money are unable to meet their basic needs, on the other hand, people who possess money have a problem regarding where to invest it. Bank deposits, funds, stocks, gold, or real estate may be some investment options for those who have enough money to invest, but among the 7.84 billion population of the world, 1.7 billion individuals have no access to banking services, and 24% of the world population do not have a bank account (McCharty, 2018).

Governments are applying minimum wage rates to at least provide a minimum living standard to their citizens. The fewer people who earn the minimum wage, the more the living standards of the citizens of these countries are better. For instance, the rate of people who work at or below the minimum wage is low in developed countries; 1,5% in the US, which dropped from 15.1% within the last 40 years, but high in developing economies, such as 42% in Türkiye in 2020 (Statista, 2020; Veripie, 2022). As Worldpopulationreview reports (2022a, b), Australia, Luxembourg, and New Zealand are listed as the top countries which pay approximately more than USD 13 per hour for skilled labor. While the minimum hourly wage is USD 7.25 in the US, Türkiye and Mexico pay less than USD 2 per hour. Despite many countries in the world having minimum wage policies, even an estimated 266 million employees earn less than the minimum wage globally (Ellerbeck, 2022).

Bandelj et al. (2017) question the meaning of money in their book "Money Talks" from different perspectives including the historical, political, and social foundations of money, the way people and corporates use it, the things money shouldn't buy, and the impact of the new twenty-first-century currencies on social relations.

The way the money is earned, the person who earns it, where it is spent, and by whom it is spent making the quality of money as important as its quantity. Today, even though money is very important for everybody, it is a piece of paper, indeed. What makes money important is the value that the human gives to it, their addiction, and the will to have it more and the ambitions to make it more. From that perspective, the real value (worthless) of money is understood when it cannot buy peace, happiness, health, youth, and life; in summary when it does not provide benefit to the person who has it or in general to the society. A very much-loved and admired Turkish businessman Mr. Sakıp Sabancı, who passed away in 2004 had a well-known and touching interview about his disabled son. He was saying that:

> I have established automobile factories, but my son has never asked me to buy him one (Youtube, 2022).

It is true that with money you can buy a house, but that may not guarantee you a peaceful home, you can buy a doctor, but there is no guarantee for your health, you can have insurance, but that does not protect you from accidents and make you hundred percent safe.

As Benjamin Franklin says "Money has never made man happy, nor will it, there is nothing in its nature to produce happiness. The more of it one has the more one wants" (Goodreads, 2022). In that context, yes, money is important for transactions, and yet it is not more than an instrument that makes it insignificant. The important point is how we add value to money and where we use it. From a happiness perspective, it is now time to find an answer to the question of what makes us happy.

What Makes People Happy?

Lyubomirsky (2007) defines happiness as one of the most significant dimensions of human experience and emotional life due to its yield of several rewards for the individual, and its positive effects on creating a better, healthier, and stronger society. Happiness is a sense of well-being and enjoyment as a result of success, safe, or luck. The reasons or level of happiness is different from one person to another, but people tend to repeat doing or experiencing the things that make them happy. While asking the question about what makes people happy, it is also important to find answers to why some people are happier than others. While some people are happy even when they are in stress or face a negative issue and Liberman et al. (2009) underline that actual happy people read life events and situations in ways that seem to preserve their happiness, while unhappy individuals interpret experiences in ways that seem to strengthen sadness.

Although it differs from person to person, the main thing that makes humans happy is providing them the self-actualization (Maslow, 1943). Establishing a mechanism that helps people to actualize self-expectations, discover their potential, and help them use it to make people happy both individually and as a society. Happiness has several positive results for individuals, families, communities, and society at large. Higher income, greater productivity, a better quality of work, and more social rewards such as more satisfying marriages, more friends, stronger social support, richer social interactions, better physical health, and even longer life are considered the benefits of happiness. Happy individuals are more imaginative, supportive, generous, and self-confident, and have better auto-control and self-discipline (Lyubomirsky et al., 2015). Eventually, happy people create a happy society, and a happy society provides the conditions to make people happy individually.

Social and cultural factors are also important regarding the perception of happiness. While harmony and contentment are more important in cultures where collectivist ideals are important, feelings of excitement and joy are more valuable in individualistic-minded Western type of cultures (Tov et al., 2017).

From a social perspective, various research exhibit that helping others is a key to happiness (Farino, 2017). Indeed, several factors measure happiness. Based on the GDP per capita, social support, healthy life expectancy, generosity, perception of corruption, and dystopia criterion of the World

Happiness Report Index (2022), Finland, Denmark, Iceland, Switzerland, and the Netherlands are the top five happiest countries in the world; the citizens of Zimbabwe, Lebanon, and Afghanistan are the least happy people. The same report also underlines that stress of people, worry, and sadness had increased, and enjoyment of life decreased compared to previous years. One of the main reasons for such a decline seems to be the globally increased conflicts, so it is also important to discuss how to resolve conflicts among individuals and societies.

How the Conflicts Among Individuals and Societies Can Be Avoided?

Bonta (1996) defines conflict as mismatched needs, dissimilar demands, opposing wishes and beliefs, or diverging interests that produce interpersonal resentment and hostile behaviors. Conflicts can be in the content dimension such as disagreeing about an action, an issue, or a plan; can be in the relationship dimension where the disagreement is caused by the nature of the relationship itself or a combination of both. While relationship conflict is personal, content conflict can be more impersonal. There are different types of conflicts. These are ego conflicts where everything is taken very personally, and the issues are resulted in a "zero-sum game" where one party wins and the other party loses; a pseudo conflict which is a minor disagreement that can be resolved quickly; belief conflict which is a disagreement due to the different views of parties on an issue; value conflict which is about ranking issues based on their relative importance; action conflict which refers to behaviors or policies; and meta-conflict which is a disagreement over how the conflict is being addressed instead of what the conflict is about. Providing a solution about how to control the egoistical approach of people and states due to their never-ending wills and how to avoid or manage the conflicts among the egos is quite difficult. Indeed, bringing a solution to this conflict is the solution to today's global political and economic problems.

To manage conflicts, people may use different methods such as defensiveness, withdrawing/avoiding, accommodating, compromising, forcing, and collaborating. Although collaborating is the best way to resolve conflicts with a win–win approach, forcing the other party by using power is a very common way that the stronger parties use. Indeed, power is perceived, and it changes depending on how we perceive the other party. In addition, the party that has the least interest has more power over the other party, and the more power a party has, the less it follows the rules, norms, and regulations (Verderber & MacGeorge, 2016).

Learning how to manage and resolve the conflict also starts in the early childhood years. Teaching moral values from childhood and implementing the value of conscience is the main solution in that context. People who have strong moral values and free consciences and who are listening to their inner voice and heart may avoid or at least decrease the disputes and conflicts in a society. The first step for this is structuring a social, systematic, and fair system that creates justice from individuals to society and from society to individuals is the main solution to avoid such conflicts. When this is actualized, the negative consequences of individuality and the ego of people can be converted to positive benefits for society and individuals.

References

Badenochandclark. (2022). *Flexibility is the key to workplace happiness for 33% of employees*. https://www.badenochandclark.com/~/media/uk/inspiringinclusionintheworkplace.pdf/. Last Accessed on January 14, 2023.

Bandelj, N., Wherry, F. F., & Zelizer, V. A. (2017) *Money talks: Explaining how money really works*. Princeton University Press. https://doi.org/10.23943/princeton/9780691168685.001.0001, ISBN(s): 9780691168685, 9781400885268.

Bonta, B. C. (1996). Conflict resolution among peaceful societies: The culture of peacefulness. *Journal of Peace Research, 33*(4), 403–420.

Chartlon, E. (2019). *This is the critical number that shows when housing breaks down*. https://www.weforum.org/agenda/2019/01/here-s-a-way-of-predicting-when-homelessness-is-likely-to-rise/. Last Accessed on January 14, 2023.

Chomsky, N. (2020). https://www.euractiv.com/section/economy-jobs/interview/chomsky-on-covid-19-the-latest-massive-failure-of-neoliberalism/. Last Accessed on March 20, 2022.

Economist.com. (2017). *Global Access to Healthcare*. https://impact.economist.com/perspectives/sites/default/files/Globalaccesstohealthcare-3.pdf. Last Accessed on March 05, 2023.

Ellerbeck, S. (2022). *Which countries have the highest minimum wages in the OECD?*. https://www.weforum.org/agenda/2022/08/highest-minimum-wage-countries-oecd/. Last Accessed on January 14, 2023.

Elshurafa, D. (2012). Islamic capitalism—An imminent reality or a hopeful possibility for Islamic finance? *Arab Law Quarterly, 26*(3), 339–360.

Farino, L. (2017). New research shows that helping others may be the key to happiness. https://www.go-cdc.org/2017/new-research-shows-that-helping-others-may-be-the-key-to-happiness/. Last Accessed on January 14, 2023.

Forbes. (2022). *How quiet quitting became the next big phase in the great resignation.* https://www.forbes.com/sites/forbeshumanresourcescouncil/2022/11/09/how-quiet-quitting-became-the-next-big-phase-in-the-great-resignation/?sh=94dbb872dae4. Last Accessed on January 14, 2023.

Freedomhouse.org. (2022). *Freedom in the World 2022.* https://freedomhouse.org/sites/default/files/2022-02/FIW_2022_PDF_Booklet_Digital_Final_Web.pdf. Last Accessed on March 05, 2023.

Goodreads. (2022). *Benjamin Franklin > Quotes.* https://www.goodreads.com/quotes/3189290-money-never-made-a-man-happy-yet-nor-will-it. Last Accessed on January 14, 2023.

Habitat.org. (2017). *Statement by Habitat for Humanity about the future of the United Nations Human Settlement Programme*, UN-Habitat. https://www.habitat.org/newsroom/2017/statement-habitat-humanity-about-future-unitednations-human-settlement-programme-un. Last Accessed on March 05, 2023.

Hopkins, J. L., & Bardoel A. (2022). *Three emerging trends in a post-pandemic hybrid work era.* https://www.smartcompany.com.au/people-human-resources/remote-work/three-emerging-trends-post-pandemic-hybrid-work/. Last Accessed on January 14, 2023.

Klotz A. C., & Bolino M.C. (2022). *When quiet quitting is worse than the real thing*. https://hbr.org/2022/09/when-quiet-quitting-is-worse-than-the-real-thing. Last Accessed on January 14, 2023.

Liberman, V., Boehm, J. K., Lyubomirsky, S., & Ross, L. D. (2009). Happiness and memory: Affective significance of endowment and contrast. *Emotion, 9*(5), 666–680. https://doi.org/10.1037/a0016816

Lyubomirsky, S. (2007). *Why are some people happier than others?* https://sonjalyubomirsky.com/. Last Accessed on January 14, 2023.

Lyubomirsky, S., King, L., & Diener, E. (2015). The benefits of frequent positive affect: Does happiness lead to success? *Psychological Bulletin, 131*(6), 803–855. https://doi.org/10.1037/0033-2909.131.6.803

Maslow, A. H. (1943). A theory of human motivation. *Psychological Review, 50*(4), 430–437.

McCharty, N. (2018). *1.7 Billion adults worldwide do not have access to a bank account.* https://www.forbes.com/sites/niallmccarthy/2018/06/08/1-7-billion-adults-worldwide-do-not-have-access-to-a-bank-account-infographic/?sh=733061454b01. Last Accessed on January 14, 2023.

Nelson, A. (2020). COVID-19: Capitalist and postcapitalist perspectives. *Human Geography, 13*(3), 305–309.

Neve, J., & Ward, G. (2017). *Happiness at work*. LSE Research Online Documents on Economics.

PwC. (2022). *Survey of over 52,000 workers indicates the Great Resignation is set to continue as pressure on pay mounts*. https://www.pwc.com/gx/en/newsroom/press-releases/2022/global-workforce-hopes-and-fears-survey-2022.html. Last Accessed on January 14, 2023.

Statista. (2020). *Share of wage and salary workers in the United States paid hourly rates at or below the prevailing federal minimum wage from 1979 to 2020*. https://www.statista.com/statistics/188206/share-of-workers-paid-hourly-rates-at-or-below-minimum-wage-since-1979/. Last Accessed on January 14, 2023.

Thestorytellers. (2022). *The businessman and the fisherman*. https://thestorytellers.com/the-businessman-and-the-fisherman/. Last Accessed on January 14, 2023.

Tov, W., Ling, Z., & Nai, S. (2017). Cultural differences in subjective well-being how and why. In *Well-being and life satisfaction* (1st edn). Routledge, eBook ISBN9781351231879.

UNESCO. (2022). *New methodology shows that 258 Million children, adolescents and youth are out of school*. http://uis.unesco.org/sites/default/files/documents/new-methodology-shows-258-million-children-adolescents-and-youth-are-out-school.pdf. Last Accessed on January 14, 2023.

United Nations Refugee Agency. (2022). *Figures at a glance*. https://www.unhcr.org/figures-at-a-glance.html. Last Accessed on January 14, 2023.

Van Apeldoorn, B., & de Graaf, N. (2022). The state in global capitalism before and after the Covid-19 crisis. *Contemporary Politics, 28*(3), 306–327. https://doi.org/10.1080/13569775.2021.2022337

Verderber, K. S., & MacGeorge, E. L. (2016). *Inter-act: Interpersonal communication concepts, skills, and contexts*. Oxford University Press.

Veripie. (2022). Türkiye'nin %42'si Asgari Ücretle Çalışıyor! https://www.veripie.com.tr/turkiyenin-42si-asgari-ucretle-calisiyor/. Last Accessed on January 14, 2023.

Visionofhumanity. (2022). *Global peace index, 2022*. https://www.visionofhumanity.org/wp-content/uploads/2022/06/GPI-2022-web.pdf. Last Accessed on January 14, 2023.

WHO. (2022). *Current health expenditure (CHE) as percentage of gross domestic product (GDP) (%)*. https://www.who.int/data/gho/data/indicators/indicator-details/GHO/current-health-expenditure-(che)-as-percentage-of-gross-domestic-product-(gdp)-(-). Last Accessed on January 14, 2023.

Wordbank. (2022). *Government expenditure on education, total (% of GDP)*. https://data.worldbank.org/indicator/SE.XPD.TOTL.GD.ZS. Last Accessed on January 14, 2023.

Wordhappiness. (2022). *World happiness report (2022)*. https://worldhappiness.report/ed/2022/. Last Accessed on January 14, 2023.
Worldjusticereport. (2022). *World justice project, rule of law index 2021*. https://worldjusticeproject.org/sites/default/files/documents/WJP-INDEX-21.pdf. Last Accessed on January 14, 2023.
Worldpopulationreview. (2022a). *Homlessness by country*. https://worldpopulationreview.com/country-rankings/homelessness-by-country. Last Accessed on January 14, 2023.
Worldpopulationreview. (2022b). *Minimum Wage by Country 2023*. https://worldpopulationreview.com/country-rankings/minimum-wage-by-country. Last Accessed on January 14, 2023.
Youtube. (2022). *Sakıp Sabancı—Para Saadet Getirmez—oğlunu Anlatıyor*. https://www.youtube.com/watch?v=k4T8Y8j3e_Q. Last Accessed on January 14, 2023.

CHAPTER 7

The New Sustainable Approach

The world needs a new economic and financial system. Two world wars, the cold war, many ongoing regional wars, the 1929 Great Depression, the 2008 global financial crisis, and numerous economic and financial crises that repeat very often, the COVID-19 pandemic and various serious diseases that humanity is facing resulted in increased financial risks, widened income inequality, and decreased overall happiness globally. Economists are trying to find alternatives to current global economic and financial systems which create a crisis repetitively, and COVID-19 expedited the research in this area. 170 researchers in the Netherlands proposed five policies for a post-COVID-19 economic development model. They proposed a change of mind from GDP growth-focused development to investing in critical public sectors, clean energy, education, and health; an economic model that focuses on redistribution of income and wealth including fewer working hours and job sharing; regenerative agriculture; reduction of luxury and wasteful consumption and debt cancellation especially for small businesses, laborers, and for low-income countries (Leiden University, 2020). Rethinking the current global economic growth model, the circular economy model is also considered an alternative model in a tough post-COVID-19 world (Ibn-Mohammed et al., 2021).

L. Sümer, *The World Economy and Financial System*,
https://doi.org/10.1007/978-3-031-27530-2_7

In light of the recent development and the risks mentioned in other chapters, this chapter discusses the current alternative tools and approaches and proposes a new model.

Does Economic Growth Really Matter?

The quick answer to this question is "yes" because it is expected that GDP growth stimulates higher income and better living standards. When GDP goes up, the economy is generally thought to be healthy and doing well, on the other hand, weak growth gives a sign of a poor economy. GDP falls may result in a decrease in income and consumption as well as an increase in job losses and unemployment, but there are important questions to be answered such as how the GDP growth rate is calculated, how it is related to the population increase, how the resources are used and how sustainable is the growth. Without finding concrete answers to these questions, simple economic growth may not be for the benefit of society.

GDP is calculated based on spending or income methods. While spending-based GDP is calculated by the sum of the total of consumer spending, business investment, government spending, and net exports, income-based GDP calculation consists of the sum of all the production factors that make up an economy including the wages paid to laborers, the rent earned by land, the return on capital in the form of interest, and the enterprise profits. Sales and property taxes, depreciation, and net foreign factor income are also included in the sum. If we adjust these sums for inflation, we find the real GDP of a country.

Many countries are using public or external debts to sustain growth. Past studies reveal that there is a negative relation between external debts and growth rates (Cunningham, 1993; Deshpande, 1997; Geiger, 1990; Krugman, 1988), so decreasing the external debts is important for increasing the growth rate (Bilginoğlu & Aysu, 2008). On the other hand, while public debt has a positive impact on growth in developed economies, there is a negative relationship between growth and public debt (Yildirim & Erdogan, 2022). Studies about the macro-financial effects of households from a global perspective including emerging and developed economies exhibit a negative relationship between household debt growth and future GDP growth. The probability of a future banking crisis due to household credit booms is also reported (Abd Samad et al.,

2020; Alter et al., 2018). Although household debt increases consumption and GDP growth in the short run, mostly within one year, a 1% increase in the household debt-to-GDP ratio tends to lower growth in the long run by 0.1% (Lombard et al., 2017), so growing by debt is not sustainable.

The use of the resources also matters in terms of GDP growth. According to the United Nations Environment Programme Report, as of the end of 2019, the use of natural resources has more than tripled since 1970 and continues to grow (United Nations Environment Programme, 2019). Global resources are being consumed very fast mostly by upper-income countries. If no concerted action such as decoupling of natural resource-related environmental impacts from GDP mostly by the developed economies is taken urgently, rapid growth and inefficient use of natural resources may result in unsustainable consequences on the environment.

The global population has doubled since 1970, but the total GDP of the world increased from USD 3 trillion to USD 96.1 trillion within the same period (Worldbank, 2023). The relationship between economic growth and an increase in population is controversial. High population growth in low-income countries is likely to slow their development, and in contrast, low population growth in high-income countries may cause social and economic problems. Despite opposition, international migration is recommended to adjust these imbalances (Peterson, 2017). For instance, according to the Bureau of Labor Statistics, the rate of Hispanics and Latinos accounted for 18% of the US labor force in 2020. This rate is 43.6% in New Mexico and 37.7% in California states. In 2021, the share of the US civilian labor force that is foreign-born rose to 17.4%, half of them were Hispanic and one-quarter were Asian. Service occupations, natural resources, construction and maintenance, production, transportation, and material moving occupations were more likely performed by foreign-born workers compared to native-born workers (US Bureau of Labor Statistics, 2021).

It is also important to note that economic growth does not always bring economic development. The economic growth is measured by the increase in the monetary value of all the goods and services produced in the economy, and the economic development is defined as the overall health, well-being, and quality of life in a nation, which also includes economic growth. While GDP is the main measurement tool of economic growth, the Human Development Index (HDI) which covers many parameters including the creation of job opportunities, technological advancements, standard of living, living conditions, per capita income, quality of life, improvement in self-esteem needs, GDP, industrial and infrastructural development are the keys for economic development. (King & Levine, 1994).

What Are the Alternatives?

Economists have been seeking alternatives to change the current world economic and financial order. Among these searches, circular economy, sharing economy, digital economy, and Islamic economy and finance are the most popular and promising approaches which are currently being implemented.

Circular Economy

According to United Nations (2022) projections, the world population will reach 9.7 billion in 2050 which will increase global demand and consumption, double material usage, and put serious environmental pressures on Earth such as climate change, all types of pollution, and change of land use. It is estimated that if no action is taken, by 2050, three times of current resources of Earth will be needed to meet the world's consumption (European Commission Report, 2020).

To change the negative effects of the linear economy which is known as the traditional model where there is no concern for the ecological footprint and consequences of the extraction, production, and disposal methodology, the Circular Economy (CE) emerged in the 1970s from the idea of reducing the consumption of inputs for not only the industrial production but also potentially use of any resource (Arruda et al., 2021; Ekins et al., 2019). In that context, CE is defined as a model of production and consumption which involves sharing, leasing, reusing, repairing, refurbishing, and recycling existing materials and products to extend the life cycle of products. Material efficiency (resource-efficient housing and construction), the substitution of chemicals and the use of less hard-to-recycle materials, the durability of housing, vehicles, and products, eco-design, asset utilization by reducing travel, excess consumption and floor space, recyclability and recycling build up the main concept of CE according to Goldman Sachs Research conducted in 2022. The same report, as well as Lacy and Rutqvist (2015), underline the USD 4.5

trillion and USD 25 trillion economic output of CE by 2030, and 2050 respectively (Goldmansachs, 2022).

The relationship between circular economy and sustainability is also important to underline. While sustainability has three dimensions including the economic, social, and environmental aspects, the circular economy stresses the importance of environmental sustainability while also emphasizing its potential positive outcomes on the economy (Ekins et al., 2019). It is noted that, according to the World Economic Forum estimations, recycling, reusing, and remanufacturing could help the economy worth USD 1 trillion a year in resource savings. The CE has the potential of changing the mindsets of people in terms of how they look at their relationships while doing business, dealing with customers, and using natural resources. This may be an opportunity for sustainable economic growth.

Sharing Economy

Ownership of an asset or wealth has always been an important indicator of happiness, freedom, and social and self-esteem of people. While the early studies on happiness were focusing more on psychological and sociological perspectives, happiness has also become popular among economists who investigate the relationships between happiness and income, happiness and unemployment, and happiness and sociodemographic characteristics in later research.

Although the relationship between the wealth of nations and happiness has also been an interesting research topic for many scholars, the studies about the happiness and wealth of individuals are limited. Past studies reveal that there is a positive relationship between income level and happiness but the relationship between debt and happiness is negative (Jantsch & Veenhoven, 2018; Plug, 1997). There is a saturation level of income level that brings happiness to people which is determined as USD 10,000 per capita. For instance, despite the increase in the average income in the US and Netherlands the level of happiness has remained constant (Veenhoven & Timmermans, 1998). On the other hand, while ownership of an asset such as homeownership may increase life satisfaction (Rohe & Basolo, 2016; Rohe & Stegman, 1994), it may also have a negative effect on life satisfaction if there is a high financial cost of homeownership (Zumbro, 2014). It is also remarkable to note that while homeownership may bring happiness for low-income level people due to the future potential risks of retirement years in case their income will not be enough to cover their rental expenses, homeownership may not bring happiness in higher-income countries as Hofmann and Umbricht (2019) concluded for Switzerland.

People work to make money to get the power to purchase their needs which makes them happy when satisfied. Instead of buying a new one, they sometimes prefer to buy a secondhand one or even rent their needs due to a lack of enough financial resources, the short period of their requirements, and sensibility to environmental or social issues (Akan & Tepeler, 2022). In that context, sharing economy emerged as an alternative model defined as a collaborative way of consumption by highlighting the preference of individuals to rent or borrow goods rather than buy and own them, especially very common among the new young generation due to the need for flexibility, decreased stability of the labor market, unstable economic conditions, rise in commodity prices and difficulties to access to loans (Csizmady & Kőszeghy, 2022; Gansky, 2010).

The term sharing economy was used by Lessig (2008) who defines it as the lack of interest in monetary gain to participate. Indeed, from the word sharing which implies a moral economy of "sharing in" within a small community as a non-market-based way of supply, the term sharing economy drifted toward a commercialized and business-like activity aiming at larger and long-distance communities (Miguel et al., 2022). While Airbnb and Uber are the entities that come to mind first when talking about sharing economy, the origins of the sharing economy date to 1995 with the establishment of eBay and Craigslist which were largely used by almost two decades of acquisition of cheap imports and selling of unwanted items (Schor, 2014).

The rental preferences of customers created new business models in transportation, accommodation, tourism, education, entertainment, and many other industries, and new companies such as Uber, Airbnb, Netflix, Spotify, and Udemy grew rapidly. Those companies indeed did not have the assets to rent but were at intersection points of people with common interests where one party was willing to rent its good while the other was a candidate to rent it. The business model works not only in rental ideas but also in secondhand sales and periodic subscriptions. The sharing economy is also criticized from legal, social, environmental, and economic perspectives such as inadequate legal framework, taxation problems, unfair competition with local entities, reproducing social hierarchy, cybersecurity, privacy, and increase in damages to the environment (Čavalić &

Bećirović, 2017, Koczetkow & Klimczuk, 2022; Schor, 2014). Despite the criticism of sharing economy, it is estimated that the size of the sharing economy will reach USD 335 billion in 2025, with a rapid growth rate compared to its size in 2014 which was USD 14 billion (Yaraghi & Shamika, 2017).

Digital Economy

The sharing economy is defined as a scalable socioeconomic system that uses technology-enabled platforms that provide customers with access to resources that may be crowdsourced (Eckhardt et al., 2019). Although crowdsourcing is a key element in this definition, there is a fact that sharing economy is built on the digital economy (Chen & Wang, 2019). Digital transformation is reshaping everything in the world including the global economy. People, businesses, devices, data, and processes are connected by the internet of things and mobile technologies. In that context, the digital economy is defined as "a broad range of economic activities that include using digitized information and knowledge as the key factor of production, modern information networks as an important activity space, and the effective use of information and communication technology as an important driver of productivity growth and economic structural optimization" (G20 2016 Summit in China).

The digital economy is structured on three main components which are e-business infrastructure including hardware, software, telecom, networks, human capital, e-business, and e-commerce (Mesenbourg, 2001). Data collection, networkability, cloud computing, big data analytics, and artificial intelligence are the core technologies of the digital economy (Sturgeon, 2021). Many industries adopted digital technologies in their business models. The COVID-19 pandemic also boosted digital adaption across a wide range of consumer-facing industries. Figure 7.1 shows the increase in digital adoption by consumers within 2021. As shown in the figure, the rate of utilities and insurance had the highest rate of increase with a 46% growth rate.

According to the 2022 statistics of the US Department of Commerce Bureau of Economic Analysis, the digital economy produced USD 3.70 trillion in current-dollar gross output in 2021, with a 10% yearly growth rate. Priced digital services represent the largest activity in the digital economy in 2021, with 43.1% of total gross output followed by infrastructure with 31,5% and e-commerce with 25.4% shares, respectively

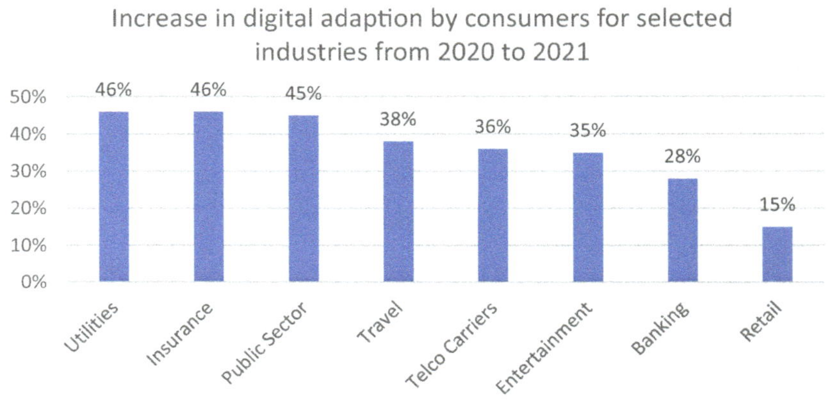

Fig. 7.1 Digital adoption by consumers for selected industries (Statista, 2022b)

(Highfill & Surfield, 2022). In 2020, the top players in technology including Amazon, Apple, Samsung, AT&T, Google, Microsoft, Huawei, JD, Alibaba, Facebook, and Tencent generated USD 1.87 trillion in revenues, equivalent to the GDP of Italy. After the outbreak of the COVID-19 pandemic, the e-commerce market grew by 28% globally in 2020. It is expected that this accelerated trend is likely to continue in the upcoming years and the revenue to be reached USD 4 trillion by 2025. In the digital economy, the key players dominate the market. For instance, the top-seven players generate two-thirds of the global e-commerce transaction volume (Statista, 2022a, b, c, d, e, f). On the other hand, the digital economy is also critiqued as intangible capitalism which increases inequality and social separation. According to Haskel and Westlake (2017), intangible assets such as branding, design, and technology are preferred over machinery, hardware, or property.

Digital interaction may be disrupted across our economy and society by blockchain technology, which is defined as a shared, immutable ledger that eases the process of recording transactions and tracking tangible or intangible assets in a business network by reducing risk and cutting costs. There are different types of blockchain networks including public, private, permissioned, and consortium blockchains. Although Bitcoin which is an unregulated digital currency comes to mind when discussing blockchain, this technology has been widely used in areas including supply chain, healthcare, government, retail, media and advertising, oil and gas, telecommunications, manufacturing, insurance, financial services, travel, and transportation. Its distributed ledger, decentralization, and information openness are considered the main advantages of blockchain. Financial technologies (fintech) developed under blockchain technology are considered to transform the traditional practices of the finance industry in terms of operations management, payment systems, lending, and deposit services (Xu, 2022). Property technology (proptech) which is defined as the intersection point of fintech, sharing economy, and smart buildings is also another practice area of blockchain technology (Baum, 2020).

Islamic Economics and Finance

Islamic economics is an alternative model which is structured on Islamic moral rules and values about individual and social economic behavior. Ibn Khaldun is known as one of the founders of Islamic economic theory who defines sharia, government, society, ownership, and free and fair economic activity as the five-key concept of Islamic economics. While the Islamic economic system aims to guarantee individual freedom, private property, and enterprise, it also ensures economic development and social justice in society. Compliance with Shariah (Islamic law and regulations), zakat, an important pillar of Islam defined as a charitable contribution which is a mandatory tax for wealthy Muslims calculated over 2.5% of their total wealth, prohibition of gharrar (uncertainty), riba (interest), gambling and non-Shariah compliant investments such as alcohol, pornography, etc., and voluntary measures such as sadaqah (donation) and waqf (foundation) are the key important measures of Islamic economy (Asutay, 2011).

Islamic finance is a financial system that is structured under the rules of Islamic law. The core concepts of the Islamic financial system are promoting trading and commerce with fairness and social justice (Alrifai, 2015). According to Islamic finance principles, no one can profit from something immoral, sharing the risk is a must to share the reward, it is not allowed to sell something one does not own, and the price of the good and its specification need to be clear at any transaction to remove any speculation and ensure value-enhancing activities (Asutay, 2011). The risk-sharing and speculation-free policies of Islamic finance protected Islamic financial institutions from the 2008 global financial crisis. This situation increased interest-free investment vehicles (Alawode, 2015).

Islamic finance is an important tool that is used both in Muslim countries as well as the states including the UK, Luxembourg, South Africa, and Hong Kong. The roots of Islamic banking back to the early 1960s in Egypt in its modern form. Dubai Islamic Bank was established as the first major Islamic commercial bank in the United Arab Emirates, and Islamic Development Bank (IsDB) was founded in 1975 just after the establishment of the Dubai Islamic Bank (Hussain et al., 2015). Islamic finance is considered a trending phenomenon that has already been mainstreamed as an alternative to traditional finance within the global financial system. In many Muslim countries, the growth rate of Islamic banking assets exceeds the growth rate of conventional banking assets. Islamic finance which is considered a sustainable and ethical finance tool is backed by assets. Islamic finance links the financial sector and the real economy by valuing risk-sharing and emphasizing social welfare with its environmentally and socially responsible perspective. Islamic funds provide socially responsible and ethical investment opportunities to many institutional investors by using many Sharia-compliant financial tools (Sümer, 2017). In Islamic finance, being converted into a productive activity is the main condition for money to make money (Alrifai, 2015). According to World Bank Report 2015, the rate of bank users among 1.6 billion Muslims is just 14%. Islamic finance is an option and opportunity to respond to the requirements of people who do not prefer to use conventional systems due to religious concerns.

Murabaha, ijara, mudaraba, ijara, musharaka, bai'muaccal, bai'salam, and sukuk are the main instruments of Islamic financing. Murabaha (cost plus financing) is a property purchasing transaction with a free and clear title. A percentage is added as profit which is not considered an interest-bearing loan for the purchased asset on behalf of the client. The ownership of the property or the asset remains with the purchaser until the client pays the loan completely. Ijara (leasing) means the sale of the right to use an asset for a determined period. In ijara transactions, the leased asset is owned by the lessor until the end period of the lease. Assets are purchased by a bank on behalf of the client, and they can be used for a fixed rental payment. The financial institution keeps the ownership of the assets but may progressively transfer them to the client who may ultimately become the possessor (Sümer, 2017).

Mudaraba (profit sharing) is defined as a trust financing contract. It is a partnership where the mudarib provides the know-how and labor, and the other party is responsible for providing the financing. In mudaraba, the parties share the profit in accordance with a predetermined ratio, and return is not guaranteed for the investor, yet they may bear financial losses if any. Musharaka means a profit-loss partnership, not necessarily about contributions, but the parties share the losses in percentage to their capital contributions. Bai'Muajjal means deferred payment sale contract. At Bai'Muaccal, no delayed payment is requested from the buyer in which the seller makes a profit on the purchase he made for the buyer where he receives his payment at future date at once or in installments. At Bai'Salam, the payment is made in advance, but the delivery of the product is made later. Istisna'a is a contractual agreement used for financing construction projects including houses, plants, bridges, roads, and highways. The customer/investor pays the contractor in installments for the build delivered (State Bank of Pakistan, 2022).

Sukuk are called the certificates of ownership which give the investor a share of an asset, along with the appropriate cash flows and risk by following Islamic laws. Sukuk is defined as a project financing instrument issued in accordance with the Shariah principles in the Islamic capital market. The Arabic origin of the term sukuk is the plural of the word sak which means certificate or certificate of property (Saripudin et al., 2012). Sukuk is recognized as an alternative tool for financing and investment that follows Islamic laws. Sukuk is based on tangible assets (Hussin et al, 2012). As of the end of 2021, the total size of Islamic finance reached almost USD 4 trillion and is projected to be USD 5.9 trillion in 2026 according to Islamic Finance Development Indicator Report 2022. Islamic Banking has the largest share among Islamic finance institutions with USD 2.8 trillion, and this is followed by sukuk with USD 713 billion outstanding sizes. Islamic funds, the third main sector of Islamic finance reached USD 238 billion in assets under management with a 34% growth rate. Outstanding ESG sukuk and ESG Islamic funds with a total of USD 24 billion sizes also rose sharply in 2021. Islamic financial technology companies, investment firms, financing companies, leasing and microfinance firms, and brokers and traders, categorized under other financial institutions' asset size also reached USD 169 billion in 2021. Despite its 17% growth rate, Islamic insurance named as Takaful is the smallest sector of the Islamic finance industry, with a USD 73 billion size. Figure 7.2 shows the yearly size of Islamic Finance and the breakdown of Islamic finance according to the Islamic financial institutions is exhibited in Fig. 7.3.

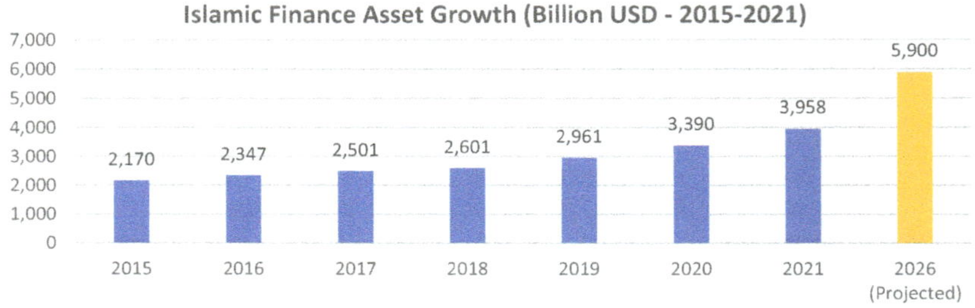

Fig. 7.2 The size of Islamic finance (Refinitiv, 2022)

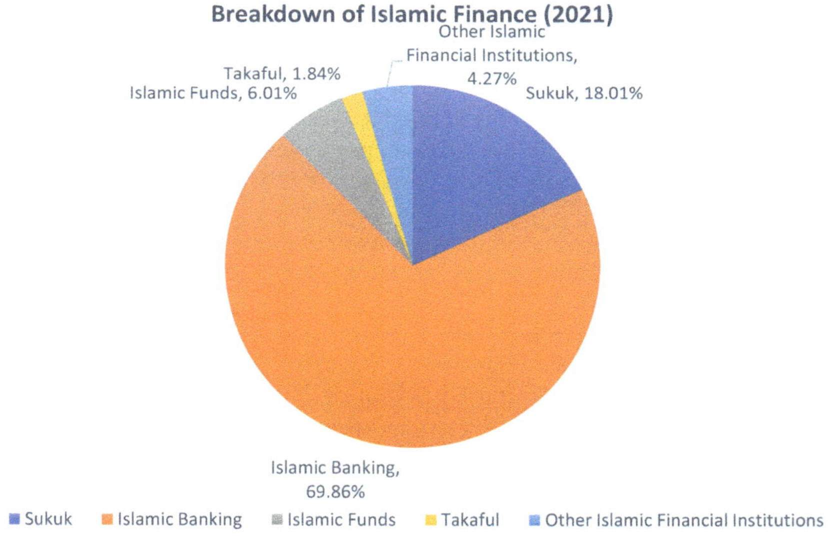

Fig. 7.3 The breakdown of Islamic finance (Refinitiv, 2022)

The New Approach

The abovementioned alternative economic models are independently useful approaches to resolve some of the flaws of the currently used economic systems. For instance, while the circular economy is focusing on the efficient use of resources, reducing waste, and using clean energy that helps to save the planet, the sharing economy replaces buying with renting by aiming to decrease overspending. On the other hand, while the utilization of technology is one of the major pillars of the digital economy which helps to ease of doing business worldwide and bring comfort to society, Islamic finance and economics are underlying the moral values and the importance of social cooperation together with replacing the interest-based financial system with the asset-backed approach. Despite the benefits of these alternatives, they are also criticized from different perspectives including the increase in inequality due to the capitalist implementation of the digital/sharing economy, or the high correlation of Islamic banking with conventional banking systems. Thus, the new model I developed is not aiming to combine all but is not limited to the benefits of the alternative approaches in one ecosystem, but also bringing solutions to the criticized parts. To achieve this, the pillars of the economic policies shall be restructured to change the paradigms of the economic systems and increase the welfare of the societies in a balanced way by ***"creating new sharing ecosystems that aim the social justice and cooperation"***. That may only be possible by shifting the focus of the economic systems from the current ambitions-oriented mindset to a collective, collaborative, and sustainable approach.

Main Pillars: Developing, Balancing, Saving, and Sharing

A new economic model shall address the main issues of society. A better life standard is the desire of everybody, and that can be achieved through continuous development. People need to work to develop, but also, need to rest, so there is a need for balance in every phase of life, not just at the micro-individual level but also macro-corporate, national, and international levels, a balance among societies. On the other hand, people think about their future regarding how they can sustain their welfare in their retirement years. That makes them save money for their main needs such as accommodation, health, and nourishment in the future. Finally, people live in a society, where they are not unconcerned about the environmental and social issues around them, and that makes them share their ideas, values, contentment, sadness, and money to help create collaborative prosperity. The new approach proposed in this book structures the model under developing, balancing, saving, and sharing pillars.

Pillar 1: Developing

Individualism is important for capitalist systems, and people are encouraged to possess more as an individual, but that materialist approach is not working when considering the social part of humans. It is almost impossible for humankind to live alone. The more people have common values in a society, the more they feel happy. Developing common values and communities may bring people together with the same aims, thus money in that sense becomes just a tool that serves the common goals of society.

In that sense, ***(1) developing a human and society-focused financial system*** is essential. Fukuyama (2018) mentions the term Society 5.0 intends to realize a society where people enjoy life the most, and where economic growth and technological advancement serve that goal but not for the benefit of a limited few groups. In addition, Clark (2020) and Nesbitt (2022) emphasize the importance of human-centered finance which may shape the future of the financial sector. The 2021 future of financial services report of Deloitte also underlines the customer-led economic transformation. The report also highlights the important role of financial services companies in addressing major social issues to generate profit in support of shareholder interests together in collaboration with various other stakeholder communities by accelerating the emerging human-centric ecosystems reshaping the economy.

Yes, a new economy model shall be human-oriented and customer-led, but that does not mean consumption shall be the main driver of the economy. Contrary to capitalism, which is based on consumerism, a new system shall be based on production, so the society shall be ***(2) production oriented***. To avoid any misconception, what I mean by a production-oriented society is not producing more than the needs of people and trying to market the excessively produced goods to people to make them consume more than they need, but in contrast, to engage the society to become a producer instead of being dependent to other producers.

Post-normal periods characterized by complication, chaos, inconsistencies, and uncertainties are the main concepts that we need to take into consideration to manage the transition from the analytic thinking-based knowledge economy to a human-centered economy characterized by using creativity, character, and passion. A sustainable and innovative education system should prepare the generations for the constantly changing dynamics of the world (Çepni, 2017). Societies that aim to create a sustainable education system shall intersect the theory and practice in a ***(3) collective education approach*** and the system should provide opportunities for the people to explore and use their skills.

The first and the most important goal of an education system shall be raising individuals by teaching them moral values, who are respectful to others' rights, who are beneficial to themselves and society, and who have self-esteem, self-confidence, and self-respect. A happy individual creates a happy society, and a happy society makes individuals happy. The first step to achieving this is to start teaching these values to our children at the preschool education level. The system should be built on the education of good morals and respect for human rights (in fact, respect for the world, including all the living in this world). Furthermore, incepting the idea of being an individual who is aiming to succeed in a team is essential for a collective education system. A talented person may be successful individually but being part of a team and succeeding together may motivate her more. Sharing knowledge, target magnification, and defending an idea in a team without causing a major conflict or being capable of resolving disputes in a respective way help the individuals develop themselves and the society better. Instead of serving the knowledge ready to take, encouraging the kids to make research, question and compare, be patient and find relations between the causes and results to reach the knowledge at an early age is the key to developing a producer—rather than a consumer—society. Talent-focused perspective is also another key to a sustainable education system that may enhance the productivity of society. A well-known anonymous quote describes the standardized and competition-based education models very well:

> *Everybody is a genius. but if you judge a fish by its ability to climb a tree, it will live its whole life believing that it is stupid.*

It is also important to note that equality is not always the key to providing justice. Offering the same aid may not result in equal success. Instead, giving different supports may help different groups to be treated better, but the best approach is removing the barriers for all groups to get rid of the reasons for inequity and provide justice to society.

While providing education at schools, it is also important to open a path for generations to start up their businesses and ***(4) become entrepreneurs***, especially to develop the technology. The world is in a digital revolution era and technology is developing very fast. The financial systems, transportation, manufacturing, and many other industries are shaping their future based on new technological developments including connectivity, robotics, and artificial intelligence. Humankind is discussing how machines may think and act like humans but does not see that humans are more likely to behave like machines. Leonhard (2018) discusses the fight of humanity against technology and focuses on how to get the benefit of technology without sacrificing our humanity. Technology is needed to be considered as ***(5) a tool that increases the welfare of society*** and developing new technologies without being its slave and creating a perception of using the technology for the benefit of the society shall be the main approach to develop the technology.

Pillar 2: Balancing

The development of technology made it easy for people to reach products/goods they want, and to travel from one place to another, shortly, to get whatever they want easily. The more people can get their needs satisfied, the more imbalance between consumption and expenditures increases. Easily access to credit cards, installments applied to cards to increase purchasing powers which in reality is increasing the debt, attractive products in windows of luxury stores, consumption pressures imposed by the social status of people caused a drastic change in the consumption behaviors of people.

Diderot Effect

A French philosopher Denis Diderot (1713–1784) wrote an essay named "Regrets on Parting with My Old Dressing Gown" and described how a gift of a beautiful scarlet dressing gown led him to an unexpected result that plunged him into debt. Starting from the point he received and liked the gift, he changed all his belongings including the decoration of his house to fit everything all together. He expresses his regret with these meaningful words:

> I was an absolute master of my old dressing gown, but I have become a slave to my new one … Beware of the contamination of sudden wealth. The poor man may take his ease without thinking of appearances, but the rich man is always under a strain.

The Diderot effect, which was coined by a scholar of consumption patterns, Grant McCracken, in 1988, is accepted as a social fact related to consumer goods which are based on two ideas. While the first one underlines the alignment of goods purchased by consumers with their sense of identity which complements one another as a result, the second idea states the process of spiral complementary consumption initiated by the introduction of a new possession. Thus, such consumption behaviors result in negative environmental, psychological, and social impacts.

Especially, whenever there was an increase in the income level of people, their lifestyle, neighborhood, homes, furniture, clothes, and even friends change. In the past, when the supply and diversity of the products were less and incomes were lower, people would "put their feet up on their quilts", avoid bank loans, and endure great hardships to own something—for example, a house or a car. In the past, the sense of cooperation in the social structure was at a better level than it is today (because nowadays people are paying mortgages, credit card bills, etc., and either they don't have saved money to lend, or they don't want to lend the money they saved); there would be many people who would give a helping hand when someone was in need. This situation is very rare in today's economic conditions. The competition-oriented conditions of capitalism encourage people to earn and consume more, and COVID-19 showed the drawbacks of a hyper-consumption model of economic growth and development (Everingham & Chassagne, 2020). The selfness and the ambitions of humans compare themselves with others and always ask for more. The never-ending wills of humans consume limited resources rapidly. A society that ***(6) does not purchase and consume more than it needs*** may open a door for ***(7) balancing the unfair income distribution among nations and countries.***

According to the World Bank statistics, as of the end of 2021, the average GDP per capita of the world is USD 12.263. While the average of G20 countries is around USD 30,000 and the Euro area is USD 36,352, the country with the largest GDP per capita in Africa is Seychelles with USD 15,713. There are 19 countries in Africa with less than only USD 1,000 GDP per capita (Tradingeconomics, 2022). There is a fact that some parts of the world are in great wealth, and some other parts are just struggling to survive. While each day 25,000 people, including more than 10,000 children die from hunger and related causes, nearly 33% of all food produced annually is wasted. Around 854 million people worldwide are estimated to be malnourished, and another 100 million people are in poverty and hunger risks due to high food prices. Around USD 1 trillion worth of food is wasted yearly and only a quarter of the wasted food amount can feed 840 million hungry people in the world (Holmes, 2021).

Acting with the philosophy of not wasting a single loaf of bread, feeling the spiritual peace of relieving someone's distress instead of getting the pleasure of material feelings coming with excess consumption, and believing in the fact that what is shared will increase are the core approaches solutions of inequality problems.

Working hard is important for human beings to invent, discover, produce, and develop. Working long but non-productive hours without taking into consideration the social and personal needs of humans brings nothing but unhappiness and loss of health. While people used to work in offices for long hours before COVID-19, now by working from home, the situation is even worse as people are always online no matter whether it is late at night or weekend. Studies reveal that remote working has a positive effect on mental well-being, work-life balance, and job satisfaction (Irawanto et al., 2021; Yuceol et al., 2021). On the other hand, people feel more time pressure while working at home (Hjálmsdóttir & Bjarnadóttir, 2020).

As COVID-19 stayed in our lives for longer periods, and companies restructured their working policies including hybrid models, the definition of the workplace is being rewritten. In that sense, regulations about employment policies which are important columns of a healthy economy shall be structured on a ***(8) balance between work and private life***. Work-life balance is defined as the ability to meet work and family responsibilities, as well as other non-work duties and activities (Delecta, 2011).

As mentioned in previous chapters, the main reason for the trade war declared by the US against China was the trade imbalance between the countries in favor of China. Under the current slowed down of globalization caused by extended trade wars among many states, the impacts of the COVID-19 pandemic, and thereafter the energy and food crisis caused by the ongoing war between Russia and Ukraine, countries tend to ***(9) balance their imports and exports*** especially to decrease their current account deficit. For instance, agriculture is evaluated as a "national security" priority by countries and COVID-19 made the states more cautious on the food issue as many import-dependent states suffered from the inadequateness of consumer goods during the COVID-19 pandemic, and the abovementioned war (Beckman & Countryman, 2021). In that context, an alternative economy model shall balance the trade of a state by making them less dependent on other countries.

Pillar 3: Saving

Savings provide sources for the economies and help the economic growth of a country (McKinnon, 1973; Ribaj & Mexhuani, 2021; Solow, 1956). When there are not enough savings within the country, economies tend to seek external debts which is one of the major problems of the current economic systems defined in the previous chapters. Whenever the expenditures increase, the savings decline and the use of credit cards reduces saving habits and increases the amount of spending (Ersin & Eti, 2017). By using credit cards for payment, people also tend to buy more expensive goods and give larger tips. Paying with credit cards reduces the pain of payment and creates the pleasure of purchasing (Banker et al., 2021). According to Shift Credit Card Processing Report, as of August 2021, there are 2.8 billion credit cards in use worldwide and 1.06 billion in the US, respectively. 83% of Americans use a credit card, 14% of Americans have at least 10 credit cards, and while the average credit card per person in America is 2.7, the average outstanding credit card debt is USD 5,315 (Shiftprocessing, 2022).

The ease of payment methods triggers more spending appetite, and this may result in more household debts. There is a trade-off between current and future consumption based on saving and spending relations. While spending today may increase the current living standards, it may put a question mark on the future standards of individuals as it leaves less to be invested for future income. On the other hand, high savings may slow down economic activities. Considering the mid- and low-income countries, people may indeed not be capable enough to save for the future, as their current income may not be enough or may be barely sufficient to cover their daily needs. As a result of the balance between production and consumption, people may prevent unnecessary spending by making saving the surplus of their real needs. The money accumulated in saving accounts, for instance in pension funds, may be invested into different companies which may stimulate long-term growth in stock markets as well as the real economy.

Making savings is also directly related to poverty and according to Burgess and Pande (2005), ***(10) significant increases in savings*** may reduce poverty. People who make savings may share their savings with people in need even in some circumstances without seeking a profit. ***(11) Pension and insurance systems, charities, and foundations may be restructured*** in that context. As of the end of 2020, within 10 years, the total size of the pension funds has reached from USD 27.06 trillion to USD 56 trillion more than doubling an 11% increase compared to the end of 2019 (OECD Pension Market in Focus, 2021). In addition, the global insurance market size is expected to grow from USD 5.4 trillion in 2021 to USD 5.94 trillion in 2022 at a compound annual growth rate of 10.4%. The market is expected to grow to USD 8.4 trillion in 2026 at a CAGR of 9.1% (Prnewswire, 2022). That means that people have money in their accounts, are insuring themselves or their belongings such as cars, houses, etc., making savings, and it is critical to direct these savings, contributions, and premiums for the mutual benefit of people and society. This indeed structures the main economic system based on the direct contribution of the savings of the people into the economy.

Pillar 4: Sharing

Sharing economy is a new concept that is focused on utilizing resources by shifting from the possession of goods to the accessibility of people. While it is considered an opportunity to replace capitalism-driven high consumption with a sustainable form of access-based use (Botsman & Rogers, 2011), it is, on the other hand, evaluated as a new form of liberalism that is not aiming to shape the global economy from a better life perspective, yet it also does not focus on the needs of the middle class (De Grave, 2014; Morozov, 2013). If taken from a positive side, ***(12) sharing economy*** may play an important role, especially in terms of decreasing the expenditures of excess own-centric consumption and replacing it with a buy or rent—if really needed—mindset.

Sharing economy can be an important sub-pillar of a new economic model if it mainly focuses on taking care of the people who need help. Spending money on others rather than the human may bring more happiness, and spending on others is considered the most satisfying way of using money. This may be derived from the fundamental component of human nature (Dunn et al., 2014). If people internalize the idea of sharing with others, then ***(13) their savings may be directed to human-focused and environment-friendly investments*** such as funding

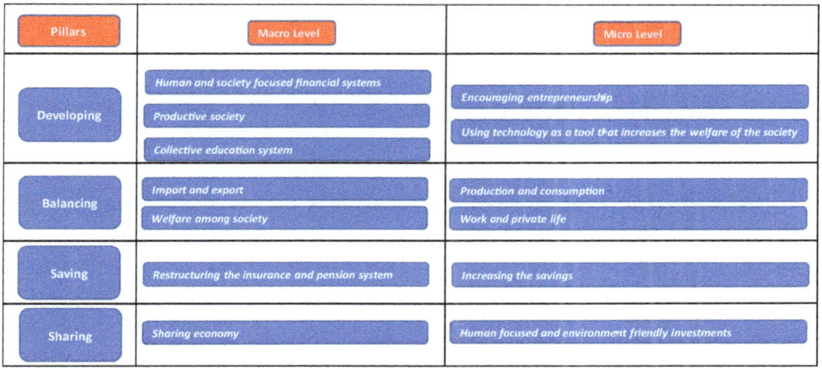

Fig. 7.4 The 4 main and 13 sub-pillars of the new economy approach (by author)

entrepreneurs, involvement in sustainable projects, green energy, circular economy, organic farming, socially responsible projects, etc.

In light of the abovementioned points, the 4 main and 13 sub-pillars of the new economy approach under macro and micro levels are shown in Fig. 7.4.

The Model Framework of the New System

While structuring a new economic and financial system, the most critical point is the positive practical implementation of the model in our daily lives and the explanation of its differentiation from the current flawed systems. In other words, the practical use of the new approach that covers the 4 main and 13 sub-pillars shall be designed in a way that shifts the focus of the policymakers on how they include the involvement of people more into the economic system and how the people and the society can get more benefit of their participation and contribution.

From Debt-Oriented Deadlock to Partnership-Tailored Solution Approach

The past economic and financial crisis revealed that the rise in total debt in every category is impeding the economic and financial system into a deadlock, so a new system shall first bring a solution to this major problem. Even though structuring a debt-free system is a utopia under the current economic and financial rules of the world, an alternative approach may decrease the dependency of people, companies, and states on debts. In that context, a question rises about how debt can be replaced and what the future of the current conventional banking system shall be in the case we structure a non-debt-focused system.

The first and foremost issue that we need to find an answer to is how to replace the trust mechanism of the banking system because we all know that people or companies are using banks because they think that their money is secured there, and fixed interest rates protect their savings against any potential decrease in their wealth due to inflation, or any financial shock. On the other hand, banks are indeed intermediary financial institutions that transfer the deposit of an entity to another entity by getting a commissioning fee over the adjusted interest rates they apply to borrowers and lenders. Thus, if we can build an alternative trustable system in that people may confidently deposit their savings, the dependency on debt may decrease. Investing through capital markets and funds may change the rule of the game and in that context, the role of banks may change in the financial system. Blockchain technology and fintech have already initiated this shift. Currently, the users of the banking system are evaluated by the number of people who have bank accounts, who have credit cards, and the number of Automated Teller Machines (ATMs). In the near future, the determinants of the banking system will be the number of people who have digital currency accounts, and the people who use mobile apps and Quick Response (QR) codes to withdraw money or make payments.

In the second phase, instead of depositing money to bank accounts no matter if this account is interest-bearing or not, the money shall flow from banks to capital markets and be directed to different investment funds. These funds may provide financing for different investment projects, firms, and even social responsibility projects, and that may open a path to the use of money for the benefit of society. The more digital channels are used such as being an investor of these funds through the mobile apps of the banks, the more the role of banks changes as they will provide an infrastructure and a platform to access these funds. Indeed, it is possible to make all these transactions by using the mobile apps of the banks, but there are some limitations and restrictions. The more the digital systems provide flexibility for users, the more the banks will first maintain and then reshape their roles in the new economic and financial system. Another determinant of the implementation of the new system is the level of financial literacy of people. The rate of financial literacy varies from 13 to 71% in different countries according to the survey of S&P Financial Literacy Survey conducted in 2014. Globally, 38% of account-owning people are financially literate, and while this rate is 57% in developed economies, it is only 30% in major emerging economies. The increase in the level of financial literacy may open a path for more involvement of people in the financial system (Klapper et al, 2014).

The Model Framework

Imagine an umbrella fund established under the Treasury of a State which is named ***"Partnership Economy Fund".*** People are encouraged to deposit their savings in their bank accounts, pension accounts, money stored at home in their safe, etc., to the sub-funds established under this umbrella fund. These sub-funds may be related to agriculture, livestock, energy, infrastructure, health, education, urban transformation, innovation, technology, etc., or a combination of them. People or companies may be investors of these funds and finance different projects or become shareholders of the firms through these funds. Figure 7.5 shows the general outline of the model proposed. The motivation behind the model is the idea of ***shared responsibility and returns***. The more people are involved in these funds, the more they use their money for the benefit of others, and as a result, they increase their returns.

What Are the Sources of Money for the New System?

Since the system is putting the partnership in the center, the source of the money comes from the savings of the people and the profits of companies. The model is bringing individuals, firms, professional portfolio management companies, fund managers, and funds together under the regulation of the treasury. It is important to note that, to attract people more into

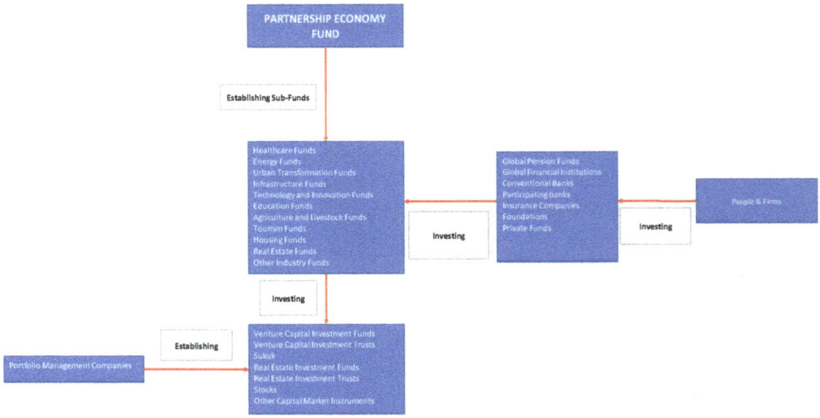

Fig. 7.5 General outline of the model (by author)

the system, the Treasury shall also support the established funds by establishing the sub-funds and depositing initial investment amounts directly or through Sovereign Wealth Fund, which is defined as an investment way for countries to invest excess capital into markets or other investments.

Sovereign Wealth Funds

Sovereign wealth funds are state-owned financial assets including stocks, bonds, real estate, precious metals, and other financial instruments. Fostering socioeconomic development, hedging against the aging population problem, and protecting the economy against sudden shocks are the primary objectives of SWFs which are funded by foreign-exchange reserves accumulated through excess capital. As of June 2022, Norway Sovereign Wealth Fund, with its USD 1.36 trillion asset value is the largest SWF in the world. That is followed by China Investment Corporation and State Administration of Foreign Exchanges with 1.22 and 0.98 USD trillion asset sizes, respectively. Table 7.1 shows the largest SWFs in the world.

The history of Sovereign Wealth Funds dates back to 1953 when Kuwait Investment Authority was established in 1953 to manage the surplus oil income (Alheshel, 2015). The total asset size of the SWFs reached USD 10.3 trillion according to the Sovereign Wealth Institute. Fixed income constitutes 53% of the asset allocation of the SWFs, and

Table 7.1 Largest SWFs (Statista, 2022c)

Largest sovereign wealth funds	*Size (in USD trillion)*
Norges Bank Investment Management (Norway)	1.362
China Investment Corporation (China)	1.222
State Administration of Foreign Exchanges (China)	980
Abu Dhabi Investment Authority (UAE)	829
Government of Singapore Investment Corporation (Singapore)	799
Kuwait Investment Authority (Kuwait)	693
Public Investment Fund (Saudi Arabia)	620
Hong Kong Monetary Authority (Hong Kong)	587
National Council for Social Security Fund (China)	452
Qatar Investment Authority (Qatar)	445
Investment Corporation of Dubai (UAE)	300
Mubadala (UAE)	284
Temasek (Singapore)	283
Korea Investment Corporation (Korea)	205
Future Fund (Australia)	183

this is followed by equity, infrastructure/real estate, and hedge fund investments with 34, 8, and 5%, respectively. While 71.5% of the investments are made in foreign countries, developed economies get a 92.5% share of the global SWF investments (International Forum of Sovereign Wealth Funds, 2016). If we make it possible to direct the investments from developed economies to more emerging markets, and if we can achieve to decrease the fixed income investments and increase the shares of asset-backed investments, the SWFs may be a good source for the new economic and financial approach.

Pension Funds

People seek to keep their comfortable lives in their retirement ages. Although nobody knows when they will die, it is a common reflex of people to save money and invest it in different investment instruments such as real estate, gold, stocks, and funds to get either a one-time lump-sum payment or monthly income in their retirement years. Pension funds which are defined as collective monetary payments to provide retirement benefits are very widely accepted in many countries for future investments. Pension assets exceeded USD 56 trillion worldwide at the end of 2020 according to the Pension Markets in Focus Report published by OECD in 2021.

A faster increase in pension assets over GDP highlights the increasing significance of retirement savings. For instance, while the assets of 9 out of 38 OECD countries exceeded their GDP at the end of 2020, 7 of the 38 OECD countries held more than 90% of the total pension assets. As of the end of 2021, the rate of the total pension fund assets over the total GDP of all OECD countries reached 66.9%. The United States has the largest pension market within the OECD, with assets worth USD 35.5 trillion. The United Kingdom with USD 3.6 trillion, Canada with USD 3.1 trillion, the Netherlands with USD 2.1 trillion, Australia with USD 1.8 trillion, Japan with USD 1.6 trillion, and Switzerland with USD 1.3 trillion follow the US. While these 7 countries hold 90.5% of the total pension assets, the remaining 31 countries hold only 9.5% of the total assets. Figure 7.6 shows the geographical distribution of pension assets in OECD countries.

Bonds and equities accounted for around 75% of the total pension fund investments with 48.1 and 26.1% on average, respectively. Bonds are usually one of the major investment tools in the portfolios of pension

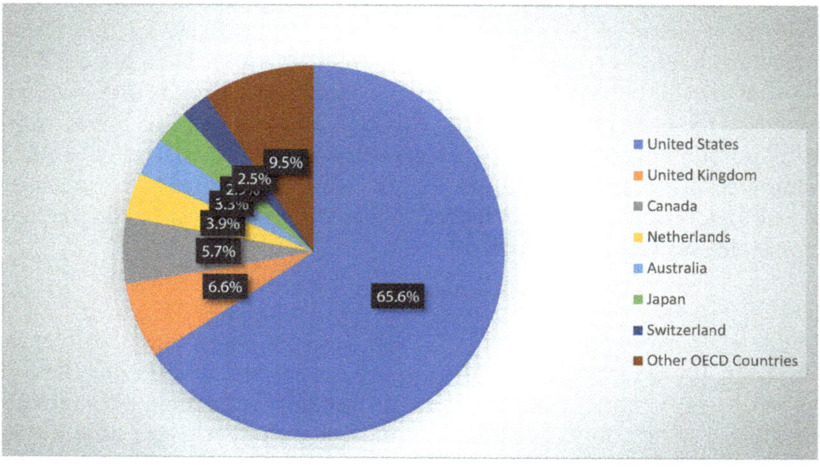

Fig. 7.6 Geographical distribution of pension assets in the OECD area (OECD, 2022b)

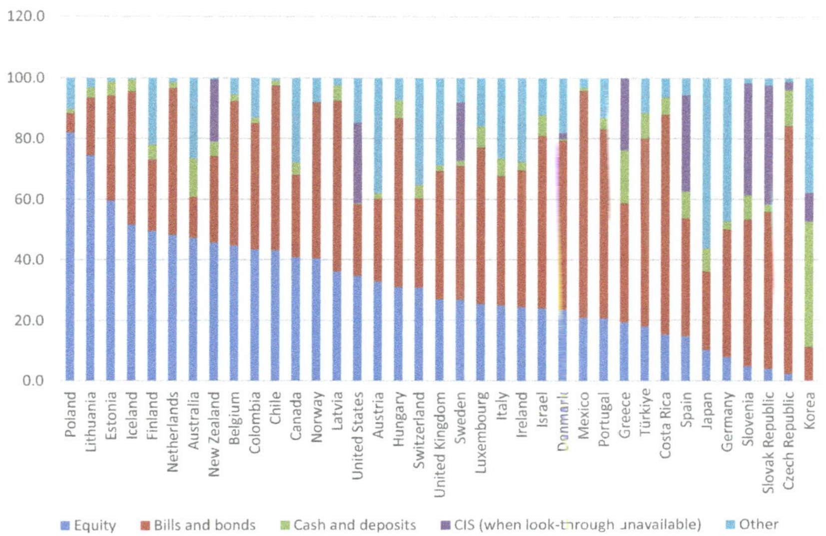

Fig. 7.7 The asset allocation of pension funds at the end of 2021 (OECD, 2022b)

funds, accounting for more than 50% of investments in 30 reporting territories, and even more than 90% in Albania (91.5%), the Maldives (93.2%), and Uruguay (93.1%).

On the other hand, 18 countries including Australia, Canada, the Netherlands, Switzerland, and the US invest more in equities compared to bonds. Cash and deposits are accounting for 9% of pension fund investments on average at the end of 2021. Figure 7.7 shows the investment breakdown of selected OECD and non-OECD countries. The pension funds are considered the largest source of financing for the new model suggested. If we can direct a notable portion of the investments into the suggested funds in the novel approach, it may change the paradigm of the pension concept.

Insurance
Individuals and firms protect themselves by using the insurance mechanism. From health to life, from motor vehicles to travel, from property to construction or transportation, in almost every phase of our lives, the

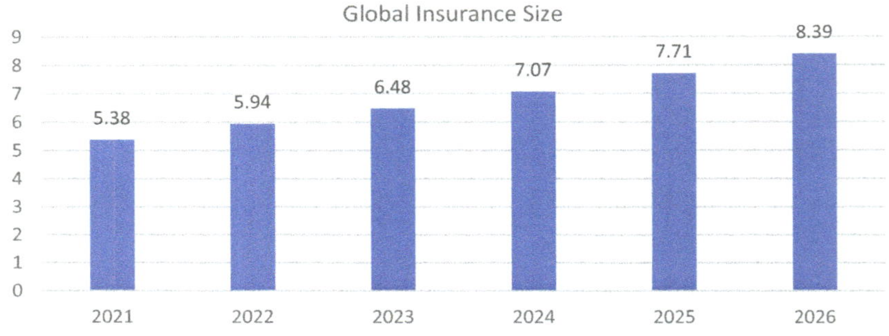

Fig. 7.8 The size of the insurance industry (Statista, 2022g)

insurance system is commonly used. Access to insurance is an important indicator of the balanced distribution of wealth. As shown in Fig. 7.8, the size of the insurance industry is around USD 6 trillion now and is forecasted to reach almost USD 8.4 trillion in 2026 (Statista, 2022a, b, c, d, e, f).

On the other hand, Swartz and Coetzer (2010) reported that among the world's 2.5 billion poor people, only eighty million are insured with some form of microinsurance. 0.3% of the poor in Africa, 3% of the poor in India and China are insured, and no microinsurance is identified in 23 of the 100 poorest countries in the world. The insurance companies collect the premiums and direct the money they accumulated to different investment tools including debt securities such as bonds and redeemable preferred stock, equity securities including common stock, mutual fund shares, and non-redeemable preferred stock, short-term investments such as certificates of deposit, mutual funds, and money market funds, repos, swaps, options, futures, and forwards. In that context, insurance companies help the stability of financial systems as they are large investors with the money they accumulate. If it is possible to direct these premiums to the model proposed in this book, individuals and firms may indirectly contribute to the new economic approach. That may lead us to create a new insurance mechanism.

Mutual Funds

Mutual funds are investment funds managed by professional asset management companies in which the capital is pooled from different investors and then used to purchase securities such as stocks, bonds, or money market instruments. As of 2021, there are around 7,500 mutual funds domiciled in the US and 131,808 funds globally. The total global net assets of mutual funds in the US amounted to nearly USD 27 trillion in 2021, five times more than their value in 1998, around USD 5.53 trillion (Statista, 2022a, b, c, d, e, f).

Hedge Funds

Hedge funds are a special type of investment tool that aims to achieve an absolute return, but unlike conventional investment funds, they use alternative methods such as long/short equity and relative value arbitrage to gain more than the average rate of return. As shown in Fig. 7.9, the hedge fund industry started growing in the 1990s, and the value of assets managed by global hedge funds grew progressively until 2007. Due to the global financial crisis, the value fell significantly in 2008 and got recovered by 2013. As of the first quarter of 2022, the value of hedge funds reached over USD 5.13 trillion (Statista, 2022a, b, c, d, e, f).

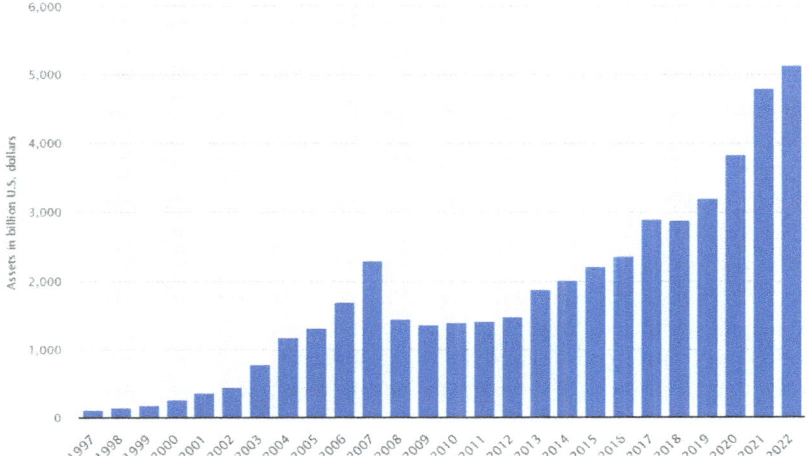

Fig. 7.9 The size of hedge funds (Statista, 2022f)

Venture Capital Investment Funds

Venture capital (VC) funds are pooled investment funds that focus on a very specific type of early state investments including start-ups and small- to medium-sized enterprises especially high-tech companies with strong growth potential. These investments are generally described as risky investments with high-return opportunities. VC funds take a seat on board and are actively involved in the management and operations of the companies in their portfolio. The investors of the VC funds get their returns through an exit strategy including an IPO, merger, or acquisition. By investing in the firms, the VC funds provide some sort of interest-free financing to start-ups and provide leverage to the investments required for their growth strategies. According to the Allied Market Research Report, the total size of the VC funds is USD 173.1 billion in 2021 and is expected to exceed USD 1 trillion in 2031. VC funds are good examples of the economic system proposed as the investors seek returns over the investment, they make directly to companies through the VC funds (Alliedmarketresearch, 2022).

Real Estate Investment Funds

Real estate investment funds are mutual funds that enable investors to invest in real estate without the need to own, operate, or finance properties. Real estate funds focus on annual profits and value increases through appreciation and provide good alternatives to long-term investors. As shown in Fig. 7.10, starting from 2014, the global real estate investment management sector grew rapidly and the total assets under management (AUM) held by the largest 100 firms reached approximately Euro 3.52 trillion in 2020 (Statista, 2022a, b, c, d, e, f). By investing in real estate funds, the investors become a shareholder of the fund which direct the investments to purchase different assets aiming for regular rental income and capital gains. The size of the investments is determined by the invested amount accumulated in the fund and the more investors are involved in the fund, the more money is directed to a larger scale of real estate investments which provide a cooperative and shared return to stakeholders.

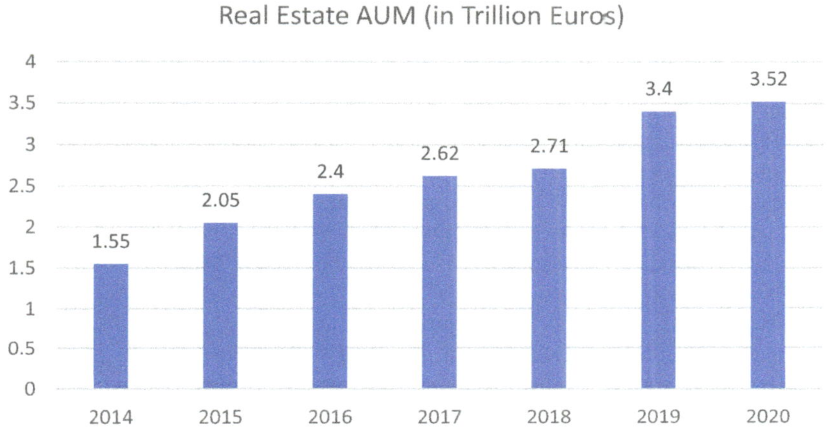

Fig. 7.10 Total real estate assets under management (Statista, 2022a)

How Can the Model Be Implemented?

The new approach is a game changer. The new model suggests an alternative housing financing model, replaces debt financing with cooperative financing, opens a path for investors to become shareholders of companies through venture capital funds, switches fixed-interest financing with interest-free financing, changes the rule of games in the insurance industry, and combines it with the pension fund approach which means also changing the paradigm in the pension systems.

An Alternative Housing Financing Model

The housing financing models currently used are very dependent on bank loans. The interest rate policies of central banks are interrelated with housing demand and prices. The rapid rise in housing prices and the increase in outstanding mortgage loans jeopardize the future of the housing industry in the post-COVID-19 period. While the total global debt keeps increasing, and central banks are increasing the interest rates, any potential default in the repayment of the mortgage loans which exceeded USD 18 trillion in the US may trigger a new mortgage crisis. Developing alternative home financing models is a must in that context. As shown in Fig. 7.11, according to the model I developed, a real estate investment fund (housing fund) is established and potential home buyers directly or indirectly, through pension funds, become investors in this fund. The house is rented to the investor and the investor (lessee) starts paying rent to the fund and keep contributing to the housing fund through the pension fund or directly. An Islamic financing model, diminishing musharaka (partnership) is also integrated into the model from an interest-free finance and sharing economy perspective.

To make it clear, we can describe the model by an example. Let's consider a potential home-purchaser who has USD 100,000 in savings and is willing to buy a house with a USD 500,000 sales price. Instead of using a bank loan, the home purchaser may invest USD 100,000 as a down payment of the house to the housing fund directly or through the pension fund and becomes the fund participant to purchase her specific house. Based on her monthly income, each month she deposits money to the fund as she contributes to the pension fund account. The housing fund rents the house to her, and she may move into the house as soon as she becomes a fund participant. Her financing costs will be the monthly rent of the house, which will be assessed each year by a professional valuation company. The value of the house will also be evaluated yearly, and the share rate of both parties will be updated. The more she pays to the fund, the more her share will increase, and the rental fee will decrease. Once the full value of the house is paid, she may get her title deed and

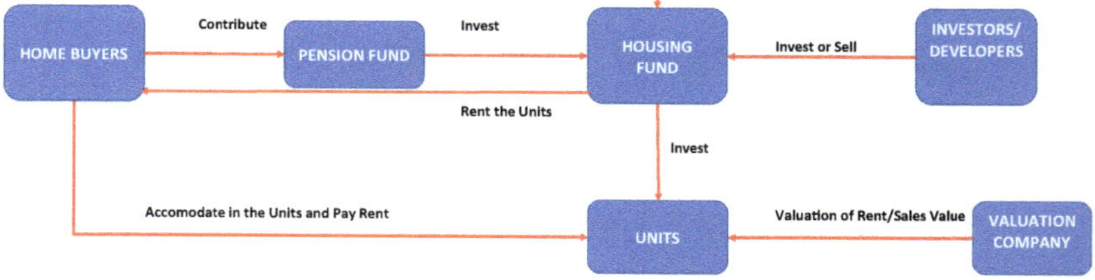

Fig. 7.11 An alternative interest-free home financing model (Modified from Sümer, 2021)

exit the fund or may keep being a fund participant and get a return from the fund by comparing it with her monthly rent (Sümer, 2021).

This alternative model developed is a bank loan-free approach and is not affected by market interest rates directly. It is transparent as the fund is established by an asset management company under the regulations of capital market boards, and combines the real estate investment funds, pension fund, and interest-free housing financing approach in one ecosystem. Sharing economy is also integrated into the model by diminishing the partnership idea. The existence of independent valuation companies which determine the rent, and the sales prices of the units also enhance the model and protect it from any price speculations.

An Alternative Approach to Replace Debt Financing

Companies need a different source of financing to grow. While some of them use bank loans, others prefer issuing bonds and providing fixed returns to investors on a specific period. Sometimes governments provide guarantees for bank loans or give tax incentives. Depending on the size of the companies, equity financing is also an option where the stocks of the firms circulate in the stock market. Small or middle size enterprises (SMEs) are not that lucky to be traded on the stock market, nor may they find cheap loans from banks. These SMEs face financial difficulties and usually use bank loans. While debt financing is a solution during low interest-rate periods, it is difficult when the interest rates are increasing, the economies are contracting, and the returns are diminishing. Not only SMEs but also large enterprises need alternative sources of financing.

As an alternative to lending to ease their cash flows, strengthening the capital structures of SMEs may be a sustainable solution. As shown in Fig. 7.12, establishing a Partnership Fund fed from different financing sources including pension funds, insurance companies, foundations, etc., assigning independent board members to ensure that their interim management is transparent, efficient, and successful, and giving them the option to trade in the stock market at the end of the interim management period may bring another bank-loan free and sustainable solution to millions of enterprises worldwide. The model suggested can also be applied to companies that are involved in strategic investments for the growth of the country. In that case, the treasury directly or indirectly by establishing a specific fund invests in such strategic companies mainly in the crisis period. At first sight, this idea may sound similar to one

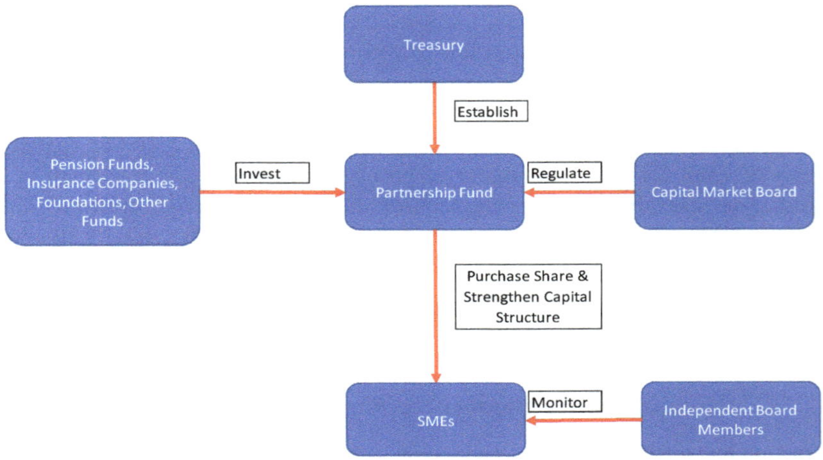

Fig. 7.12 Partnership fund (by author)

of the most criticized approaches "too big to fail" but the structure of my suggestion is different. If the company is critical for the economy and providing strategic services and facing difficulties due to the unforeseen effects of a crisis, the government may intervene in the situation and instead of providing debt to the company, may raise funds to strengthen the capital of the company and become its shareholder through the fund. The involvement of people directly or indirectly through pension funds or other investment vehicles may enhance the shared responsibility and return mindset in that context.

An Alternative Project Financing Model: Public-Private-People Partnership (4P Model)

Governments need financing for public investment projects. Taxes, fees, a surplus of public services, fines and penalties, printing money, and borrowing are the main sources of financing for governments. Public-private partnership (PPP) is also an important model which involves cooperation between a government agency and a private-sector firm to finance, build, and operate investment projects including infrastructure, bridges, tunnels, airports, power plants, roads, hospitals, etc., to be completed with private funding. While the private sector develops or uses technology and innovation, the public sector provides incentives to complete the projects within schedule and budget. The private firms carry the commercial and technical risks, on the other hand, the public sector accepts the deviation between the planned and actual incomes such as not being able to collect the total revenue of the toll fees due to the number of actual vehicles used on a highway or a bridge. Despite their advantages, public-private partnerships are often criticized for concealing the lines between legitimate public purposes and private for-profit activity, and for perceived corruption of the public due to self-dealing and rent-seeking that may occur. For instance, in Türkiye, while PPP is evaluated as a successful financing model that the government completed many investment projects without using its budget, the model is extremely criticized due to long-term guarantees provided to contractors that may be more costly to the public budget and eventually on taxpayers over years (Sonmez, 2019). Another criticism is about the public banks' involvement in the financial consortium of the project financing which underlines the indirect participation of the treasury in project funding. There is also criticism about the governance of the system including, lack of transparency, divided legal and regulatory framework, weak institutional capability and limited accountability, discrepancies in risk-sharing, non-affordable public services, and neglection for environmental sustainability (Ayhan & Üstüner, 2022).

In 2017, I proposed an alternative project financing model which suggested directing the savings in the pension funds to capital market instruments issued by special purpose vehicles (SPVs) to be founded for each public investment project. For each specific investment project (city hospitals, energy investments, infrastructure projects, technology, and innovation investments, etc.), Based on the general outline of the model shown in Fig. 7.5, I recommended establishing specific sub-funds to invest in infrastructure, healthcare, technology, innovation, industrial, social responsibility, education facilities, renewable energy, agriculture, real estate, tourism, and urban transformation projects. Then, for specific projects, I suggested various capital market instruments including sukuk, green bonds, revenue partnership shares, project-based SPV stocks, real estate investment trusts, real estate investment funds, and venture capital investment funds to be issued, and the current and future savings of the participants in the pension funds directed to these new pools of investment instruments to the abovementioned funds. For instance, let's consider that the government will make a new hospital investment. First,

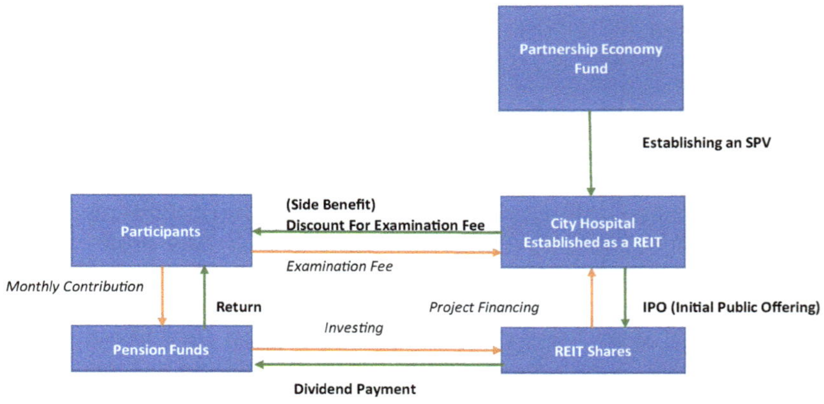

Fig. 7.13 Project financing through 4P Model (Modified from Sümer & Özorhon, 2019)

an SPV, a hospital real estate investment trust (REIT) will be founded, and the shares of this company will be traded in the stock market. Individuals will buy the stocks through their pension accounts and the return of this hospital will be shared with individual investors. There may also be side benefits such as receiving a discount for the examination fee.

We can name this approach Public-Private-People Partnership Model (4P Model). As exhibited in Fig. 7.13, the public is involved as the regulator, the private sector is undertaking the construction operations receiving their profit over their commercial offer for the construction contract amount only, and people are financing the project and getting the long-term sustainable profit over the savings they directed into pension funds. Depending on the size of the project, additional sources of financing institutions such as global pension funds, insurance companies, and private banks may also be involved with the condition to be a shareholder of the fund instead of providing a loan.

Redesigning the Pension and Insurance Systems

Insurance and pension plans are defined as two different models purposed for two different aims: insurance against unexpected situations and pension plans for retirement years, respectively. While people enroll in pension systems by making savings to protect themselves against future risks, they also insure themselves or their goods to get protection for their daily risks. Combining both the pension and insurance systems in one ecosystem and integrating the social cooperation approach would bring a new perspective to both systems. One of the main principles of the model proposed in this book is sharing, which requires the distribution of wealth equally among society. In that context, focusing on the insurance and pension systems and suggesting an innovative approach by combining the idea of saving, the other pillar of the model suggested, protection and social cooperation in one investment ecosystem would contribute to a wider implication area of the new model.

There are many important criteria for pension fund contributors when making investments in different tools. While some of the fund participants seek higher returns by taking more risks, some of them target moderate but sustainable incomes. Financial education is important for pension plan participants about their decisions of investment tools they are willing to direct their savings (Akgiray, 2019). On the other hand, insurance companies are directing the premiums of the policyholders to different investment tools. Each year, depending on the damage ratios, the policyholders are paying a premium without gaining any return on the money they spent because, within the limits of their policy, they are purchasing the potential risks. Despite technical losses they declare due to the increase in global risks, especially during the COVID-19 period, the insurance companies are financially profitable considering their financial profits made over the premiums they directed to different investment instruments.

Considering the saving and sharing pillars of the model I proposed, changing the paradigm in insurance and pension systems may be another serious game changer in the global financial system. Since 2017, I have been emphasizing the contribution of people to the economic system in many aspects and see pension assets as the largest source of funding. Justifying my studies, a recent publication by OECD about strengthening asset-backed pension systems in a post-COVID world published in 2022 underlines how investing in new infrastructure projects such as hospitals, schools, renewable energy, and digital networks could provide good returns, create jobs, and deliver tangible assets that will help long-term economic growth. Furthermore, the report also emphasizes real estate as a promising asset class and suggests governments use pension funds to finance investment projects as I have been suggesting for many years including in the models I proposed in this chapter.

The current conventional insurance system protects the policyholders against potential risks the people or the organizations may face. While the damages are paid from the premiums of the people, the potential loss or profit belongs to the insurance company. From a social perspective, neither the pension system nor the insurance system contributes to social justice because both systems are individuals-oriented and direct the savings and premiums mostly to debt instruments such as bonds and bills, so in their current forms, both the pension and insurance systems do not solve the social problems. If we can combine the pension and insurance systems in one ecosystem, we may develop an alternative way to protect the insurance policyholders/pension participants now and then. We can also integrate a social dimension into the new approach.

Consider a new insurance system in which the premiums of the policyholders are automatically invested in different asset-backed investment tools such as venture capital investment funds, real estate investment funds, sukuk, etc., and the policyholders get a share of return over the money they paid depending on their damage ratios. On the other hand, the same approach can be applied to pension accounts and the contributions of people may be directed to similar asset-backed investment instruments. The insurance fund and pension fund can be combined in one single fund of funds and the premiums, and the contributions of the participants may be directed to various investment tools that may finance projects, help the pension account owner/policyholder buy his house, enhance the capital structure of different firms by investing in them, etc. The returns may be used for different aims such as spending, donating, or providing interest-free loans to those in need. Figure 7.14 shows the general outline of the model.

The suggested model is a game changer and requires a mindset shift because integrating the insurance and pension systems needs a paradigm change and re-writes the whole scenarios of the debt-oriented finance industry. Creating a strong legal framework and governance, and increasing awareness and perceptions of people to a combined model are important steps to be taken before implementing such model. The model also helps people to use their savings without waiting until they get retired. With this approach, the returns and the risks of the insurance companies are shared with the policyholders under strong regulations issued and monitored by the government. The size of the pension funds also increases as people get the flexibility of spending their returns whenever they need to under certain rules and regulations.

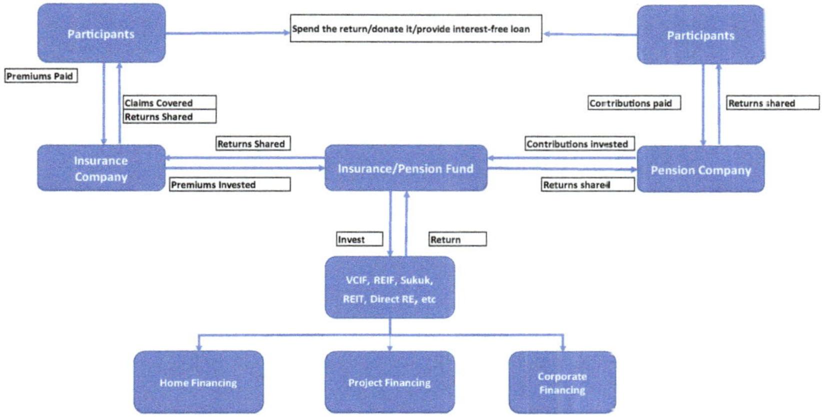

Fig. 7.14 Combined pension/insurance model (by author)

A New Tax System

Tax policies and structures have always been important factors that directly have relations with the social and economic activities of any nation. One of the critical issues needed to be structured decisively in a good financial system is the taxation system. In a good tax structure, the revenues needed to finance government expenditures are raised in an equitable, simple, and growth-friendly manner. While even Albert Einstein defines income tax as the hardest thing to understand, Benjamin Franklin mentioned tax and death together which are certain (Quoteinvestigator, 2022, Waverton, 2022). High taxes were one of the ignites of the French Revolution in 1879. According to Smith (1876), the taxes shall be proportioned to the incomes of the individuals, the taxes shall be certain, and the payment time and type shall be predetermined, taxes shall be collected in a period that is convenient for taxpayers, and taxes shall be reasonable for both the individuals and the states.

Sometimes, the governments provide tax incentives, decrease the rates to stimulate economic activities, and use debts to finance such incentives which are criticized by David Ricardo. This temporary solution eventually creates bigger problems, and the taxpayers have to pay more taxes in the future. On the other hand, increasing the taxes may result in a decrease in working hours or transferring their wealth to tax haven countries. Gale and Krupkin (2016) from Brooking Institute classify the five big improvement areas of the US tax system as long-term revenue raising, increase in environmental taxes, corporate tax reforming, equitable and efficient treatment of low- and middle-income earners, and ensuring appropriate taxation of high-income households. On the other hand, Gerçek (2019) suggests rewriting the basic tax laws, simplifying the tax system, and making it understandable and justifiable is essential for tax reform in Türkiye, an emerging economy.

The governments collect income tax, corporate tax, property tax, value-added tax, social security tax, value appreciation tax, inheritance tax, customs tax, and many other types of taxes to finance public services. According to the Tax Revenue Statistics Report of OECD (2022a, b), average tax revenues as a percentage of GDP (the tax-to-GDP ratio) increased from 33.6 to 34.1% in 2021. The more the welfare of the country increase, the more tax rates increase. For instance, Denmark had the highest tax-to-GDP ratio in 2021 (46.9%), and that is followed by France with a 45.1% ratio. On the other hand, Mexico had the lowest tax-to-GDP ratio (16.7%) and the rate in Türkiye was 22.8% in 2021.

A strong, sustainable, and reliable tax system shall help to decrease poverty, reduce income inequality, and build social justice in society. Balancing the collected taxes depending on the income level of the individuals has always been a motto of many politicians, but the regular citizens are carrying the burden of tax systems while the systems in many countries enable the large capital owners to pay less tax.

Different countries apply different tax systems. For instance, only the US and Eritrea tax their citizens based on their citizenship which means the taxpayers pay taxes even though they live in a country outside of their home country. Residential taxation which is based on applying taxes to the residents over the income they gained worldwide and territorial taxation which collects tax over the income within the country of residence only are the two most used tax systems. While more than 130 countries including most of the EU countries, Canada, Australia, Japan, and other developed countries use a residential tax system, around 40 countries use the territorial taxation system. 23 countries, either because they have a low quality of life, or they try to limit migration do not charge any direct taxes. Only a few companies such as the UK and Ireland apply a non-dom taxation system, which is a hybrid model of residential and taxation systems, and the tax is collected based on the durations spent at the place of residency and living (Globalisationguide, 2022).

A new tax system is required for a sustainable economic and financial system. First and the foremost step to be taken in this regard is structuring the system free of tax applied to the basic needs of people. For instance, the governments shall not collect property tax from homeowners who own only one house with a maximum square meter, let's say not exceeding 150 m^2. The same approach can be applied to other basic needs of people including automobiles, mobile phones, etc., depending on the engine power, price range, etc. If the taxpayer or his spouse would like to have more than one house, a car, etc., then the second and the other goods shall be subject to taxation which may also increase gradually. Second, the tax system shall be structured over the total wealth of people. A good example of that is the zakat tax in Islamic finance which 2.5% of tax is collected yearly over the total wealth of people and distributed to people who need financial aid most.

This approach can help to structure a balanced tax system as wealthy people will pay more taxes than ones who have less. Upper-income individuals are paying around 2–3% management fees to professional asset management companies over the total money/asset they let them manage. These rates match the zakat tax rates. Third, corporate tax shall be designed incrementally. The companies may first pay a fixed tax determined based on the size of the gross income and other predetermined criteria such as the number of employees, the gross profit, the size of the loans used, the payback period, and other financial ratios. Then, the more the companies increase their gross sales and profit, the more tax rates may increase. The tax amount may also be limited while the companies are reaching an acceptable level of tax payment. Collecting tax from all the liable stakeholders is one of the main problems of the governments. Using tax exemptions for basic needs, applying fixed tax amounts until to a certain level of income, using gradually increased or decreased ranges, and limiting the tax paid under certain circumstances may increase the tax-to-GDP ratios of countries and help create a more equal society.

References

Abd Samad, K., & Mohd Daud, S. N., Mohd Dali R.N.S. (2020). Early warning indicators for systemic banking crises: Household debt and property prices. *Jurnal Ekonomi Malaysia, 54*(1), 121–134. https://doi.org/10.17576/JEM-2020-5401-9

Akan, M., & Tepeler, M. İ. (2022). Sürdürülebilirlik ve Güven Ekseninde Paylaşım Ekonomisi, *30*(53), 447–464. https://doi.org/10.17233/sosyoekonomi.2022.03.22

Akgiray, V., Peksevim, S., & Sener, E. (2016). Pension funds and financial stability: Lessons from Chile and Turkey. *Journal of Finance & Banking Studies, 5*(2, Special Issue), 1–20.

Alrifai, T. (2015).*Islamic finance and the new financial system: An ethical approach to preventing future financial crises*. Wiley. ISBN: 978-1-118-99063-6

Alawode, A. A. (2015). *Islamic finance*. https://www.worldbank.org/en/topic/financialsector/brief/islamic-finance. Last Accessed on January 15, 2023.

Alheshel, B. (2015). Sovereign wealth funds: A literature review. *Journal of Economics and Business, 78*, 1–13.

Alliedmarketresearch. (2022). *Venture capital investment market research, 2031.* https://www.alliedmarketresearch.com/venture-capital-investment-market-A19435. Last Accessed on January 15, 2023.

Alter, A., Feng, A. X., & Valckx, N. (2018). *Understanding the macro-financial effects of household debt: A global perspective* (IMF Working Paper WP/18/76).

Akgiray, V. (2019). *Good Finance: Why we need a new concept of finance*. Bristol University Press, University of Bristol. ISBN 978-1-5292-0000-3

Arruda E. H., Pita R. A., Melatto B., Levy W., & Conti D. M. (2021). Circular economy: A brief literature review (2015–2020). *Sustainable Operations and Computers, 2*, 79–86. ISSN 2666-4127, https://doi.org/10.1016/j.susoc.2021.05.001

Asutay M. (2011). *An introduction to Islamic Moral Economy (IME).* https://tkbb.org.tr/Documents/EgitimVeKonferans/DIFAS-2011-IST-PR%2001-ASUTAY.pdf. Last Accessed on January 15, 2023.

Ayhan, B., & Üstüner, Y. (2022). Turkey's public-private partnership experience: A political economy perspective. *Southeast European and Black Sea Studies*. https://doi.org/10.1080/14683857.2022.2065622

Banker, S., Dunfield, D., & Huang A. (2021). Neural mechanisms of credit card spending. *Science and Reports, 11*, 4070, https://doi.org/10.1038/s41598-021-83488-3

Baum, A. (2020). *PropTech 2020: The future of real estate*. https://www.sbs.ox.ac.uk/sites/default/files/2020-02/proptech2020.pdf. Last Accessed on January 15, 2023.

Beckman, J., & Countryman, A. M. (2021). The importance of agriculture in the economy: Impacts from COVID-19. *American Journal of Agricultural Economics, 103*(5), 1595–1611.

Bilginoğlu, M. A., & Aysu, A. (2008). Dış Borçların Ekonomik Büyümede Etkisi: Türkiye Örneği. *Erciyes Üniversitesi İktisadi ve İdari Bilimler Fakültesi Dergisi, Sayı, 31*, 1–23.

Botsman, R., & Rogers, R. (2011). *What's mine is yours: How collaborative consumption is changing the way we live*. Collins.

Bureau of Economic Analysis. (2022). *Digital economy*. https://www.bea.gov/data/special-topics/digital-economy. Last Accessed on January 15, 2023.

Burgess, R., & Pande, R. (2005). Do rural banks matter? Evidence from the Indian social banking experiment. *The American Economic Review, 95*(3), 780–795.

Čavalić, A., & Bećirović, D. (2017). Sharing economy: A critical review. *6th International Scientific Symposium Economy of Eastern Croatia-Vision and Growth*.

Çepni, E. (2017). Transforming education for a transition into human-centered economy. *CADMUS, 3*(3), 24–41.

Chen, Y., & Wang, L. (2019). Commentary: Marketing and the sharing economy: Digital economy and emerging market challenges. *Journal of Marketing, 83*, 28–31. https://doi.org/10.1177/0022242919868470

Clark, M. (2020). *Human-centered finance*. Available at https://worldpositive.com/human-centered-finance-dd755d71e82a. Last Accessed on January 15, 2023.

Csizmady, A., & Kőszeghy, L. (2022). 'Generation rent' in a super homeownership environment: The case of Budapest, Hungary. *Sustainability, 14*(14), 8929. https://doi.org/10.3390/su14148929

Cunningham, R. T. (1993). The effects of debt burden on economic growth in heavily indebted nations. *Journal of Economic Development, 18*(1), 115–126.

De Grave, A. (2014). *The sharing economy: Capitalism's last stand?* Available at https://basicincome.org/news/2014/05/arthur-de-grave-the-sharing-economy-capitalisms-last-stand/. Last Accessed on March 20, 2022.

Delecta, P. (2011). Work-life balance. *International Journal of Current Research, 3*(4), 186–189.

Deshpande, A. (1997). The debt overhang and the disincentive to invest. *Journal of Development Economics, 52*(1), 169–187.

Diderot, D. (1769). *Regrets for my Old Dressing Gown*. Available at https://www.marxists.org/reference/archive/diderot/1769/regrets.htm. Last Accessed on January 15, 2023.

Dunn, E., Aknin, L., & Norton, M. I. (2014). Prosocial spending and happiness: Using money to benefit others pays off. *Current Directions in Psychological Science, 23*(1), 41–47.

Eckhardt, G. M., Houston, M. B., Jiang, B., Lamberton, C., Rindfleisch, A., & Zerva G. (2019). Marketing in the sharing economy *Journal of Marketing*, 1–23. https://doi.org/10.1177/0022242919861929journals.sagepub.com/home/jmx

Ekins, P., Domenech, T., Drummond, P., Bleischwitz, R., Hughes, N., & Lotti, L. (2019). The circular economy: What, why, how and where. Background paper for an OECD/EC Workshop on 5 July 2019 within the workshop series "Managing environmental and energy transitions for regions and cities", Paris.

Ersin, I., & Eti, S. (2017). Measuring the waste-conscious and saving habits of the youth in Turkey: The sample of Istanbul. *International Journal of Islamic Economics and Finance Studies, 3*, 41–49. https://doi.org/10.25272/j.2149-8407.2017.3.3.04.

EU Commission. (2020). *Circular economy fact sheet*. https://ec.europa.eu/environment/enveco/pdf/FACT_SHEET_iv_Circular_Economy.pdf. Last Accessed on January 15, 2023.

Everingham, P., & Chassagne, N. (2020). Post COVID-19 ecological and social reset: Moving away from capitalist growth models towards tourism as Buen Vivir. *Tourism Geographies, 22*(3), 555–566.

Fukuyama, M. (2018). *Society 5.0: Aiming for a new human-centered society*. Available at https://www.jef.or.jp/journal/pdf/220th_Special_Article_02.pdf (jef.or.jp). Last Accessed on January 15, 2023.

G20 China. (2016). *G20 Summit 2016, China*. http://www.g20chn.org/English/China2016/G202016/201512/P020151210392071823168.pdf. Last Accessed on January 15, 2023.

Gale, W. G., & Krupkin, A. (2016). *Major tax issues in 2016*. https://www.urban.org/sites/default/files/publication/78771/2000528-major-tax-issues-in-2016.pdf. Last Accessed on January 15, 2023.

Gansky, L. (2010). *The mesh: Why the future of business is sharing*. Penguin.

Geiger, L. T. (1990). Debt and economic development in Latin America. *The Journal of Developing Areas, 24*(2), 181–194.

Gerçek, A. (2019). The need for reform in Turkish tax system: Main problems and recommendations. *International Public Finance Conference/Turkey*, Vol. 34, pp. 99–105. https://doi.org/10.26650/PB/SS10.2019.001.015

Globalisationguide. (2022). *The different income tax systems worldwide*. https://globalisationguide.org/tax/world-taxation-systems/. Last Accessed on January 15, 2023.

Goldmansachs. (2022). *The evolution towards a circular economy*. Goldman Sachs Research. https://www.goldmansachs.com/insights/pages/gs-research/gs-sustain-circular-economy/report.pdf. Last Accessed on January 15, 2023.

Haskel, J., & Westlake, S. (2017). *Capitalism without capital: The rise of the intangible economy* (p. 9780691175034). Princeton University Press.

Highfill, T., & Surfield, C. (2022). *New and revised statistics of the U.S. digital economy, 2005–2020*. https://www.bea.gov/system/files/2022-05/New%20and%20Revised%20Statistics%20of%20the%20U.S.%20Digital%20Economy%202005-2020.pdf. Last Accessed on January 15, 2023.

Hjálmsdóttir, A. & Bjarnadóttir, V., (2020). "I have turned into a foreman here at home": Families and work–life balance in times of COVID-19 in a gender equality paradise. *Gender Work and Organization*. https://doi.org/10.1111/gwao.12552.

Hofmann, R., & Umbricht, R. (2019). Homeownership and happiness: Evidence for Switzerland. *Swiss Real Estate Journal, 19*, 4–12. https://doi.org/10.21256/zhaw-18640

Holmes, J. (2021). *Losing 25,000 to hunger every day*. https://www.un.org/en/chronicle/article/losing-25000-hunger-every-day. Last Accessed on January 15, 2023.

Hussain, M., Shahmoradi, A., & Turk, R. (2015). *An overview of Islamic Finance* (IMF Working Paper).

Hussin, M. Y. M., Muhammed, F., Awang, S. A., & Mohammad, A. A. S. (2012). Development of Sukuk Ijarah in Malaysia. *Journal of Islamic Economics, Banking and Finance, 8*(2), 91–102.

Ibn-Mohammed, T., Mustaphab, K. B., Godsella, J., Adamuc, Z., Babatunded, K. A., Akintadef, D. D., Acquayeg, A., Fujiih, H., Ndiayei, M. M., Yamoahj, F. A., & Kohk, S. C. L. (2021). A critical analysis of the impacts of COVID-19 on the global economy and ecosystems and opportunities for circular economy strategies. *Resources, Conservation and Recycling, 164*, 105–169.

International Forum of Sovereign Wealth Funds. (2016). *Trends in sovereign wealth funds' asset allocation over time: a survey*. https://www.ifswf.org/trends-sovereign-wealth-funds-asset-allocation-over-time-survey. Last Accessed on March 05, 2023.

Irawanto, D. W., Novianti, K. N., & Roz, K. (2021). Work from home: Measuring satisfaction between work–life balance and work stress during the COVID-19 pandemic in Indonesia. *Economies, 9*, 96. https://doi.org/10.3390/economies9030096

Jantsch, A., & Veenhoven, R. (2018). *Private wealth and happiness a research synthesis using an online findings-archive* (EHERO Working Paper 2018/03 310714-01)

King, R. G., & Levine, R. (1994). Capital fundamentalism, economic development, and economic growth. *Carnegie-Rochester Conference Series on Public Policy, 40*, 259–292.

Klapper, L., Lusardi, A., & Oudheusden, P. (2014). Financial literacy around the world: Insights from the standard & poor's ratings services global financial literacy survey. https://www.cssf.lu/wp-content/uploads/S_P_Survey.pdf. Last Accessed on January 15, 2023.

Koczetkow, B., & Klimczuk, A. (2022). The context of public policy on the sharing economy. In V. Česnuitytė, A. Klimczuk, C. Miguel & G. Avram (Eds.), *The sharing economy in Europe: Developments, practices, and contradictions* (pp. 41–64). Palgrave Macmillan.

Krugman, P. (1988). *Financing vs. forgiving a debt overhang* (NBER Working Paper, No. 2486, National Bureau of Economic Research).

Lacy, P., & Rutqvist, J. (2015). *Waste to wealth: The circular economy advantage* (1st ed.). Palgrave Macmillan. 9781137530684 ISBN-13978-1137530684.

Leiden University. (2020). *170 scientists sign manifesto with five policy proposals for a post-COVID-19 development model*. https://www.universiteitleiden.nl/en/news/2020/04/170-scientists-sign-manifesto. Last Accessed on March 20, 2022.

Leonhard, G. (2018). *Technology vs. Humanity: The coming clash between man and machine*. Springfield Collectibles. ISBN: 9780993295829.

Lessig, L. (2008). Two economies: Commercial and sharing. In *Remix: Making art and commerce thrive in the hybrid economy* (pp. 117–176). Bloomsbury Academic.

Lombard, M., Mohanty, M., & Shim, I. (2017). *The real effects of household debt in the short and long run* (BIS Working Papers, No 607), Monetary and Economic Department

McCracken, G. D. (1988). *Culture and consumption: New approaches to the symbolic character of consumer goods and activities*. Indiana University Press.

McKinnon, R. I. (1973). *Money and capital in economic development*. Brookings Institution Press. ISBN: 9780815756132

Mesenbourg, T. L. (2001). *Measuring electronic business*. Economic Programs U.S. Bureau of the Census. https://www.census.gov/content/dam/Census/library/working-papers/2001/econ/ebusasa.pdf. Last Accessed on January 15, 2023.

Miguel, C., Avram, G., Klimczuk, A., Simonovits, B., Balázs, B., & Česnuitytė, V. (2022). The sharing economy in Europe: From idea to reality. In V. Česnuitytė, A. Klimczuk, C. Miguel, & G. Avram (Eds.), *The sharing economy in Europe*. Palgrave Macmillan. https://doi.org/10.1007/978-3-030-86897-0_1

Morozov, E. (2013). The 'sharing economy' undermines workers' rights. *Financial Times*. https://www.ft.com/content/92c3021c-34c2-11e3-8148-00144feab7de. Last Accessed on March 20, 2022.

Nesbitt, P. (2022). *The future of finance is human-centered*. https://www.forbes.com/sites/forbesfinancecouncil/2022/06/23/the-future-of-finance-is-human-centered/?sh=7b03f8f73ba8. Last Accessed on January 15, 2023.

OECD. (2022a). *Strengthening asset-backed pension systems in a post-COVID world*. OECD Publishing. https://doi.org/10.1787/288cb3cf-en.

OECD. (2022b). *Revenue statistics 2022 the impact of COVID-19 on OECD tax revenues*. https://www.oecd.org/tax/tax-policy/revenue-statistics-highlights-brochure.pdf. Last Accessed on January 15, 2023.

Peterson, E. W. F. (2017). The role of population in economic growth. *SAGE Open, 7*(4). https://doi.org/10.1177/2158244017736094

Plug, E. J. S. (1997). *Leyden welfare and beyond* (PhD thesis). Thesis Publishers.

Prnewswire. (2022). Global Insurance Market Report 2022: Market is expected to grow to $8,398.11 billion in 2026—Long-term forecast to 2031. https://www.prnewswire.com/news-releases/global-insurance-market-report-2022-market-is-expected-to-grow-to-8-398-11-billion-in-2026---long-term-forecast-to-2031--301588937.html. Last Accessed on January 15, 2023.

Quoteinvestigator. (2022). *The hardest thing in the world to understand is income taxes*. https://quoteinvestigator.com/2011/03/07/einstein-income-taxes/. Last Accessed on January 15, 2023.

Refinitiv. (2022). *Islamic Finance Development Report 2022: Embracing change*. https://www.refinitiv.com/en/resources/special-report/islamic-finance-development-report-2022#form. Last Accessed on January 15, 2023.

Ribaj, A., & Mexhuani, F. (2021). The impact of savings on economic growth in a developing country (the case of Kosovo). *Journal of Innovation and Entrepreneurship, 10*(1), 1–13.

Rohe, W., & Basolo, V. (2016). Long-term effects of homeownership on the self perceptions and social interaction of low-income persons. *Environment and Behavior, 29*, 793–819.

Rohe, W., & Stegman, M. A. (1994). The effects of homeownership. On the self-esteem, perceived control and life satisfaction of low-income people. *Journal of the American Planning Association, 60*, 173–184.

Saripudin, K. J., Mohamad, S., Nazif, N. F. M., Abdullah, L. H., & Abdul Rahman, N. N. (2012). Case study on Sukuk Musharakah Issued in Malaysia. *Middle-East Journal of Scientific Research, 12*(2), 168–175.

Schor, J. (2014). *Debating the sharing economy*. Great Transition Initiative. https://greattransition.org/images/Schor-Debating-Sharing-Economy.pdf. Last Accessed on January 15, 2023.

Shiftprocessing. (2022). *Credit card statistics*. https://shiftprocessing.com/credit-card/. Last Accessed on January 15, 2023.

Smith, A. (1876). *The Wealth of Nations*. Bibliomania.com Ltd.

Solow, R. M. (1956). A contribution to the theory of economic growth. *The Quarterly Journal of Economics, 70*(1), 65–94.

Sonmez, M. (2019). *Turkey's taxpayers in dark over bill of big investment projects*. http://mustafasonmez.net/turkeys-taxpayers-in-dark-over-bill-of-big-investment-projects-al-monitor-december-9-2019/. Last Accessed on January 15, 2023.

State Bank of Pakistan. (2022). *Glossary on Islamic banking*. http://www.sbp.org.pk/IB/Gloss.asp. Last Accessed on January 15, 2023

Statista. (2022a). *Assets under management of leading real estate investment managers worldwide from 2014 to 2020*. https://www.statista.com/statistics/1193071/aggregate-assets-under-management-aum-leading-real-estate-investment-managers-globally/. Last Accessed on January 15, 2023.

Statista. (2022b). *E-commerce worldwide—Statistics & facts*. https://www.statista.com/topics/871/online-shopping/#topicOverview. Last Accessed on January 15, 2023.
Statista. (2022c). *Largest sovereign wealth funds worldwide as of June 2022, by assets under management*. https://www.statista.com/statistics/276617/sovereign-wealth-funds-worldwide-based-on-assets-under-management/#:~:text=The%20world's%20largest%20sovereign%20wealth,oil%20in%20the%20North%20Sea. Last Accessed on January 15, 2023.
Statista. (2022d). *Leading mutual fund groups globally as of March 2022, by assets under management*. https://www.statista.com/statistics/255864/top-global-fund-groups-worldwide-by-assets/. Last Accessed on January 15, 2023.
Statista. (2022e). *Share of professionals from companies prioritizing digital manufacturing platforms in 2022, by sector*. https://www.statista.com/statistics/1300611/digital-manufacturing-platform-company-adoption-by-sector/. Last Accessed on January 15, 2023.
Statista. (2022f). *Value of assets managed by hedge funds worldwide from 1997 to Q1 2022*. https://www.statista.com/statistics/271771/assets-of-the-hedge-funds-worldwide/. Last Accessed on January 15, 2023.
Statista. (2022g). *Forecast of the global insurance market in 2021 and 2022, with forecasts from 2023 to 2026(in billion U.S. dollars)*. https://www.statista.com/statistics/1192960/forecast-global-insurance-market/. Last Accessed on January 15, 2023.
Sturgeon, T. J. (2021). Upgrading strategies for the digital economy. *Global Strategy Journal, Special Issue: Digitalization and Global Strategy, 11*(1), 34–57.
Sümer, L. (2017). *Developing a real estate-pension fund investment ecosystem: Turkey real estate fund* (Ph.D. Thesis), Boğaziçi University.
Sümer, L. (2021). An alternative interest-free home financing model. *International Journal of Housing Markets and Analysis*, 1753-8270. https://doi.org/10.1108/IJHMA-02-2022-0027
Sümer, L., & Özorhon, B. (2019). The shortcomings of pension system in Turkey: Solutions with a new model proposed. *International Journal of Islamic Economics and Finance Studies, 5*(2), 23–48. https://doi.org/10.25272/ijisef.559898
Swartz, N. P., & Coetzer, P. (2010). Takaful: An Islamic insurance instrument. *Journal of Development and Agricultural Economics, 2*(10), 333–339.
Tradingeconomics. (2022). *GDP per Capita*. https://tradingeconomics.com/country-list/gdp-per-capita. Last Accessed on March 05, 2023.
United Nation. (2022). *World population prospects 2022*. https://www.un.org/development/desa/pd/sites/www.un.org.development.desa.pd/files/wpp2022_summary_of_results.pdf. Last Accessed on January 15, 2023.

United Nation Environment Programme. (2019). *We're gobbling up the earth's resources at an unsustainable rate*. https://www.unep.org/news-and-stories/story/were-gobbling-earths-resources-unsustainable-rate. Last Accessed on January 15, 2023.

US Bureau of Labor Statistics. (2021). *Hispanics or Latinos made up over one-fourth of the labor force in six states in 2020*. https://www.bls.gov/opub/ted/2021/hispanics-or-latinos-made-up-over-one-fourth-of-the-labor-force-in-six-states-in-2020.htm. Last Accessed on January 15, 2023.

Veenhoven, R., & Timmermans, D. (1998). Welvaart en Geluk (affluence and happiness). *Economisch Statistische Berichten, 83*, 628–631.

Waverton. (2022). *Nothing is certain except death and taxes'—Benjamin Franklin, 1789*. https://www.waverton.co.uk/media-centre/insights/nothing-is-certain-except-death-and-taxes-benjamin-franklin-1789. Last Accessed on January 15, 2023.

Worldbank. (2023). *World GDP*. https://data.worldbank.org/indicator/NY.GDP.MKTP.CD. Last Accessed on January 15, 2023.

Xu, J. (2022). *The future and FinTech: ABCDI and beyond*. World Scientific. https://doi.org/10.1142/12686, ISBN: 978-981-125-089-7.

Yaraghi, N., & Shamika, R. (2017). *The current and future state of the sharing economy* (Brookings India IMPACT Series No. 032017).

Yildirim S., & Erdogan, K. S. (2022). The impact of public debt on growth: A panel analysis in selected countries. *Finansal Araştırmalar ve Çalışmalar Dergisi, 14*(27), 362–378. ISSN: 2529-0029, https://doi.org/10.14784/marufacd.1145693

Yuceol, N., Urfa, A. M., Sarp, P., & Binici, C. M. (2021). The impact of work-life balance on mental well-being of remote working generation Y academicians due to the COVID-19 pandemic in Turkey. *Marmara Üniversitesi İktisadi ve İdari Bilimler Dergisi, 43*(2), 266–284. ISSN: 2587-2672, https://doi.org/10.14780/muiibd.1052073

Zumbro, T. (2014). The relationship between homeownership and life satisfaction in Germany. *Housing Studies, 29*, 319–338.

CHAPTER 8

What Is Next?

The world is in a transition period. The post-pandemic world is characterized by populism, nationalism, and limited individual freedoms which also damaged globalization and free trade (Bhusal, 2020). Although the health-related consequences of the COVID-19 pandemic are still unpredictable, the focus of the states has been shifted to economic effects as the negative impacts of the pandemic are combined with political risks. The global economy is struggling with the negative effects of the COVID-19 pandemic and started to get recovered gradually, but the political developments including the ongoing war between Russia and Ukraine and its potential threats to the security of the world increased the pressure on the risks of the global economy. The rise in inflation rates in the world including the US and the Eurozone, the energy supply problems, limited access to food, trade barriers, and sanctions are seemed to be the crucial issues to be resolved immediately to keep the world economy stable.

Governments started to limit food exports, seek alternative energy sources to decrease their dependencies on oil and gas, deciding to keep using nuclear energy or even build new ones. To fight against inflation, the central banks started increasing the interest rates which may slow down the economies, but on the other hand, if they fail to decrease the inflation in short term, there is a potential stagflation risk. In that context, it can be said that the current financial system is very fragile because the

L. Sümer, *The World Economy and Financial System*,
https://doi.org/10.1007/978-3-031-27530-2_8

financial system is built on a boom-and-bust cycle where financial crises are frequent and part of the system's design (Alrifai, 2015).

A new system is urgently needed as the world may face a new global financial crisis where its effect may be the heaviest ever. This book proposed a paradigm change and mindset shift from the quite common use and acceptance of capitalism-driven economy models based on consumption and growth to a new perspective focusing on ***creating new sharing ecosystems that aim the social justice and cooperation*** structuring under developing, balancing, saving, and sharing pillars.

At a macro level, the new model is suggesting developing a human and society-focused financial system, a productive society, and a collective education system. The countries need to balance their imports and exports and decrease income inequality by balancing the welfare of the society. Managing the savings by restructuring the pension and insurance system and emphasizing the sharing economy are the other macro-level steps suggested by the model. At a micro level, developing a system that encourages entrepreneurship, using technology as a tool that increases the welfare of society, and balancing production and consumption and work and private life are essential for a sustainable model. Increasing the savings but directing these savings to human-focused and environment-friendly investments is highly recommended.

By following these pillars, and combining the pension and insurance systems, a game-changer approach, was designed. With the new design, the savings of people were evaluated as the main contributor to the new economic model. A new housing financing model that combines the pension funds, real estate investment funds, and diminishing partnership approach, a new project financing model that replace debt financing with asset-backed financing and directs the pension funds to invest in interest-free capital market instruments, strengthening the capital structures of firms instead of providing debt to them were also some important implication areas of the model suggested in this book. Considering the flaws of the tax system, a new tax system that protect the lower income group provides an exemption for the basic needs of people, uses a fixed tax amount, and increases it gradually based on the wealth of stakeholders may increase the tax amount the governments collect, decrease the income inequality, and contribute to social justice.

The world is in a transition period. The signs are pointing out that a new global financial crisis is nearing or worse, and the world is on the edge of a new world war. The paradigms are changing, the rules of the games are being rewritten and the cards are dealt with again. The new concept of the world requires a mindset shift from the traditional approach to a sustainable human-oriented approach. The development of technology is very fast and is bringing permanent changes to our lives. The use of artificial intelligence, production with robots, trillions of data produced, mobility, and connectedness are the new normal of our lives. The finance industry is being shaped by technology and blockchain technology, where fintech and digital currencies are the undeniable facts of the future of the finance world. That emphasizes the importance of the digital economy. The energy crisis caused by the Russia-Ukraine war is forcing us to focus more on renewable energy. The finance industry is also issuing debt and equity instruments that are "green". Circular economy, as an extension of sustainability, in that context, becomes more important than ever.

On the other hand, while we are discussing sustainability and digitalization in one part of the world, in the other part, millions of people are dying just because of hunger. While these people have all the required underground and aboveground resources including mines, natural gas, rivers, wind, sun, etc., they have no access to clean water, energy, infrastructure, and other basic needs of humans which is a big dilemma and a big failure of humanity. Thus, this situation underlines the value of sharing economy. The resources of the earth are not endless, and the income level of individuals is not always constant. A saving economy is essential in that context.

The new approach I presented is a starting point for redesigning the economic and financial system. Putting the individuals in the center of the economic and financial system, removing the debt-oriented systems from our lives, and sharing the returns of the enterprises or projects with people who contributed to its financing will initiate the change of paradigms.

References

Alrifai, T. (2015). *Islamic finance and the new financial system: An ethical approach to preventing future financial crises*. Wiley. ISBN: 978-1-118-99063-6.

Bhusal, M. K. (2020). The world after COVID-19: An opportunity for a new beginning. *International Journal of Scientific and Research Publications, 10*(5), 735–741.

Index

L. Sümer, *The World Economy and Financial System*, https://doi.org/10.1007/978-3-031-27530-2

GPSR Compliance
The European Union's (EU) General Product Safety Regulation (GPSR) is a set of rules that requires consumer products to be safe and our obligations to ensure this.

If you have any concerns about our products, you can contact us on

ProductSafety@springernature.com

In case Publisher is established outside the EU, the EU authorized representative is:

Springer Nature Customer Service Center GmbH
Europaplatz 3
69115 Heidelberg, Germany

www.ingramcontent.com/pod-product-compliance
Ingram Content Group UK Ltd.
Pitfield, Milton Keynes, MK11 3LW, UK
UKHW022222051026
15624UKWH00002B/304
9783031275296